Fourth Workshop on Resources for African Indigenous Languages (RAIL 2023)

Dubrovnik, Croatia
6 May 2023

ISBN: 978-1-7138-9061-4

Printed from e-media with permission by:

Curran Associates, Inc.
57 Morehouse Lane
Red Hook, NY 12571

Some format issues inherent in the e-media version may also appear in this print version.

Printed with permission by Curran Associates, Inc. (2024)

For permission requests, please contact the Association for Computational Linguistics at the address below.

Association for Computational Linguistics
209 N. Eighth Street
Stroudsburg, Pennsylvania 18360

Phone: 1-570-476-8006
Fax: 1-570-476-0860

acl@aclweb.org

Additional copies of this publication are available from:

Curran Associates, Inc.
57 Morehouse Lane
Red Hook, NY 12571 USA
Phone: 845-758-0400
Fax: 845-758-2633
Email: curran@proceedings.com
Web: www.proceedings.com

RAIL 2023

Fourth workshop on Resources for African Indigenous Languages (RAIL)

Proceedings of the Workshop

May 6, 2023

Preface

Africa is a multilingual continent with an estimation of 1500 to 2000 indigenous languages. Many of the languages currently have no or very limited language resources available and are often structurally quite different from more well-resourced languages, therefore requiring the development and use of specialized techniques. To bring together and emphasize research in these areas, the Resources for African Indigenous Languages (RAIL) workshop series aims to provide an interdisciplinary platform for researchers working on resources (data collections, tools, etc.) specifically targeted towards African indigenous languages. These events provide an overview of the current state-of-the-art and emphasize the availability of African indigenous language resources, including both data and tools.

With the UNESCO-supported Decade of Indigenous Languages, there is currently much interest in indigenous languages. The Permanent Forum on Indigenous Issues mentioned that "40 percent of the estimated 6,700 languages spoken around the world were in danger of disappearing" and the "languages represent complex systems of knowledge and communication and should be recognized as a strategic national resource for development, peace building and reconciliation."

This year's RAIL workshop is the fourth in a series. The first workshop was co-located with the Language Resources and Evaluation Conference (LREC) in 2020, whereas the second RAIL workshop, in 2021, was co-located with the Digital Humanities Association of Southern Africa (DHASA) conference. Both of these events were virtual. The third RAIL workshop was co-located with the tenth Southern African Microlinguistics Workshop and took place in person in Potchefstroom, South Africa.

Previous RAIL workshops showed that the presented problems (and solutions) are typically not only applicable to African languages. Many issues are also relevant to other low-resource languages, such as different scripts and properties like tone. As such, these languages share similar challenges. This allows for researchers working on these languages with such properties (including non-African languages) to learn from each other, especially on issues pertaining to language resource development.

For the fourth RAIL workshop, in total, nineteen very high-quality submissions were received. Out of these, fourteen submissions were selected for presentation in the workshop using double blind review. Additionally, one presentation that is published in EACL's Findings proceedings is incorporated in the programme as well. The RAIL workshop took place as a full day workshop in Dubrovnik, Croatia. It was co-located with the EACL 2023 conference, the seventeenth Conference of the European Chapter of the Association for Computational Linguistics. Each presentation consisted of 25 minutes (including time for discussion).

This publication adheres to South Africa's DHET's 60% rule, authors in the proceedings come from a wide range of institutions.

The workshop has "Impact of impairments on language resources" as its theme, but submissions on any topic related to properties of African indigenous languages were considered. In fact, several suggested topics for the workshop were mentioned in the call for papers:

- Digital representations of linguistic structures
- Descriptions of corpora or other data sets of African indigenous languages
- Building resources for (under resourced) African indigenous languages
- Developing and using African indigenous languages in the digital age
- Effectiveness of digital technologies for the development of African indigenous languages

- Revealing unknown or unpublished existing resources for African indigenous languages
- Developing desired resources for African indigenous languages
- Improving quality, availability and accessibility of African indigenous language resources

The goals for the workshop are:

- to bring together researchers who are interested in showcasing their research and thereby boosting the field of African indigenous languages,
- to create the conditions for the emergence of a scientific community of practice that focuses on data, as well as tools, specifically designed for or applied to indigenous languages found in Africa,
- to create conversations between academics and researchers in different fields such as African indigenous languages, computational linguistics, sociolinguistics, and language technology, and
- to provide an opportunity for the African indigenous languages community to identify, describe and share their Language Resources.

We would like to mention explicitly that the term "indigenous languages" used in the RAIL workshop is intended to refer to non-colonial languages (in this case those used in Africa). In no way is this term used to cause any harm or discomfort to anyone. Many of these languages were or still are marginalized and the aim of the workshop is to bring attention to the creation, curation, and development of resources for these languages in Africa.

The organizers would like to thank the authors who submitted publications and the programme committee who provided feedback on the quality and the content of the submissions.

The RAIL organizing committee and editors of the proceedings:

- Rooweither Mabuya, South African Centre for Digital Language Resources
- Don Mthobela, Cam Foundation
- Mmasibidi Setaka, South African Centre for Digital Language Resources
- Menno van Zaanen, South African Centre for Digital Language Resources

Organizing Committee

Organizers

Rooweither Mabuya, South African Centre for Digital Language Resources
Don Mthobela, Cam Foundation
Mmasibidi Setaka, South African Centre for Digital Language Resources
Menno Van Zaanen, South African Centre for Digital Language Resources

Program Committee

Chairs

Rooweither Mabuya, South African Centre for Digital Language Resources
Don Mthobela, Cam Foundation
Mmasibidi Setaka, South African Centre for Digital Language Resources
Menno Van Zaanen, South African Centre for Digital Language Resources

Program Committee

Gilles-Maurice De Schryver, Ghent University
Febe De Wet, Stellenbosch University
Sibonelo Dlamini, University of KwaZulu-Natal
Roald Eiselen, Centre for Text Technology, North-West University
Tanja Gaustad, Centre for Text Technology, North-West University
Marissa Griesel, University of South Africa
Ayodele James Akinola, Chrisland University
C. Maria Keet, University of Cape Town
Papi Lemeko, Central University of Technology Free State
Vukosi Marivate, University of Pretoria, Lelapa AI
Muzi Matfunjwa, South African Centre for Digital Language Resources
Dimakatso Mathe, University of Limpopo
Innocentia Mhlambi, University of the Witwatersrand
Emmanuel Ngue Um, University of Yaoundé I
Makanjuola Ogunleye, Virginia Polytechnic Institute and State University
Tunde Ope-davies, Centre for Digital Humanities, University of Lagos
Sara Petrollino, Leiden University
Pule Phindane, Central University of Technology
Mpho Raborife, University of Johannesburg
Lorraine Shabangu, Wits University
Johannes Sibeko, Nelson Mandela University
Hussein Suleman, University of Cape Town
Elsabe Taljard, University of Pretoria
Valencia Wagner, Sol Plaatje University
Friedel Wolff, South African Centre for Digital Language Resources

Table of Contents

Program

Saturday, May 6, 2023

08:30 - 09:00 *Registration and opening remarks*

09:00 - 10:15 *Morning Session 1*

IsiXhosa Intellectual Traditions Digital Archive: Digitizing isiXhosa texts from 1870-1914
Jonathan Schoots, Amandla Ngwendu, Jacques De Wet and Sanjin Muftic

Preparing the Vuk'uzenzele and ZA-gov-multilingual South African multilingual corpora
Richard Lastrucci, Jenalea Rajab, Matimba Shingange, Daniel Njini and Vukosi Marivate

Automatic Spell Checker and Correction for Under-represented Spoken Languages: Case Study on Wolof
Thierno Ibrahima Cissé and Fatiha Sadat

10:15 - 10:55 *Morning tea break*

10:55 - 12:30 *Morning Session 2*

SpeechReporting Corpus: annotated corpora of West African traditional narratives
Ekaterina Aplonova, Izabela Jordanoska, Timofey Arkhangelskiy and Tatiana Nikitina

Analyzing political formation through historical isiXhosa text analysis: Using frequency analysis to examine emerging African Nationalism in South Africa
Jonathan Schoots

Unsupervised Cross-lingual Word Embedding Representation for English-isiZulu
Derwin Ngomane, Rooweither Mabuya, Jade Abbott and Vukosi Marivate

Investigating Sentiment-Bearing Words- and Emoji-based Distant Supervision Approaches for Sentiment Analysis
Ronny Mabokela, Mpho Roborife and Turguy Celik

12:30 - 14:00 *Lunch break*

14:00 - 15:40 *Afternoon Session 1*

Saturday, May 6, 2023 (continued)

	Towards a Swahili Universal Dependency Treebank: Leveraging the Annotations of the Helsinki Corpus of Swahili Kenneth Steimel, Sandra Kübler and Daniel Dakota
	Evaluating the Sesotho rule-based syllabification system on Sepedi and Setswana words Johannes Sibeko and Mmasibidi Setaka
	Deep learning and low-resource languages: How much data is enough? A case study of three linguistically distinct South African languages Roald Eiselen and Tanja Gaustad
	Comparing methods of orthographic conversion for Bàsàá, a language of Cameroon Alexandra O'neil, Daniel Swanson, Robert Pugh, Francis Tyers and Emmanuel Ngue Um
15:40 - 16:20	*Afternoon tea break*
16:20 - 18:00	*Afternoon Session 2*
	Natural Language Processing in Ethiopian Languages: Current State, Challenges, and Opportunities Tolúlọpẹ́ Ògúnrẹ̀mí, Dan Jurafsky and Christopher D. Manning
	Natural Language Processing in Ethiopian Languages: Current State, Challenges, and Opportunities Atnafu Lambebo Tonja, Tadesse Destaw Belay, Israel Abebe Azime, Abinew Ali Ayele, Moges Ahmed Mehamed, Olga Kolesnikova and Seid Muhie Yimam
	A Corpus-Based List of Frequently Used Words in Sesotho Johannes Sibeko and Orphée De Clercq
	Vowels and the Igala Language Resources Mahmud Momoh
18:00 - 18:05	*Closing statements*

Automatic Spell Checker and Correction for Under-represented Spoken Languages: Case Study on Wolof

Thierno Ibrahima Cissé
Université du Québec à Montréal
cisse.thierno_ibrahima@courrier.uqam.ca

Fatiha Sadat
Université du Québec à Montréal
sadat.fatiha@uqam.ca

Abstract

This paper presents a spell checker and correction tool specifically designed for Wolof, an under-represented spoken language in Africa. The proposed spell checker leverages a combination of a trie data structure, dynamic programming, and the weighted Levenshtein distance to generate suggestions for misspelled words. We created novel linguistic resources for Wolof, such as a lexicon and a corpus of misspelled words, using a semi-automatic approach that combines manual and automatic annotation methods. Despite the limited data available for the Wolof language, the spell checker's performance showed a predictive accuracy of 98.31% and a suggestion accuracy of 93.33%.

Our primary focus remains the revitalization and preservation of Wolof as an Indigenous and spoken language in Africa, providing our efforts to develop novel linguistic resources. This work represents a valuable contribution to the growth of computational tools and resources for the Wolof language and provides a strong foundation for future studies in the automatic spell checking and correction field.

1 Introduction

Linguistic diversity in Natural Language Processing (NLP) is essential to enable communication between different users and thus the development of linguistic tools that will serve the inclusion of diverse communities. Several research studies for low-resource languages have emerged; however spoken Indigenous and Endangered languages in Africa have been neglected, even though the cultural and linguistic richness they contain is inestimable.

The Wolof language, a popular language in west Africa spoken by almost 10 million individuals worldwide, is an immensely popular lingua franca in countries on the African continent, such as Senegal, Gambia and Mauritania. It serves as the primary dialect of Senegal (Diouf et al., 2017), hailing from the Senegambian branch of Niger-Congo's expansive language family. Furthermore, the language has been officially acknowledged in West Africa (Eberhard et al., 2019). It is therefore not surprising that the intensive use of Wolof within the region has allowed it to be recognized as being of paramount importance.

Like several Indigenous and spoken languages of Africa, Wolof presents many challenges and issues, among which is the lack of linguistic resources and tools. Moreover, it is distinguished by its distinct tonal system which uses nasal vowels. The Wolof script is comprised of a total of 45 consonant phonemes, which are further subdivided into categories (Cissé, 2004). Table 1 illustrates the various Wolof consonants and their respective classifications.

Consonants		
Weak	Strong	
	Geminate	Prenazalized
p, t, c, k, q, b, d, j, g, m, n, ñ, ŋ, f, r, s, x, w, l, y	pp, tt, cc, kk, bb, dd, jj, gg, ŋŋ, ww, ll, mm, nn, yy, ññ, qq	mp, nt, nc, nk, nq, mb, nd, nj, ng

Table 1: Wolof Consonants and Classifications

Furthermore, the Wolof writing system integrates a set of 17 vowel phonemes (Cissé, 2004) complementing the already existing 45 consonant phonemes. Table 2 provides an overview of the Wolof vowels and their respective classifications.

As writing becomes increasingly important due to our digital age, automatic spell checking plays a vital role in making sure written communications are both efficient and accurate. Despite the lack of standardization in their orthography, there has

Proceedings of the Fourth workshop on Resources for African Indigenous Languages (RAIL 2023), pages 1–10
May 6, 2023 ©2023 Association for Computational Linguistics

Vowels	
Short	**Long**
a, à, ã, i, o, ó, u, e, ë, é	ii, uu, éé, óó, ee, oo, aa

Table 2: Wolof Vowels and Classifications

been a surge of interest to develop spell checkers for African Indigenous languages due to their growing importance in education, commerce, and diplomacy. Consequently, the development of spell checkers for these languages is slowly increasing.

Our main contribution in this paper, is the development of new resources for the Wolof language. Specifically, we have created a spell checker for the autocorrection of Wolof text, as well as a corpus of misspelled words that will enable researchers to evaluate the performance of future autocorrection systems. Additionally, we have developed a Wolof lexicon that can be leveraged for a range of tasks beyond autocorrection, such as neural machine translation, automatic speech recognition, etc.
The resources that have been developed over the course of this study are made publicly accessible on GitHub[1], thereby enabling wider dissemination and facilitating the reproducibility of the research findings.

The remainder of our paper is structured as follows: in Section 2, we conduct a brief literature review and discuss some published studies. In Section 3, we describe our proposed methodology and the novel linguistic resources, we developped. In Section 4, we present results and evaluations of our study. In Section 5, we show the limitations of our system through an error analysis. Finally, section 6 concludes the paper and show some promising perspectives for the future.

2 Background

Spelling correction consists in suggesting valid words closer to a wrong one. In order to create an automatic spelling correction system, it is imperative to comprehend the root causes of spelling errors (Baba and Suzuki, 2012).
Several studies about spelling errors have been done, with a notable contribution from (Mitton, 1996) who thoroughly analyzed different types of spelling mistakes for English and described methods to construct an automatic spelling correction system. (Kukich, 1992), on the other hand, presented a survey on documented findings on spelling error patterns and categorized spelling errors into two groups:

- Lexical errors: Result of mistakes applied to individual words, regardless of their context within a sentence (Ten Hacken and Tschichold, 2001).

- Grammatical errors: Include both morphological and syntactical errors. Morphological errors involve deficiencies in linguistic elements such as derivation, inflection, prepositions, articles, personal pronouns, auxiliary verbs, and determiners. Syntactical errors result from issues in linguistic components, including passive voice, tense, noun phrases, auxiliary verbs, subject-verb agreement, and determiners (Gayo and Widodo, 2018).

The causes of spelling errors are diverse and can stem from both cognitive and typographical sources (Peterson, 1980). Cognitive errors arise when an individual lacks the proper understanding of the correct spelling of a word while typographical errors take place when incorrect keystrokes are made when typing. Literature in the field of spelling correction has typically approached these error types separately, with various techniques developed specifically to address each type (Kukich, 1992).
Despite the significance of language processing, there has been a shortfall of focus on the creation of automatic spelling correction tools for low resource languages especially. While some attempts have been made to apply standard automatic spelling correction techniques to a few African indigenous languages (Boago Okgetheng et al., 2022; M'eric, 2014; Salifou and Naroua, 2014), no such efforts have been made for the Wolof language. As far as we are aware, the only research solely dedicated to the correction of Wolof is (Lo et al., 2016), which provides an overview of the state of the art and outlines potential solutions for developing a tailored orthographic corrector for Wolof. This research adopts commonly used approaches in the field and assesses the performance of our system using various known evaluation metrics.

3 Methodology

The system outlined in this study aims to identify and correct non-word errors in Wolof language.

[1]https://github.com/TiDev00/Wolof_SpellChecker

To achieve this objective, we designed and implemented the flowchart in Figure 1.

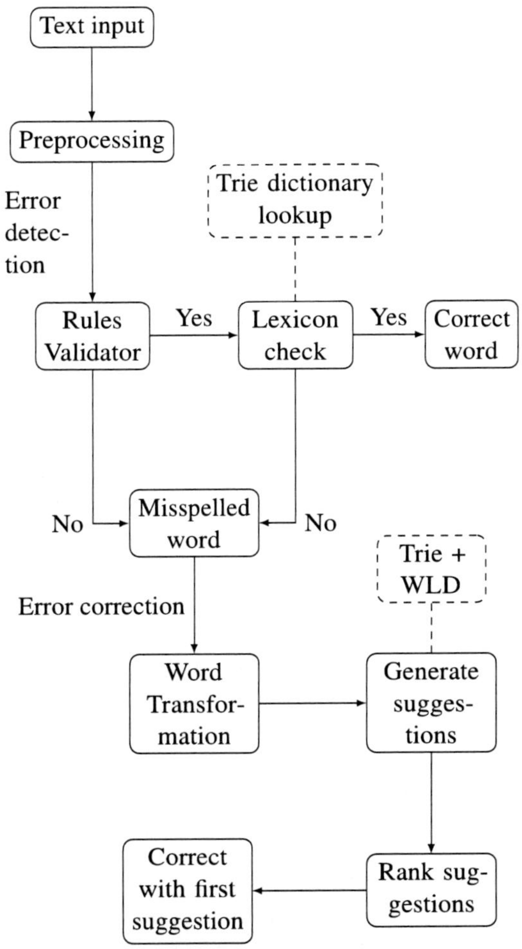

Figure 1: Flowchart of the spell checker

The flowchart in Figure 1 provides a visual representation of the various components and processes involved in the proposed spell checker system. The system includes input and output mechanisms, algorithms for error detection and correction, as well as data structures and models that aid in its functionality. The aim of the system is to accurately identify and rectify non-word errors in the Wolof language. Through the presentation of the system's overall architecture, the reader will be able to comprehend the workings of the system and its design principles aimed at detecting and correcting invalid words in the Wolof language.

3.1 Wolof Lexicon Generation

Our approach to generating a reliable Wolof lexicon involves the combination of manual annotation and automatic extraction methods.

First, manual annotation was performed on a corpus of Wolof text (James Cross et al., 2022) to identify unique words and extract them into a list. This methodology provides a thorough examination of the Wolof language and ensures the precision of the lexicon by enabling manual control over the inclusion of words.

Second, an automatic extraction was performed using Optical Character Recognition (OCR) methods and implemented in the form of Python scripts, applied to several Wolof-French dictionaries (Fal et al., 1990 and Diouf and Kenkyūjo, 2001). This methodology facilitates the expansion of the lexicon's coverage and enables the identification of additional words that may not have been captured through the manual annotation alone.

Finally, to ensure the lexicon's accuracy, the overall resulting data underwent proofreading. This step validated the correctness of the words and their spellings and allowed for any necessary revisions before the final lexicon was generated.

It is important to note that due to the limited availability of Wolof resources, the resulting lexicon only contains 1410 different words. Despite this constraint, the combination of manual annotation and automatic extraction methods allowed the generation of a reliable Wolof lexicon.

3.2 Preprocessing

Our spell checking system implements a preliminary stage, which entails the removal of inputs that contain numerical characters, punctuation marks, or borrowed words from foreign languages. The outcome of this step serves as the basis for the detection of non-word errors in the text.

The preprocessing phase consists of three primary operations: the elimination of punctuation marks, normalization of the input, and segmentation of the text into individual words.

3.2.1 Punctuation Removal

The goal of the punctuation removal in our preprocessing step is to eliminate any non-essential punctuation marks present in the input text. These marks can hinder the efficiency of the spell checking process and may cause confusion during the analysis of the text (Rahimi and Homayounpour, 2022). By removing these marks, we ensure that the subsequent stages of the spell checking system can process the text more effectively and efficiently. The algorithm employed in this stage scans the input text and removes all instances of punctuation marks, including commas, periods, exclamation marks, and question marks. The output of this step is a cleaned text that is free of the extraneous elements and ready for focused analysis in subsequent stages of the system.

3.2.2 Normalization

The normalization phase in our preprocessing step transforms the input text into a standardized form by converting all alphabetic characters to lowercase and removing any words outside of the Wolof language.

The conversion to lowercase is essential as many NLP techniques treat words in different cases as separate entities, and converting the text to lowercase eliminates this case sensitivity impact on the analysis (HaCohen-Kerner et al., 2020).

By removing words from foreign languages, we aim to ensure that the text being analyzed is only in the target language and minimize the effect of words that may not hold semantic significance in the context of the Wolof language. This enhances the accuracy of the analysis and reduces the likelihood of introducing errors into the results.

3.2.3 Word Tokenization

Tokenization is a critical step in the automatic spell checking process, as it segments the input text into smaller units referred to as tokens.

There is a range of techniques used for tokenization that vary depending on the language and task at hand. These may include splitting on whitespace and punctuation, using regular expressions, or utilizing dictionaries and morphological rules (Dalrymple et al., 2006).

The tokenization process results in units that can range from individual characters or words to phrases or even full sentences. However, word tokenization is the most commonly used form of segmentation in spell checking systems, as it separates the text into individual words and provides a solid foundation for the identification of spelling errors (Mosavi Miangah, 2013; Rahman et al., 2021; Abdulrahman and Hassani, 2022).

Word tokenization not only enhances the accuracy and efficiency of the spell checking process but also allows for an analysis of the context in which each word appears. This enables the spell checking system to make more informed suggestions for appropriate spelling corrections, ultimately improving the accuracy of the results.

In the current investigation, we are implementing the process of tokenization with a focus on word-level segmentation.

3.3 Error Detection

The error detection stage in our spell checking system is designed to identify non-word errors in the text. This is achieved through a two-step process, consisting of validation against Wolof writing rules and comparison with a constructed lexicon.

3.3.1 Rules Validator

The spelling of words in the Wolof language follows certain conventions, as described by the CVC and CVCV(C) forms for monosyllabic and disyllabic words, respectively (Merrill, 2021). These conventions specify that the final consonant and vowel of a syllable cannot both be long, and strong consonants cannot appear after a long vowel or at the beginning of a word, except for prenasalized consonants.

Our error detection stage includes a validation step that rigorously checks each word in the input text against these writing conventions. If a word is found to be in compliance with these rules, it will move on to the next stage of validation. Conversely, if the word is determined to be non-compliant, it will be flagged as invalid and require correction.

3.3.2 Lexicon Check

In the lexicon verification phase, the spell checking system assesses each word in the input text against the Wolof lexicon to determine its validity. The lexicon, being a large repository of words, can pose challenges for quick and efficient searches. To address this, various techniques such as hash tables (Kukich, 1992), binary search (Knuth, 1998), tries data structure (Bentley and Sedgewick, 1997), and bloom filter (Bloom, 1970) have been developed to enable fast dictionary lookups.

In the present spell checker, the system uses the trie data structure, which organizes the lexicon into nodes that represent individual characters and the root node that represents the empty string. In this structure, searching for a word in the lexicon involves following the path through the trie that corresponds to the characters of the target word (Feng et al., 2012). If the end of the path is a terminal node, the word is considered to be in the lexicon and deemed valid. Conversely, if the path ends before reaching a terminal node, the word is considered incorrect and corrections are initiated.

3.4 Error Correction

The last stage of the spell correction procedure is to produce potential replacements for the incorrectly spelled word. Our correction techniques, described below, focus exclusively on the word and do not consider the context in which it appears. The correction process is comprised of three distinct phases: Translation of French Compound Sounds, Generation of Candidate Suggestions, and Ranking of those Suggestions.

3.4.1 Translation of French compound sounds

Prior to implementing the module responsible for translating French compound sounds into Wolof, we collected a small amount of Wolof data from various sources. This data was sourced from news websites[2], social media platforms[3] and religious websites[4]. A thorough analysis of this data was carried out to determine the most common misspellings made by Wolof speakers when writing in the language. Our findings indicated that a significant number of these errors were due to the usage of the French alphabet instead of the Wolof alphabet. This often resulted in the presence of French compound sounds or letters that are not native to the Wolof language. Furthermore, it was observed that accents, which play a crucial role in ensuring proper pronunciation and meaning of words, were frequently neglected. To showcase these findings, Table 3 presents some of the misspellings observed and their correct Wolof equivalent.

Misspellings	Correct Wolof
dadialé	dajale (to gather)
guinaw	ginnaaw (behind)
mousiba	musiba (danger)
deuk	dëkk (village)
thiossane	cosaan (tradition)
gnopati	ñoppati (to pinch)
niaar	ñaar (two)
sakhar	saxaar (train)
tank	tànk (foot)

Table 3: Misspellings and correct wolof words

Taking into consideration the common errors observed in the analysis of Wolof language data, our system is designed to assess each word for the presence of French compound sounds or letters that are extraneous to the Wolof alphabet. Should such sounds be detected, the module will translate them into their corresponding Wolof counterparts. Letters not belonging to the Wolof alphabet will be systematically eliminated. Upon completing these transformations, the output will be directed to the next phase of the correction process and candidate suggestions module.

[2]https://www.wolof-online.com/

[3]https://twitter.com/SaabalN

[4]http://biblewolof.com/

3.4.2 Generation of Candidate Suggestions

In the current system, to generate potential alternatives for misspelled words, we have implemented a lexicographical distance comparison method. This process involves determining the minimum number of edit operations, such as insertion, deletion, transposition, and substitution, necessary to change one word into another (Vienney, 2004). The more significant the disparities between two words, the greater the lexicographical distance between them. Out of various lexicographical distance metrics, the Levenshtein Distance (Levenshtein, 1965) is the most commonly utilized. It quantifies the difference between two strings based on the three fundamental string operations: substitution, insertion, and deletion.

Let $Lev_{\alpha,\beta}$ be the Levenshtein distance between the subsequence formed with the α first characters of a word W_1 and the subsequence formed with the β first characters of a word W_2. The Levenshtein distance between the two subsequences W_1 and W_2 (of length $|W_1|$ and $|W_2|$ respectively) can be recursively calculated using Formula 1 (Levenshtein, 1965).

$$Lev_{\alpha,\beta} = \begin{cases} \max(\alpha,\beta) & \textbf{if } \min(\alpha,\beta) = 0 \\ \min \begin{cases} lev_{\alpha-1,\beta} + 1 \\ lev_{\alpha,\beta-1} + 1 \\ lev_{\alpha-1,\beta-1} + 1_{(W_{1\alpha} \neq W_{2\beta})} \end{cases} \end{cases} \quad (1)$$

The Levenshtein distance, computed using its recursive equation, can be computationally expensive (Gusfield, 1997), especially for large distances as it has an exponential time complexity of $O(3^{min(|W_1|,|W_2|)})$. To address this issue, our approach combines two techniques: dynamic programming and the trie data structure.

Dynamic programming (Almudevar, 2001), as a technique for solving problems by decomposing them into more manageable subproblems and storing the solutions, helps reduce the number of redundant calculations by providing a more efficient storage of intermediate results. When applied to the Levenshtein distance, it allows for the intermediate results of partial computations to be stored in a matrix, leading to a more efficient calculation of the final result.

By combining dynamic programming and the trie data structure, our approach effectively prunes the search space and avoids redundant calculations. This provides a powerful combination for computing the Levenshtein distance in a fast and efficient manner, even for large inputs.

In the standard Levenshtein distance, all edit operations are assigned a uniform cost of 1. However, considering the findings discussed earlier, a cost matrix was introduced to allow for the assignment of varying costs to different edit operations. This allows for a more nuanced representation of the importance of each operation. The cost for insertions and deletions remains at 1 for all characters. Substitution operations between source and target characters are assigned a cost of 1 if the character couple is listed in Table 4, otherwise, a cost of 2 is assigned.

Couple	Substitution cost
('a', 'à')	1
('a', 'ã')	1
('o', 'ó')	1
('e', 'é')	1
('e', 'ë')	1
('é', 'ë')	1
('x', 'q')	1

Table 4: Substitution cost of specific couples

Our suggestion module generates potential candidate words for a given misspelled word through the computation of the edit distance between the misspelled word and each valid word in the Wolof lexicon. For each candidate word, the cost of transforming the misspelled word into the candidate word is provided.

3.4.3 Ranking of candidate suggestions

In the following phase of our methodology, the candidate words generated from the previous stage are subjected to evaluation. The ranking is performed based on the proximity of the candidate words to the misspelled word, with the candidate word having the smallest edit cost being assigned the highest rank. The candidate word with the lowest edit cost is determined to be the closest match and is therefore selected as the most likely substitution for the incorrect word.

4 Evaluations

In order to assess the performance of our spell checking system, we first constructed a corpus of misspelled words, then selected the appropriate evaluation metrics, and finally, we implemented the chosen metrics to assess the performance of the system.

4.1 Generation of a Misspelled Word Corpus

The creation of a Misspelled Word Corpus followed a similar method as the generation of the Wolof lexicon. We used a hybrid approach of manual and automatic annotation, followed by proofreading. The method involved the selection of commonly misspelled Wolof words discovered through social media, religious websites, and news websites. For each misspelling, we manually added its correction. This process resulted in the formation of a corpus consisting of 3070 words, with 1075 valid words and 1995 invalid words. The edit distance between the misspelled words and their corrected forms is presented in Table 5.

Edit Distance	Count	Percentage
1	400	20.05%
2	412	20.65%
3	445	22.31%
4	281	14.09%
5	204	10.23%
6	114	5.71%
7	67	3.36%
8	36	1.80%
9	23	1.15%
10	9	0.45%
11	2	0.1%
12	1	0.05%
13	1	0.05%
Total	1995	100%

Table 5: Edit distance of misspellings against their corrections

4.2 Selection of the Evaluation Metrics

There are various factors to consider in evaluating spelling checkers. Conventional metrics, including recall and precision, have been widely used for a considerable time to gauge the linguistic proficiency of such tools. nevertheless, from a usage-centered approach, these evaluation parameters have limitations due to the absence of certain variables intrinsic to the evaluation of spelling checkers in these metrics.

To determine the reliability of our spell checker, we employed the metrics proposed in (Starlander and Popescu-Belis, 2002), (Voorhees and Garofolo, 2000), (Paggio and Music, 1998), (Paggio and Underwood, 1998), (King, 1999) as well as the following measures:

- True positive (TP): correct word which is recognized as correct by the spell checker.
- False positive (FP): incorrect word which is recognized as correct by the spell checker.
- False negative (FN): correct word which is recognized as incorrect by the spell checker.
- True negative (TN): incorrect word which is recognized as incorrect by the spell checker.

Despite their age, these metrics remain widely used in the current state of the art for evaluating spell checkers, particularly those designed for low-resource languages such as (Abdulrahman and Hassani, 2022) and (Boago Okgetheng et al., 2022).

The other used metrics in these evlautions, are described as follows:

4.2.1 Lexical Recall or R_c

It is determined by calculating the ratio of correctly recognized valid words in the text by the spell checker, to the total number of accurate words in the same text, as shown in Formula 2 (Starlander and Popescu-Belis, 2002).

$$R_c = \frac{T_p}{T_p + F_n} \quad (2)$$

4.2.2 Error Recall or R_i

It is expressed as the fraction of incorrect words in the text detected by the spell checker, compared to the overall number of incorrect words in the text, as shown in Formula 3 (Starlander and Popescu-Belis, 2002).

$$R_i = \frac{T_n}{T_n + F_p} \quad (3)$$

4.2.3 Lexical Precision or P_c

It is calculated by dividing the total number of valid words accurately recognized by the spelling checker by the sum of valid words recognized by the spell checker and the quantity of invalid words that were not identified by the spell checker as incorrect, as shown in Formula 4 (Starlander and Popescu-Belis, 2002).

$$P_c = \frac{T_p}{T_p + F_p} \quad (4)$$

4.2.4 Error Precision or P_i

It is determined by dividing the number of accurate flags made by the spell checker by the total number of flags issued by the system, as shown in Formula 5 (Starlander and Popescu-Belis, 2002).

$$P_i = \frac{T_n}{T_n + F_n} \quad (5)$$

4.2.5 Lexical F-measure or Fm_c

It enables the calculation of the harmonic mean between lexical recall and lexical precision, as shown in Formula 6 (Starlander and Popescu-Belis, 2002).

$$Fm_c = \frac{2}{\frac{1}{R_c} + \frac{1}{P_c}} \quad (6)$$

4.2.6 Error F-measure or Fm_i

The Error F-measure is calculated by computing the harmonic mean of lexical recall and lexical precision, as shown in Formula 7 (Starlander and Popescu-Belis, 2002).

$$Fm_i = \frac{2}{\frac{1}{R_i} + \frac{1}{P_i}} \quad (7)$$

4.2.7 Predictive Accuracy or PA

It quantifies the probability of any word, whether correct or incorrect, being processed correctly by the spelling checker. It is calculated using Formula 8 (Starlander and Popescu-Belis, 2002).

$$PA = \frac{T_p + T_n}{T_p + T_n + F_p + F_n} \quad (8)$$

4.2.8 Suggestion Adequacy or SA

It measures the ability of our spell checker to suggest accurate spelling alternatives for a misspelled word. Let S denote a proper recommendation for an incorrect word and N represent the total number of misspelled words. The Suggestion Adequacy of our system is calculated using Formula 9 (Starlander and Popescu-Belis, 2002).

$$SA = \frac{1}{N} \sum_{i=1}^{n} S_i \quad (9)$$

4.2.9 Mean Reciprocal Rank or MRR

As previously stated, our spell checker systematically selects the first word in the list of recommendations as the most likely substitution for the misspelled word. However, as selecting the initial option in the recommended list may not always be the appropriate choice, we will utilize the MRR metric to assess the ranking methodology. Let N be the total number of incorrect words and $Rank_{i,c}$ be the position of the correct suggestion in the list of suggestion for the ith misspelled word in N. The MRR is computed using the Formula 10 (Voorhees and Garofolo, 2000).

$$MRR = \frac{1}{N}\sum_{i=1}^{N}\frac{1}{Rank_{i,c}} \quad (10)$$

4.3 Experiments

4.3.1 Results

The results of our spell checker, as demonstrated in Table 6, exhibit a remarkable level of proficiency in various aspects of spelling correction.

Metrics	Ratio	Percentage
R_c	1023/1075	95.16%
R_i	1995/1995	100%
P_c	1023/1023	100%
P_i	1995/2047	97.46%
Fm_c	0.9752	97.52%
Fm_i	0.9871	98.71%
PA	3018/3070	98.31%
SA	1862/1995	93.33%
MRR	0.9604	96.04%

Table 6: Performance measures of the spell checker

The recall score of 95.16% (R_c) and 100% (R_i) depicts the comprehensive nature of the lexicon utilized by the spell checker, as well as its relatively unspoiled status.

The spell checker exhibits an exceptional level of precision, with a score of 100% (P_c) and 97.46% (P_i), indicating its reliability in accurately identifying spelling errors as well as valid words.

The F-measure scores of 97.52% (Fm_c) and 98.71% (Fm_i) demonstrate the spell checker's avoidance of simplistic strategies, thereby ensuring its efficiency.

The spell checker's suggestion accuracy (SA) score of 93.33% attests to the suitability and veracity of the most probable alternative to the misspelled word presented to the end-user.

The mean reciprocal rank (MRR) score of 96.04% highlights the quality of the ranking of suggestions presented by the spell checker.

Finally, the overall linguistic performance of the spell checker, as indicated by its predictive accuracy (PA) score of 98.31%, is of a highly satisfactory nature.

4.3.2 Errors analysis

To fully understand and identify the linguistic limitations of our spell checker, we conducted an investigation into the edit distances of the misspelled words for which the system produced an incorrect suggestion. The outcome of this study is presented in Table 7.

Edit Distance	Count	Percentage
1	4	3.01%
2	17	12.78%
3	32	24.06%
4	20	15.04%
5	22	16.54%
6	13	9.77%
7	10	7.52%
8	11	8.27%
9	3	2.26%
10	1	0.75%
Total	133	100%

Table 7: Edit distance of misspellings with wrong suggestions

After a thorough examination of the results displayed, we surprisingly noted that there was no significant linear correlation between the edit distance of a misspelled word and the probability of the spell checker generating incorrect suggestions. These findings are in line with those displayed in Table 5. The majority of words in our misspelled word corpus had an edit distance of 3, which increased the likelihood of the spell checker producing a wrong suggestion for misspelled words with an edit distance of 3. Additionally, as misspelled words with edit distances of 11, 12, and 13 were under-represented in our corpus, the spell checker's suggestions for these words were all accurate. This reinforces our conclusion that the higher the frequency of misspelled words with a specific edit distance, the greater the chances of the spell checker generating inaccurate suggestions for misspelled words with that same edit distance.

5 Limitations

Despite the impressive performance and minimal processing time of our spell checker, it is important to acknowledge its limitations.
Firstly, the spell checker is restricted to the words included in the created Wolof lexicon and cannot recognize words outside of it. Secondly, the weighted Levenshtein distance algorithm used may not always accurately reflect the likelihood of different types of errors, leading to potential inaccuracies in the suggestions.
Thirdly, the dynamic programming and trie data structures utilized may result in false positive suggestions due to a lack of consideration for the semantic meaning of words. Additionally, the computational cost of our approach can be substantial, particularly for larger lexicons or words with numerous possible corrections. Finally, the lack of context awareness may result in missed errors or incorrect suggestions.

6 Conclusion

This paper presented a novel spell checker for the Wolof language, that has demonstrated its potential, owing to its effective combination of the trie data structure, dynamic programming, and weighted Levenshtein distance algorithms. The hybrid approach of manual and automatic annotation enabled the construction of a comprehensive lexicon and a robust Misspelled Word Corpus, allowing for a robust evaluation of the spell checker's potential despite the limited data available for the language. Through these efforts, we hope to advance the state of NLP research for the Wolof language and contribute to preserving the linguistic heritage of African nations, ensuring that their distinct cultural expressions are protected for future generations.
The findings of this research provide compelling evidence of the viability of the spell checker for the Wolof language, opening avenues for further improvement and exploration.

For future research, it would be of interest to study the effect of increasing the lexicon and Misspelled Word Corpus on the spell checker's performance. Furthermore, a comparison of the spell checker's performance with other spell-checking methods used in low-resource languages, such as the Indigenous African languages, could provide valuable insights into the strengths and weaknesses of the current approach. The integration of state-of-the-art techniques,taking into consideration the context, such as those based on machine learning and Deep Neural Networks, into the spell checker could also be explored to further enhance its capabilities.

Acknowledgements

We thank the anonymous reviewers for their helpful comments and feedback.
We also thank the participants of the Wolof community for giving their time, wisdom, and expertise.

References

Roshna Omer Abdulrahman and Hossein Hassani. 2022. A language model for spell checking of educational texts in kurdish (sorani). 1st Annual Meeting of the ELRA/ISCA Special Interest Group on Under-Resourced Languages, SIGUL 2022 - Held in Conjunction with the International Conference on Language Resources and Evaluation, LREC 2022 - Proceedings, pages 189–198.

Anthony Almudevar. 2001. A dynamic programming algorithm for the optimal control of piecewise deterministic markov processes. *SIAM Journal on Control and Optimization*, 40(2):525–539.

Yukino Baba and Hisami Suzuki. 2012. How are spelling errors generated and corrected? A study of corrected and uncorrected spelling errors using keystroke logs. In *Proceedings of the 50th Annual Meeting of the Association for Computational Linguistics (Volume 2: Short Papers)*, pages 373–377, Jeju Island, Korea. Association for Computational Linguistics.

Jon L. Bentley and Robert Sedgewick. 1997. Fast algorithms for sorting and searching strings. Proceedings of the Annual ACM-SIAM Symposium on Discrete Algorithms, pages 360–369.

Burton H. Bloom. 1970. Space/Time trade-offs in hash coding with allowable errors. *Communications of the ACM*, 13(7):422–426.

Boago Okgetheng, G. Malema, Ariq Ahmer, Boemo Lenyibi, and Ontiretse Ishmael. 2022. Bantu Spell Checker and Corrector using Modified Edit Distance Algorithm (MEDA). *Data Science and Machine Learning*.

Mamadou Cissé. 2004. *Dictionnaire Francais-Wolof*, 2.éd. révisée et augmentée edition. Dictionnaires des Langues O. Langues et MOndes, L'Asiatheque, Paris.

Mary Dalrymple, Maria Liakata, and Lisa Mackie. 2006. Tokenization and morphological analysis for Malagasy. In *International Journal of Computational Linguistics & Chinese Language Processing, Volume 11, Number 4, December 2006*, pages 315–332.

Ibrahima Diouf, Cheikh Tidiane Ndiaye, and Ndèye Binta Dieme. 2017. Dynamique et transmission linguistique au Sénégal au cours des 25 dernières années. *Cahiers québécois de démographie*, 46(2):197–217.

Jean Léopold Diouf and Tōkyō Gaikokugo Daigaku. Ajia Afurika Gengo Bunka Kenkyūjo. 2001. *Dictionnaire wolof : wolof-français, français-wolof.* 39. Institute for the Study of Languages and Cultures of Asia and Africa (ILCAA), Tokyo University of Foreign Studies, Tokyo.

David Eberhard, Gary Simons, and Chuck Fennig. 2019. *Ethnologue: Languages of the World*, 22nd edition edition. SIL International, Dallas, Texas.

A. Fal, R. Santos, and J.L. Doneux. 1990. *Dictionnaire Wolof-Français: Suivi d'un Index Français-Wolof*. Karthala, 22-24, boulevard Arago, 75013 Paris.

Jianhua Feng, Jiannan Wang, and Guoliang Li. 2012. Trie-join: A trie-based method for efficient string similarity joins. *The VLDB Journal*, 21(4):437–461.

Hendri Gayo and Pratomo Widodo. 2018. An Analysis of Morphological and Syntactical Errors on the English Writing of Junior High School Indonesian Students. *International Journal of Learning, Teaching and Educational Research*, 17(4):58–70.

Dan Gusfield. 1997. Algorithms on strings, trees, and sequences: Computer science and computational biology. *SIGACT News*, 28(4):41–60.

Yaakov HaCohen-Kerner, Daniel Miller, and Yair Yigal. 2020. The influence of preprocessing on text classification using a bag-of-words representation. *PloS one*, 15(5):e0232525.

James Cross, Maha Elbayad, and Kenneth Heafield. 2022. No language left behind: Scaling human-centered machine translation.

M King. 1999. Evaluation design: The EAGLES framework. In *Proceedings of the Konvens '98: Evaluation of the Linguistic Performance of Machine Translation Systems*, Bonn, Germany. Rita Nübel, Uta Seewald-Heeg, Gardezi Verlag, St. Augustin.

Donald Knuth. 1998. *Art of computer programming, the: Volume 3: Sorting and searching*, 2nd edition. edition. Addison-Wesley Professional.

Karen Kukich. 1992. Techniques for automatically correcting words in text. *Acm Computing Surveys*, 24(4):377–439.

Vladimir I. Levenshtein. 1965. Binary codes capable of correcting deletions, insertions, and reversals. *Soviet physics. Doklady*, 10:707–710.

Alla Lo, Cheikh Bamba Dione, Mathieu Mangeot, Mouhamadou Khoule, Sokhna Bao-Diop, Mame-Thierno Cissé, et al. 2016. Correction orthographique pour la langue wolof: état de l'art et perspectives. In *JEP-TALN-RECITAL 2016: Traitement Automatique Des Langues Africaines TALAF 2016*.

Jean-Jacques M'eric. 2014. A spell-checker and thesaurus for Bambara (Bamanankan) (Un v'erificateur orthographique pour la langue bambara) [in French]. *TALAf@TALN*, pages 141–146.

John T. M. Merrill. 2021. The evolution of consonant mutation and noun class marking in Wolof. *Diachronica*, 38(1):64–110.

Roger Mitton. 1996. *English Spelling and the Computer*. Studies in Language and Linguistics. Longman, London ; New York.

Tayebeh Mosavi Miangah. 2013. FarsiSpell: A spell-checking system for Persian using a large monolingual corpus. *Literary and Linguistic Computing*, 29(1):56–73.

Patrizia Paggio and Bradley Music. 1998. Evaluation in the SCARRIE project. *International Conference on Language Resources and Evaluation, Granada, Spain*, pages 277–282.

Patrizia Paggio and Nancy L. Underwood. 1998. Validating the TEMAA LE evaluation methodology: A case study on Danish spelling checkers. *Natural Language Engineering*, 4(3):211–228.

James L. Peterson. 1980. Computer programs for detecting and correcting spelling errors. *Communications of The Acm*, 23(12):676–687.

Zahra Rahimi and Mohammad Mehdi Homayounpour. 2022. The impact of preprocessing on word embedding quality: A comparative study. *Language Resources and Evaluation*.

Md. Mijanur Rahman, Hasan Mahmud, Razia Sultana Rupa, and Mahnuma Rahman Rinty. 2021. A robust bangla spell checker for search engine. In *2021 6th International Conference on Communication and Electronics Systems (ICCES)*, pages 1329–1334.

Lawaly Salifou and Harouna Naroua. 2014. Design and Implementation of a Spell Checker for Hausa Language ('Etude et conception d'un correcteur orthographique pour la langue haoussa) [in French]. *TALAf@TALN*, pages 147–158.

Marianne Starlander and Andrei Popescu-Belis. 2002. Corpus-based evaluation of a French spelling and grammar checker. Proceedings of the 3rd International Conference on Language Resources and Evaluation, LREC 2002, pages 268–274.

Pius Ten Hacken and Cornelia Tschichold. 2001. Word Manager and CALL: Structured access to the lexicon as a tool for enriching learners' vocabulary. *ReCALL*, 13(1):121–131.

S. Vienney. 2004. *Correction Automatique : Bilan et Perspectives*. Presses universitaires de Franche-Comté.

Ellen Voorhees and John Garofolo. 2000. The TREC Spoken Document Retrieval Track. *Bulletin of the American Society for Information Science and Technology*, 26(5):18–19.

Unsupervised Cross-lingual Word Embedding Representation for English-isiZulu

Derwin Ngomane[1], Vukosi Marivate[1,2,3], Jade Abbott[2,3], Rooweither Mabuya[3,4]
[1]Department of Computer Science, University of Pretoria;
[2]Lelapa AI; [3]Masakhane NLP;
[4]South African Centre for Digital Language Resources, North-West University
derwin.ngomane@gmail.com, vukosi.marivate@cs.up.ac.za,
jade.abbott@lelapa.ai, roo.mabuya@nwu.ac.za

Abstract

In this study, we investigate the effectiveness of using cross-lingual word embeddings for zero-shot transfer learning between a language with an abundant resource, English, and a language with limited resource, isiZulu. IsiZulu is a part of the South African Nguni language family, which is characterised by complex agglutinating morphology. We use VecMap, an open source tool, to obtain cross-lingual word embeddings. To perform an extrinsic evaluation of the effectiveness of the embeddings, we train a news classifier on labelled English data in order to categorise unlabelled isiZulu data using zero-shot transfer learning. In our study, we found our model to have a weighted average F1-score of 0.34. Our findings demonstrate that VecMap generates modular word embeddings in the cross-lingual space that have an impact on the downstream classifier used for zero-shot transfer learning.

1 Introduction

In the development of egalitarian Natural Language Processing (NLP) systems, cross-lingual word embeddings are gaining prominence. According to distributional theory, words that appear in comparable contexts have semantic commonalities (Villegas et al., 2016). As a result, word embeddings have paved the way for NLP technology advancement.

The use of word embedding representation has provided satisfactory performance for many NLP applications and associated applications (Gutiérrez and Keith, 2018). Word embeddings have been used for feature engineering (Tang et al., 2014) and transfer learning purposes (Bataa and Wu, 2019). Translation models, sentiment analysis tasks and classification tasks have all benefited. These improvements have been primarily in high-resource languages, such as English, due to the abundance of labelled corpora in these languages. The lack of labelled corpora in low-resourced languages has come at a disadvantage in advancing NLP technologies within this space.

Many news publications in South Africa are in English even though South Africa has eleven official languages (Marivate et al., 2020). According to the Statistics South Africa (Stats SA) Census 2011 results, isiZulu was the most spoken home language with 22.7% of the population indicating it as a home language (Statistics South Africa (Stats SA), 2012). IsiZulu forms part of the many indigenous languages in South Africa, and belongs to the Nguni family of languages (Dube and Suleman, 2019). The Nguni language family is characterised by their agglutinative morphology (Keet and Khumalo, 2016).

South Africa is a multilingual nation where the large majority of the population have a secondary language that they use on top of their primary languages. Over the post-apartheid years, the country has seen a population growth of citizens that speak English as a second language. This behaviour has also become prevalent for isiZulu, where citizens have added isiZulu as a second language (Posel and Zeller, 2020). This emphasizes the importance of advancing NLP work for low-resourced languages in South Africa.

In this work we attempt to take advantage of a high-resource corpus and a low-resource corpus in order to learn cross-lingual word embeddings for English and isiZulu. The use of cross-lingual word embeddings would allow us to perform model transfer learning from a high resource language to a low-resource language. The undertaking for isiZulu is especially challenging due to the morphological complexity of the language. Hence, we have to a handle words in a manner that can maximise syntactic and semantic representation of both English and isiZulu in the cross-lingual space.

Proceedings of the Fourth workshop on Resources for African Indigenous Languages (RAIL 2023), pages 11–17
May 6, 2023 ©2023 Association for Computational Linguistics

In this work, we aim to answer the following research questions:

- Can we use monolingual word embeddings for English and isiZulu to create cross-lingual semantic embedding vectors for both languages?
- Can we use zero-shot transfer learning in the cross-lingual space to use an English news article classifier to classify isiZulu articles?

Additionally, we introduce two new datasets:

- the Umsuka English-isiZulu dataset (Mabuya et al., 2021) which is used in the creation of the cross-lingual vectors.
- An isiZulu South African news classification dataset sourced from the South African Broadcasting Corporation (SABC) data

The remainder of the work is organised as follows: Section 2 will discuss the background and prior work. Section 3 describes the methodology used for the VecMap library and zero-shot learning classifier. Section 4 discusses the experiments and results. Finally, concluding remarks and potential next steps for future research are discussed in Section 5.

2 Background & Related Work

The popular methods that have been used to represent tokens as vectors have been Bag-of-Words (BoW), Term Frequency-Inverse Document Frequency (TF-IDF) and Pointwise Mutual Information (PMI). However, these techniques create sparse and large matrices and also create vectors that do not capture semantics (Villegas et al., 2016).

Innovative advancements have led to the emergence of new techniques using neural networks. These methods include the popular Word2Vec models (Mikolov et al., 2013) and attention based models (Vaswani et al., 2017). These models have achieved state-of-the-art performance on adaption and transfer learning tasks in NLP (Devlin et al., 2018).

The disadvantage of monolingual word embeddings is that they struggle with transferring between languages that are dissimilar (Ruder et al., 2019b). Multilingual word embeddings trained on multiple languages have also shown to perform poorly for low-resource languages (Wu and Dredze, 2020). Approaches for cross-lingual representation learning have been proposed to address this issue (Ruder et al., 2019a). There are two types of cross-lingual word embedding methods: mapping and post-hoc approaches (Ruder et al., 2019a). Initial mapping approaches required the use of a bilingual mapping dictionary between the languages of study, but recent improvements have introduced adversarial methods. Adversarial approaches presume that the input monolingual spaces are isomorphic and hence reducing the requirement of a bilingual mapping dictionary (Ruder et al., 2019a). However, it has been shown that adverserial methods perform poorly when the monolingual embeddings are not isomorphic (Søgaard et al., 2018).

Downstream NLP tasks have been proven to benefit from cross-lingual word embeddings. For example, cross-lingual word embeddings have increased the performance of machine translation (Conneau and Lample, 2019) and Part-of-Speech (POS) tagging (Kim et al., 2017) tasks as a transfer learning strategy.

VecMap has been used to create a mapping between English and Welsh and the resulting embedding were used to train a zero-shot and few-shot learning Welsh sentiment classifier (Espinosa-Anke et al., 2021). In the South African context, VecMap was used to develop a Sepedi-Setswana cross-lingual word embedding and adopted a semantic assessment method to analyse the similarity between pairs of Setswana and Sepedi terms (Makgatho et al., 2021) and used in a noisy, multilingual question-answering challenge to train an LSTM classification model (Daniel et al., 2019).

Zero-shot transfer learning has not been widely used for South African news classification. Marivate et al. (2020) used an annotated corpus of local news items to create a news classifier for Setswana and Sepedi. Instead of using static word embedding as those used by VecMap, using contextual word embeddings from a fine-tuned BERT model has achieved impressive results for a zero-shot learning Named Entity Recognition (NER) task for isiZulu (Wang et al., 2020). However, this work would require significant computing and has not been applied to news classification. To our knowledge, this is the first work that uses cross-lingual word embeddings generated from VecMap to create a news article classifier from English to isiZulu.

3 Methodology

We discuss the methodology for the development of the cross-lingual word embeddings and the downstream classifier for news classification.

3.1 Data collection & Preprocessing

The data used in this study is from the South African Centre for Digital Language Resources repository. We use this data for the purposes of training our cross-lingual embedding model. The data consists only of text data for both English and isiZulu. According to the technical documentation, the monolingual English corpus [1] contains 35 686 791 tokens while the isiZulu corpus [2] contains 451 154 tokens. We will only consider the source categories that are the same between the languages.

We also use the Umsuka English-isiZulu parallel corpus (Mabuya et al., 2021) which is a open-source, high quality isiZulu parallel corpus from a mixture of domains, taking into account both Southern African and international context. Half the dataset was a random sample of the News Crawl dataset which was then translated into isiZulu. The other half of the dataset was sampled from isiZulu newspapers (Isolezwe[3], Ilanga[4] and Ezasegagasini Metro [5] publications), spanning from 2012 to 2016, as well as novels and short stories, which were then translated into English. Professional translators were used to create the dataset. An initial pilot study of 500 sentences was performed with quality assurance done by an isiZulu linguist to ensure that the quality requirements were understood.

Table 1 presents the sources used and the number of tokens. In total, we have 1 320 393 and 2 121 127 tokens for isiZulu and English respectively.

Source	isiZulu	English
Hansard	100 392	1 758 616
Hotel Websites	156 143	197 670
Information Guides	7 658	12 564
Internet	21 001	32 857
Other	82 488	5 415
Umsuka	952 711	114 005

Table 1: Tokens by Source and Language

[1]https://repo.sadilar.org/handle/20.500.12185/466

[2]https://repo.sadilar.org/handle/20.500.12185/338

[3]https://www.isolezwe.co.za

[4]https://ilanganews.co.za/

[5]https://www.durban.gov.za/pages/government/documents

We eliminate stopwords and remove punctuation in the original corpora [6]. Additionally, we perform lemmatization on the English corpus using the WordNet lemmatizer (Miller, 1995). We trained the news classifier on British Broadcasting Corporation (BBC) news data sourced from Kaggle [7]. There are 1 490 English articles for training and 736 English articles evaluation purposes. We use SABC news articles for the isiZulu evaluation. Two isiZulu speakers annotated 219 SABC news articles, which were reviewed by an isiZulu linguist [8]. Table 2 presents the distribution of the datasets.

Category	BBC English	SABC isiZulu
Sport	346	47
Business	336	25
Politics	274	111
Entertainment	273	36
Tech	261	0

Table 2: Frequency of categories

3.2 Monolingual Word Embeddings

The processed corpora that we have described in Section 3.1, are used to develop monolingual embeddings using the Python Gensim module [9]. We make use of the FastText architecture to handle the agglutinative morphology of isiZulu (Bojanowski et al., 2017).

We generate vectors of 64 dimensions for each token in the corpus with a context window size of 3. These hyperparameters were chosen because of the limited vocabulary size of our corpora, and it has been shown that a shorter context window captures the syntactic representation of the word and a larger context window captures more topical representation (Levy and Goldberg, 2014). To demonstrate the learned representation of the corpus we use Uniform Manifold Approximation and Projection (UMAP) (McInnes et al., 2018) to visualise the 10 closest words from both the monolingual corpora. The chosen tokens are "government" for English and the isiZulu translation "uhulumeni". In Figure 1, we observe that the closest tokens to "uhulumeni" are synonyms of "uhulumeni". Similarly,

[6]List of isiZulu stopwords: https://github.com/stopwords-iso/stopwords-zu

[7]https://www.kaggle.com/c/learn-ai-bbc

[8]Data available at https://github.com/dsfsi/izindaba-zesizulu and https://zenodo.org/record/5674236

[9]https://radimrehurek.com/gensim/index.html

we also observe the same for "government".

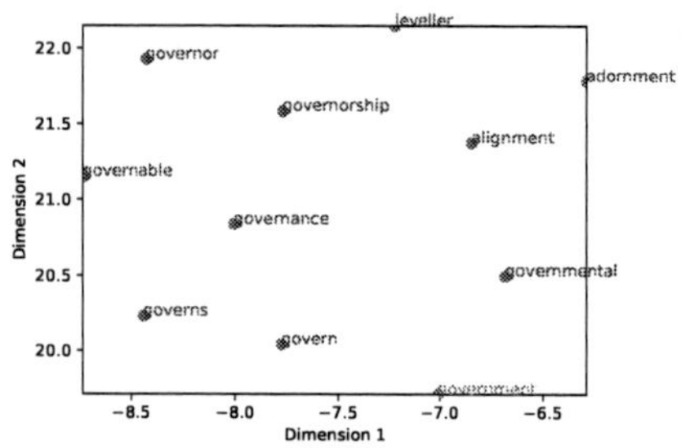

(a) Representation of "government"

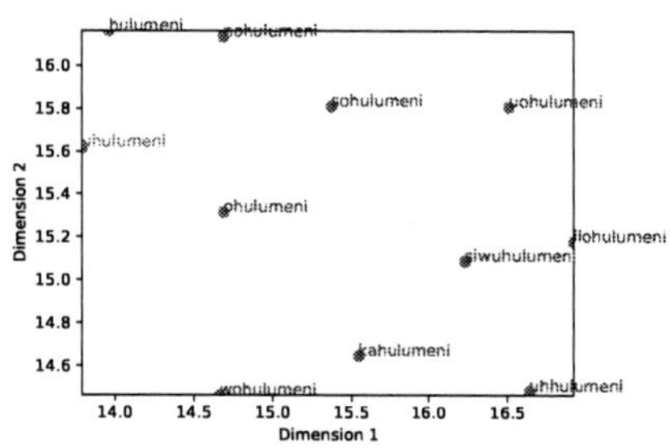

(b) Representation of "uhulumeni"

Figure 1: UMAP representation of the monolingual embeddings

3.3 News Article Classifier

The generated cross-lingual word embeddings are used to train a classifier on the English corpus. We compare four algorithms and assess their performance using cross-validation. The models we train are Naive Bayes, Support Vector Machines, Logistic Regression, and Gradient Boosted Machines. The best model is then used to classify unseen isiZulu news articles in the cross-lingual embedding space.

4 Experiments & Results

In this section of the paper we describe the experiments and outcomes conducted in an effort to answer the research questions. We describe the created cross-lingual word embeddings and the experiments undertaken to develop the news article classifier.

4.1 Cross-lingual Word Embeddings

We use the VecMap library [10] created by Artetxe et al. (2018) to generate the cross-lingual word embeddings. In VecMap, we employ the unsupervised cross-lingual learning method. The algorithm-generated UMAP representation of the 10 closest words to "government" and "uhulumeni" are depicted in Figure 2. Some of the words from the monolingual representations provided in Figure 1 were retained by VecMap. However, the algorithm developed a language-based clustering with the exception of identifying "powerfully" as being closer to isiZulu words.

Modularity is the phenomenon in which language clustering occurs in the cross-lingual space (Fujinuma et al., 2019), as depicted in Figure 2. Fujinuma et al. (2019) claim that cross-lingual embeddings that reflect modularity have a negative effect on downstream tasks.

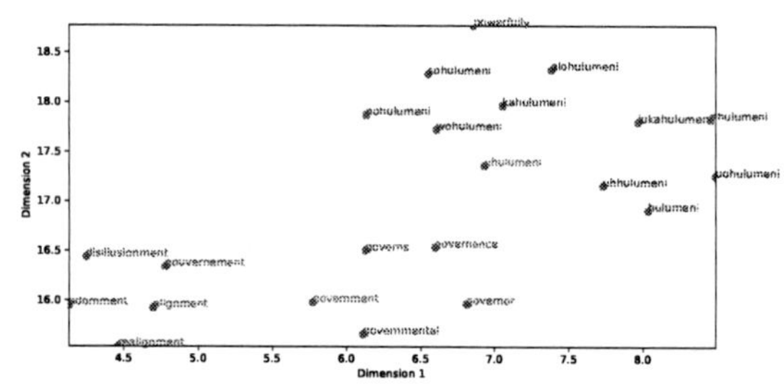

Figure 2: UMAP representation of the VecMap cross-lingual embeddings

4.2 Zero-shot transfer learning

This section presents the zero-shot transfer learning task of identifying isiZulu news headlines from an English news classifier. We initially train our model on labelled English news articles using the pre-generated cross-lingual word embeddings from the previous section.

4.2.1 Experiment Setup

The input data needs to be converted into its vector representation as per the word embeddings from VecMap. Since each token has 64 dimensions, we represent a sentence as the average of all the token vector representations. We use a 64 zero dimensional vector to represent tokens that are out of vocabulary.

We use 75% of the data for training and 25% for evaluation purposes in the English BBC data. In order to select the best model, we run a repeated 5-fold stratified cross-evaluation on the training data. Based on the cross-validation procedure, the

[10]https://github.com/artetxem/vecmap

LightGBM model outperforms all the other models.

4.2.2 Results

The LightGBM model achieves an accuracy of 76.4% on the evaluation set. The classifier achieved an above 70% accuracy for most of the classes, except for entertainment that obtained an accuracy of 68%.

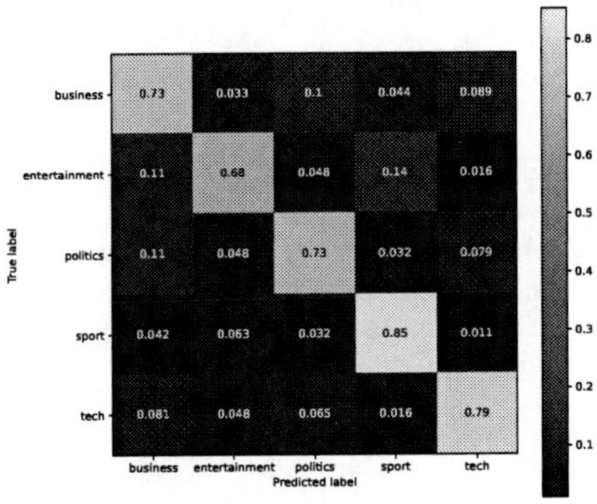

Figure 3: Confusion matrix of the evaluation set

We use the LightGBM model to classify the isiZulu news articles. The resulting performance of the model is presented in Table 3.

Category	Precision	Recall	F1-score
Business	0.07	0.04	0.05
Entertainment	0.15	0.08	0.11
Politics	0.49	0.52	0.51
Sport	0.25	0.32	0.28
Tech	0.0	0.0	0.0
weighted avg	**0.33**	**0.35**	**0.34**

Table 3: Model performance on SABC isiZulu news

The model performed unsatisfactory across all the titles. However, as depicted in Table 3 the model seems to perform better for politics related titles and getting an F1-score of 0.51. Politics contains a larger sample size in our isiZulu data. The other titles had a lower performance, which may be explained by modularity, whereby cross-lingual embeddings that cluster on language tend to perform poorly for downstream tasks (Fujinuma et al., 2019).

5 Conclusion

In this work we use VecMap to create cross-lingual word embeddings between English and isiZulu. We have shown that VecMap generates modular word embeddings in the cross-lingual space due to the monolingual word embeddings generated by FastText. Hence, we generate cross-lingual embeddings that are used to train a classifier that performs good on English news. However, we were unable to transfer the learning on unseen isiZulu news articles.

In future work, we would like to examine the performance of VecMap using a larger corpus for isiZulu. Additionally, it would also be advantageous to apply the modularity metric to optimize the hyperparameters of FastText in order to generate appropriate monolingual embeddings for the task.

Limitations

In this section of the paper we describe the limitations of the paper. We made design choices based on the corpus and the resources available for making the research possible.

The work presents a corpus that is of limited size for isiZulu. This is due to the lack of resources for the language. The other work that has attempted to build monolingual word embeddings for isiZulu is by Dlamini et al. (2021). However, the results were not published in a publicly accessible resource that would allow us to compare the embeddings generated by our work.

VecMap does not scale well without the use of a GPU, and hence hyperparameter searching was not done for this work. However, using vectors with 128 dimensions and a larger window size of 10 as suggested by Ri and Tsuruoka (2020) resulted in a performance decrease, even for the English news articles.

We also note that downstream model was trained using European news article titles and that can have an impact on the performance of identifying events that are uniquely for South African news.

Author Contributions

Derwin Ngomane: Data curation; formal analysis; investigation; methodology; writing – original draft; writing – review and editing. **Vukosi Marivate**: Conceptualization; data curation; resources; supervision; validation; writing – review and editing. **Jade Abbott**: Supervision; data curation; validation; writing – review and editing. **Rooweither Mabuya**: Supervision; data curation; writing – review and editing.

Acknowledgements

We would like to acknowledge funding from Facebook (Machine Translation Gift), the ABSA Chair of Data Science and the Google Research scholar program.

References

Mikel Artetxe, Gorka Labaka, and Eneko Agirre. 2018. A robust self-learning method for fully unsupervised cross-lingual mappings of word embeddings. In *Proceedings of the 56th Annual Meeting of the Association for Computational Linguistics (Volume 1: Long Papers)*, pages 789–798, Melbourne, Australia. Association for Computational Linguistics.

Enkhbold Bataa and Joshua Wu. 2019. An investigation of transfer learning-based sentiment analysis in japanese. *arXiv preprint arXiv:1905.09642*.

Piotr Bojanowski, Edouard Grave, Armand Joulin, and Tomas Mikolov. 2017. Enriching word vectors with subword information. *Transactions of the association for computational linguistics*, 5:135–146.

Alexis Conneau and Guillaume Lample. 2019. Cross-lingual language model pretraining. *Advances in Neural Information Processing Systems*, 32:7059–7069.

Jeanne E Daniel, Willie Brink, Ryan Eloff, and Charles Copley. 2019. Towards automating healthcare question answering in a noisy multilingual low-resource setting. In *Proceedings of the 57th Annual Meeting of the Association for Computational Linguistics*, pages 948–953.

Jacob Devlin, Ming-Wei Chang, Kenton Lee, and Kristina Toutanova. 2018. BERT: Pre-training of Deep Bidirectional Transformers for Language Understanding. *arXiv*.

Sibonelo Dlamini, Edgar Jembere, Anban Pillay, and Brett van Niekerk. 2021. isizulu word embeddings. In *2021 Conference on Information Communications Technology and Society (ICTAS)*, pages 121–126. IEEE.

Meluleki Dube and Hussein Suleman. 2019. Language identification for south african bantu languages using rank order statistics. In *International Conference on Asian Digital Libraries*, pages 283–289. Springer.

Luis Espinosa-Anke, Geraint Palmer, Padraig Corcoran, Maxim Filimonov, Irena Spasić, and Dawn Knight. 2021. English–welsh cross-lingual embeddings. *Applied Sciences*, 11(14):6541.

Yoshinari Fujinuma, Jordan Boyd-Graber, and Michael J. Paul. 2019. A resource-free evaluation metric for cross-lingual word embeddings based on graph modularity. *arXiv*.

Luis Gutiérrez and Brian Keith. 2018. A systematic literature review on word embeddings. In *International Conference on Software Process Improvement*, pages 132–141. Springer.

C. Maria Keet and Langa Khumalo. 2016. Grammar rules for the isiZulu complex verb. *arXiv*.

Joo-Kyung Kim, Young-Bum Kim, Ruhi Sarikaya, and Eric Fosler-Lussier. 2017. Cross-lingual transfer learning for pos tagging without cross-lingual resources. In *Proceedings of the 2017 conference on empirical methods in natural language processing*, pages 2832–2838.

Omer Levy and Yoav Goldberg. 2014. Dependency-based word embeddings. In *Proceedings of the 52nd Annual Meeting of the Association for Computational Linguistics (Volume 2: Short Papers)*, pages 302–308, Baltimore, Maryland. Association for Computational Linguistics.

Rooweither Mabuya, Jade Abbott, and Vukosi Marivate. 2021. Umsuka english - isizulu parallel corpus. Https://doi.org/10.5281/zenodo.5035171.

Mack Makgatho, Vukosi Marivate, Tshephisho Sefara, and Valencia Wagner. 2021. Training cross-lingual embeddings for setswana and sepedi. *arXiv preprint arXiv:2111.06230*.

Vukosi Marivate, Tshephisho Sefara, Vongani Chabalala, Keamogetswe Makhaya, Tumisho B. Mokgonyane, Rethabile Mokoena, and Abiodun Modupe. 2020. Investigating an approach for low resource language dataset creation, curation and classification: Setswana and sepedi. *arXiv*.

Leland McInnes, John Healy, Nathaniel Saul, and Lukas Grossberger. 2018. Umap: Uniform manifold approximation and projection. *The Journal of Open Source Software*, 3(29):861.

Tomas Mikolov, Ilya Sutskever, Kai Chen, Greg S Corrado, and Jeff Dean. 2013. Distributed representations of words and phrases and their compositionality. In *Advances in Neural Information Processing Systems*, volume 26. Curran Associates, Inc.

George A Miller. 1995. Wordnet: a lexical database for english. *Communications of the ACM*, 38(11):39–41.

Dorrit Posel and Jochen Zeller. 2020. *Language use and language shift in post-apartheid South Africa*, pages 288–309. Cambridge University Press Cambridge.

Ryokan Ri and Yoshimasa Tsuruoka. 2020. Revisiting the context window for cross-lingual word embeddings. In *Proceedings of the 58th Annual Meeting of the Association for Computational Linguistics*, pages 995–1005, Online. Association for Computational Linguistics.

Sebastian Ruder, Anders Søgaard, and Ivan Vulić. 2019a. Unsupervised cross-lingual representation learning. In *Proceedings of the 57th Annual Meeting of the Association for Computational Linguistics: Tutorial Abstracts*, pages 31–38, Florence, Italy. Association for Computational Linguistics.

Sebastian Ruder, Ivan Vulić, and Anders Søgaard. 2019b. A survey of cross-lingual word embedding models. *Journal of Artificial Intelligence Research*, 65:569–631.

Anders Søgaard, Sebastian Ruder, and Ivan Vulić. 2018. On the limitations of unsupervised bilingual dictionary induction. In *Proceedings of the 56th Annual Meeting of the Association for Computational Linguistics (Volume 1: Long Papers)*, pages 778–788, Melbourne, Australia. Association for Computational Linguistics.

Statistics South Africa (Stats SA). 2012. The South Africa I know, The Home I understand. https://www.statssa.gov.za/census/census_2011/census_products/NW_Municipal_Report.pdf.pdf.

Duyu Tang, Furu Wei, Nan Yang, Ming Zhou, Ting Liu, and Bing Qin. 2014. Learning sentiment-specific word embedding for Twitter sentiment classification. In *Proceedings of the 52nd Annual Meeting of the Association for Computational Linguistics (Volume 1: Long Papers)*, pages 1555–1565, Baltimore, Maryland. Association for Computational Linguistics.

Ashish Vaswani, Noam Shazeer, Niki Parmar, Jakob Uszkoreit, Llion Jones, Aidan N Gomez, Łukasz Kaiser, and Illia Polosukhin. 2017. Attention is all you need. *Advances in neural information processing systems*, 30.

María Paula Villegas, María José Garciarena Ucelay, Juan Pablo Fernández, Miguel A Álvarez Carmona, Marcelo Luis Errecalde, and Leticia Cagnina. 2016. Vector-based word representations for sentiment analysis: a comparative study. In *XXII Congreso Argentino de Ciencias de la Computación (CACIC 2016)*.

Zihan Wang, Karthikeyan K, Stephen Mayhew, and Dan Roth. 2020. Extending multilingual BERT to low-resource languages. In *Findings of the Association for Computational Linguistics: EMNLP 2020*, pages 2649–2656, Online. Association for Computational Linguistics.

Shijie Wu and Mark Dredze. 2020. Are all languages created equal in multilingual BERT? *arXiv preprint arXiv:2005.09093*.

Preparing the Vuk'uzenzele and ZA-gov-multilingual South African multilingual corpora

Richard Lastrucci[1], Isheanesu Dzingirai[1], Jenalea Rajab[2], Andani Madodonga[1], Matimba Shingange[1], Daniel Njini[1], Vukosi Marivate[1,3]
[1]Department of Computer Science, University of Pretoria
[2]School of Computer Science and Applied Mathematics, University of the Witwatersrand
[3]Lelapa AI
richard.lastrucci@tuks.co.za, ishe.dzingirai@gmail.com, jenalea.rajab@gmail.com, andanim412@gmail.com, mrosslyns@gmail.com, vukosi.marivate@cs.up.ac.za

Abstract

This paper introduces two multilingual government themed corpora in various South African languages. The corpora were collected by gathering the South African Government newspaper (Vuk'uzenzele), as well as South African government speeches (ZA-gov-multilingual), that are translated into all 11 South African official languages. The corpora can be used for a myriad of downstream NLP tasks. The corpora were created to allow researchers to study the language used in South African government publications, with a focus on understanding how South African government officials communicate with their constituents.

In this paper we highlight the process of gathering, cleaning and making available the corpora. We create parallel sentence corpora for Neural Machine Translation (NMT) tasks using Language-Agnostic Sentence Representations (LASER) embeddings. With these aligned sentences we then provide NMT benchmarks for 9 indigenous languages by fine-tuning a massively multilingual pre-trained language model.

1 Introduction

The advancement of Natural Language Processing (NLP) research in Africa is impeded due to the scarcity of data for training models for various NLP tasks (Nekoto et al., 2020) as well as availability of benchmarks and ways to reproduce them (Martinus and Abbott, 2019). For many South African languages there are still challenges finding easily available textual datasets (Marivate et al., 2020) even if there are many speakers for those languages (Ranathunga and de Silva, 2022). There is a need to focus on development of local language (Joshi et al., 2020) NLP resources.

This paper builds upon the work of Autshumato (Groenewald and Fourie, 2009; Groenewald and du Plooy, 2010) by creating automatically aligned parallel corpora from government textual data in the 11 official languages of South Africa. While the Autshumato project focused on creating Machine Translation tools for five indigenous languages, the resulting corpora lacked information about its origin or context, limiting its usefulness for other NLP tasks such as categorisation, topic modelling over time and other tasks that require contextual information of the content. Our approach provides more comprehensive data that can support a wider range of NLP applications.

Our belief is that there is a significant opportunity to create a more user-friendly data collection process that can be easily maintained and provide extraction tools for others. It is essential to preserve the data source and structure it in a way that enables extensions. Our goal is to enhance Neural Machine Translation (NMT) resources in the government data domain by including all indigenous languages and broadening the translation directions beyond English as the source language. Additionally, we recognise the importance of providing aligned data across all South African languages beyond English.

Further, this paper introduces parallel corpora datasets in the 11 official languages of South Africa, created from text data obtained from the government. These datasets are designed to facilitate the development of NMT models. The corpora are automatically aligned, and are expected to serve as a valuable resource for researchers and practitioners working in the field of machine learning.

The parallel corpora were generated using LASER encoders (Schwenk and Douze, 2017), facilitating the one-to-one alignment of tokenised sentence data. The data was sourced from credible sources such as newspapers and academic journals and covers diverse topics including health, finance, and politics.

We also provide NMT benchmarks for the parallel corpora by fine-tuning a massively multilingual model (M2M100 (Fan et al., 2021)) building on the work of Adelani et al. (2022).

This paper is structured as follows. In the fol-

Proceedings of the Fourth workshop on Resources for African Indigenous Languages (RAIL 2023), pages 18–25
May 6, 2023 ©2023 Association for Computational Linguistics

lowing section, we detail the datasets that we have compiled, including their compilation methodology and the information they contain. We then describe how we have aligned and created parallel corpora using these datasets. The subsequent section presents our NMT experiments and provides an analysis of the results obtained. Finally, we conclude the paper with our findings and make recommendations for future research.

2 Main Datasets

2.1 The Vuk'uzenzele South African Multilingual Corpus

The Vuk'uzenzele dataset was constructed from editions of the South African government magazine Vuk'uzenzele[1]. Being a magazine, the text focuses mainly on current events, politics, entertainment, and other topics related to a magazine publication. The Vuk'uzenzele dataset provides a comprehensive view of the language and topics of discussion in South Africa during the respective period, giving researchers insight into the history and culture of South Africa. The Vuk'uzenzele dataset is thus a rich resource for any researcher wanting to analyse South African politics, current events, and popular culture.

2.1.1 Creation of Vuk'uzenzele

The raw Vuk'uzenzele data is scraped from PDF editions of the magazine. The main Vuk'uzenzele edition is in the English language. Only a few of these English articles are translated into the other 10 official South African languages (Afrikaans, isiNdebele, isiXhosa, IsiZulu, Sepedi, Sesotho, siSwati, Tshivenda, Xitsonga and Setswana). As such, we created a pipeline to identify which articles should be extracted from each language pdf from a specific edition. Individual articles were extracted and placed into text files. The extracted text files still have some challenges due to PDF extraction. To clean it, a team member goes through each extracted text file and formats it as follows:

- Line 1: Title of article (*in language*)
- Line 2: *empty line*
- Line 3: Author of article (*if available. If not, defaults to Vukuzenzele Unnamed*)
- Line 4: *empty line*
- Line 5-end: *body of article*

The data is easier to analyse and visualise after being manually reviewed. The labour-intensive effort was necessary to provide a comprehensive and meaningful analysis of the magazine's content. The time-consuming process of manual review and extraction was ultimately worth it, as it provides an opportunity to create a deeper understanding of the content within Vuk'uzenzele. As of writing we have *53* editions of the newspaper spanning *January 2020 to July 2022*. More additions will be added in time by the team. Automations have been built to download and archive the PDFs, however manual effort is still required to extract and identify translated articles. The dataset, code and automated scrapers are available at at `https://github.com/dsfsi/vukuzenzele-nlp` and Zenodo[2] (Marivate et al., 2023a). We make it available in a format that allows other researchers to extend, remix and add onto it (*CC-4.0-BY-SA licence for data and MIT License for code*).

2.2 The ZA-Gov Multilingual South African corpus

The ZA-Gov Multilingual corpus dataset was constructed from the speeches following cabinet meetings of the SA government. As such, the dataset carries a variety of topics including energy, labour, service delivery, crime, COVID, international relations, the environment, and government affairs such as government appointments, cabinet decisions, etc. This provides an eye into the workings of the South African government and how it has dealt with various challenges, both internal and external.

2.2.1 Creation of ZA-Gov-multilingual

The raw ZA-Gov Multilingual data is scraped from the the South African government website (`https://www.gov.za/`), where all cabinet statements, and their translations, are posted. The data was extracted and structured into a JSON format. The JSON payload for each speech records:

- Date,
- Datetime,
- Title (*in English*),
- Url (*top url for speech*),

[1] `https://www.vukuzenzele.gov.za/`

[2] `https://doi.org/10.5281/zenodo.7598539`

- Language payload for each language (*eng, afr, nbl, xho, zul, nso, sep, tsn, ssw, ven, tso*).
  - Title (*in language*),
  - Text (*in language*),
  - Url (*for the translation*).

This structure makes it convenient for researchers and analysts to perform various natural language processing, data mining and machine learning tasks such as sentiment analysis, topic modelling, categorisation, language modelling and more. For instance, through sentiment analysis and text mining, analysts can investigate opinions of cabinet members' statements and track the evolution of these topics over time. As of writing, the dataset contains *162* cabinet statements spanning *2 May 2013 to 1 December 2022*. The dataset will update automatically when new, *translated*, statements are available on the gov.za website. The dataset, code and automated scrapers are available at at `https://github.com/dsfsi/gov-za-multilingual` and Zenodo[3] (Marivate et al., 2023b). We make it available in such a way that other researchers can extend, remix and add onto it (*CC-4.0-BY-SA licence for data and MIT License for code*).

3 The corpora as a foundation for other NLP tasks and further study

In addition to supporting the creation of NMT models (discussed in the proceeding section), our datasets have the potential to serve as a foundation for many other NLP tasks beyond translation. We believe that these datasets will be a valuable resource for the study of South African government communication, and that it can be used for direct creation of multilingual document categorisation/classification (Schwenk and Li, 2018), simplification (Lu et al., 2021; Siddharthan, 2014; Martin et al., 2022), entity extraction (Tedeschi et al., 2021; Chen et al., 2018; Pappu et al., 2017; Emelyanov and Artemova, 2019), and other NLP tasks. To further extend the dataset's usefulness, we recommend looking at work such as the Parallel Meaning Bank (Abzianidze et al., 2017), which can act as an inspiration for transferring knowledge from one language to another and provide new benchmarks that may be helpful for Southern African languages beyond South Africa. We envision these datasets as a starting point for further research in the area of multilingual NLP for South African and African languages.

[3]`https://doi.org/10.5281/zenodo.7635167`

4 Methods for Processing and Compilation

The datasets are a two way parallel corpus of the 11 official languages of South Africa, which are listed in Table 1 with their corresponding ISO 639-2code. The datasets contain texts written in the official languages of South Africa, including Afrikaans, English, isiNdebele, isiXhosa, isiZulu, siSwati, Sepedi, Xitsonga, siSwati, Tshivenda, and Setswana. As such, there are 55 ways of combining these languages into pairs, producing 55 distinct corpora in each of the datasets. The dataset uses the ISO 639-2 language codes in its naming convention, i.e., 'aligned-afr-zul.csv'. By nature of compilation, some datasets have more observations than others, which could lead to varying results, i.e., if used for NMT, then a better model can be produced for two languages from a dataset with more observations as opposed to one with fewer observations. This compilation of data allows for further exploration into the complexities of South African language and discourse, creating a multi-dimensional representation of how language is used and interpreted in South Africa. Through these datasets, the range of language usage in South Africa can be explored, providing insights into how different languages interact.

Table 1: Language List with ISO 639-2 codes

Name	Code
isiZulu	zul
isiXhosa	xho
Afrikaans	afr
English	eng
Sepedi	nso
Setswana	tsn
Xitsonga	tso
Sesotho	sot
siSwati	ssw
Tshivenda	ven
isiNdebele	nbl

4.1 Preprocessing

Preprocessing was required to refine the raw scraped data prior to LASER encoding and alignment. The preprocessing steps are listed below and differ slightly as the source data and method of scraping has an outcome on the data obtained. For example, ZA-Gov-Multilinguals involve a lot of nested points, i.e., *2.1.2*, which needed to be removed, while in contrast the Vuk'uzenzele data uses bullet points for listing.

4.1.1 Vuk'uzenzele

The raw text from the collected data was preprocessed in the following way:

- The text was set to lowercase.
- Hyphens and bullet points were removed.
- Double spaces, tabs, and newlines were replaced with a single space.
- The standard apostrophe, i.e., ", took the place of Unicode apostrophes.

4.1.2 ZA-Gov-multilingual

The raw text from the collected data was preprocessed in the following way:

- Removing the dots (or single- or multi-digit numbers) that began a line
- Inserting a period after a series of numbers in the format $x \cdot y$.
- Adding a period after a string of numbers in the format x.
- Replacing a sequence of punctuation marks, such as a period, colon, semi-colon, or a combination of these, followed by a letter with a single period.

4.2 Corpora Alignment

Once preprocessed, the text was passed to the NLTK tokeniser "punkt" which returns a vector of sentence tokens. The *n* tokenised sentences were sent to LASER encoder which encodes it into *n* sentence vectors, each of length 1024. The sentence vectors are compared and a cosine similarity algorithm was performed to produce a score from 0 to 1 on the similarity of the two vectors as described in section 4.2.1.

4.2.1 LASER Encodings

In order to compare the text for similarity, LASER encoders were utilised. LASER, which stands for Language-Agnostic Sentence Representations, is a research project by Facebook AI Research. LASER generates sentence representations by encoding sentences into a vector. The vectors serve as a machine representation of the sentence. The vectors can be compared using cosine similarity which outputs a score between zero and one. Cosine scores closer to one indicate high similarity. This score is recorded in the LASER datasets (available in the dataset repository). The observations present in each dataset with a score above 0.65, or 65% similarity, are listed in the following tables 2 and 3. Entire tables featuring the number of observations present in all datasets are featured on the READMEs of the dataset repos, `https://github.com/dsfsi/gov-za-multilingual` for ZA-Gov-Multilingual and `https://github.com/dsfsi/vukuzenzele-nlp` for Vuk'uzenzele.

Table 2: Top ten datasets with the most observations with a cosine score greater than or equal to 0.65 in Vuk'uzenzele.

Language pair	No. of observations in Vuk'uzenzele
ssw-xho	2,202
ssw-zul	2,183
xho-zul	2,102
nso-xho	2,081
nso-tso	2,071
ssw-tso	2,034
nso-ssw	2,021
tsn-tso	2,020
tsn-xho	2,009
tso-xho	2,009

Table 3: Top ten datasets with the most observations with a cosine score greater than or equal to 0.65

Language pair	No. of observations in ZAgov Multilingual
nbl-ven	18,984
nso-ssw	18,697
zul-ssw	18,563
xho-ssw	18,387
xho-zul	18,145
xho-nso	18,110
xho-tso	17,954
ssw-tso	17,880
zul-tso	17,789
zul-nso	17,630

4.3 Postprocessing

For the LASER datasets the source sentence, target sentence, and cosine score for the aligned data was written to a csv file with the naming convention 'aligned-{src_lang_code}-{tgt_lang_code}.csv', i.e. 'aligned-afr-zul.csv'. Refer to the language list in 1 for language codes used in naming the datasets.

For the simple aligned datasets the source sentence and the target sentence were written to a csv file with the same naming structure as the LASER datasets.

5 NMT Benchmarks

Minimal aligned sentence corpora, for low-resourced African languages, hinder the quality of NMT models trained from scratch (Martinus and Abbott, 2019; Nekoto et al., 2020; Adelani et al., 2022). Recently Adelani et al. (2022) approached this problem by fine-tuning massively multilingual models, including the M2M100 model (Fan et al., 2021), on a small number of aligned sentences. The M2M100 model is a Many-to-Many non-English centric language model trained to translate directly between 100 languages, including five South African official languages (Fan et al., 2021). Adelani et al. (2022) demonstrated how to effectively leverage this model for small quantities of data, to create NMT systems for languages and domains not included in pre-training.

Building on their work, we create baseline translation benchmarks for the Vuk'uzenzele and ZA-gov-multilingual datasets, in the government publication domain, by fine-tuning the M2M100 model. To provide our results in context and for comparison purposes we also fine-tune the M2M100 model on subsets of the existing Autshumato parallel corpora obtained from the South African Centre for Digital Language Resources (McKellar, (2021,2,2,2,0,2) (`https://sadilar.org`). We focus our efforts on providing NMT benchmarks for the low resource African languages in the datasets, as such Afrikaans translations are not included due to the relatively high availability of digital datasets in this language, and we leave this for future work.

5.1 Pre-processing

The aligned datasets were processed to remove duplicate and conflicting translations (in both the source and target sentences) then shuffled to remove any order bias before the train, test and dev set were created. The data splits are defined as 70% training, 20% test and 10% dev sets. For comparison, all models are fine-tuned using the 'xxx-eng' translation direction where 'xxx' represents the indigenous African source language and 'eng' is the English translation target.

The available Aushumato parallel corpora (extracted from various government resources and web-crawls (Groenewald and Fourie, 2009)) are comparable in domain to the ZA-gov-multilingual parallel corpora created, however the dataset sizes are currently much larger. We therefore extract the same number for pre-processed aligned sentences as the ZA-gov-multilingual corpora in the 'xxx-eng' translation direction, for direct NMT result comparison. The sentence and token counts of the corpora used for NMT benchmarking are provided in Appendix A.1 tables 5, 6 and 7.

5.2 Results

The M2M100 fine-tuning benchmark results for the Vuk'uzenzele, ZA-gov-multilingual and subsets of the available Autshumato parallel corpora are provided in table 4. The fine-tuning translation directions are provided, and any source languages which were not including in the original M2M100 pre-training are highlighted for references purposes. Additionally the highest BLEU score result achieved across the datasets is shown in bold. Cases where the Autshumato parallel corpora were not accessible or did not exist for a particular language are shown with a '-' symbol.

Table 4: BLEU scores for Massively Multilingual Transfer on xxx-eng translations using the Vuk'uzenzele (Vuk.), ZA-gov-multilingual (Gov.) and subsets of the available Autshumato datasets (Aut.)

Translation Direction	BLEU		
	Vuk.	Gov.	Aut.
nbl→eng	7.33	8.04	**12.24**
nso→eng	9.29	**26.50**	-
ssw→eng	4.80	**28.72**	-
sot→eng	4.55	10.21	**14.83**
tsn→eng	2.80	**29.68**	28.04
tso→eng	13.86	**35.40**	32.10
ven→eng	2.32	9.68	**17.24**
xho→eng	6.05	26.81	-
zul→eng	9.97	**30.03**	25.90

Fine-tuning on the Vuk'uzenzele datasets achieved the lowest overall BLEU scores, this is expected due to the small size of the aligned datasets in comparison to those of the ZA-gov-multilingual and Autshumato datasets. The highest BLEU scores are distributed inconsistently across the ZA-gov-multilingual and Autshumato NMT models, with the ZA-gov-multilingual models achieving a higher score for Setswana, Xitsonga and isiZulu. This could be due to the random subset selections from the Autshumato datasets, as well as a result of variations in source combinations and cleaning methods used by the Autshumato project when creating the aligned corpora. It is noted that variations in the subset selections will yield different results and an in-depth analysis is left for future work.

We achieve the highest benchmark result for Xitsonga ('tso-eng') across all datasets, which is a language that the M2M100 model has not been pre-trained on, demonstrating the effectiveness of transfer learning for new low-resource language datasets.

It is also noted that current NMT resources for the Autshumato datasets exist only in the 'eng-xxx' translation direction for Xitsonga, Setswana, Sepedi, Sesotho and isiZulu (Skosana and Mlambo, 2021). Our contributions therefore extend the benchmark translation resources (in the government data domain) to isiNdebele, isiXhosa, siSwati and Tshivenda; and broaden the translation direction beyond English as the source language.

6 Conclusion

Finally, this paper presented two multilingual corpora that are automatically aligned to facilitate the translation of texts between languages. These datasets contribute to an expanding collection of corpora for training African language NMT models that are left out or under-resourced in contemporary NLP research. It is the hope of the authors that these datasets will aid in creating NMT models for low-resource African languages and that the models can be used to facilitate access to translation services, empowering African speakers and writers to communicate more effectively in their native languages. It is also hoped that the datasets will further NLP research into the multilingualism of African languages and contribute to an understanding of the various dialects present in Africa.

7 Limitations

The NMT models discussed have been created for benchmarking the described datatsets and have not been exhaustively quality tested for production purposes. We also only tested the effectiveness of fine-tuning the M2M100 model with English as a target language and have have not extended the NMT systems to translations between indigenous South African languages, therefore further benchmarking still needs to be implemented. We would like to extend testing to include the evaluation set created by (McKellar and Puttkammer, 2020), which contains data (excluded from the Autshumato corpora) for all 11 official South African languages and could provide a more accurate comparison of the NMT models. It is noted that while the BLEU score results are promising, a qualitative linguistic analysis still needs to done on the translation models to determine if the BLEU scores for certain language translations (i.e. 'tso-eng') correlate to accurate translations within our domain. As future work we hope to collaborate with respective linguists to improve the quality and effectiveness of such NMT systems for South African Languages (Skosana and Mlambo, 2021).

8 Ethics Statement

The datasets created and used for the translation model benchmarks are taken solely from South African government resources. Therefore it is highlighted that if these models are used in production, they might ignore certain social/societal structures and will be representative of the dominant political party at the time the datasets were sourced (Bender et al., 2021). We also note that the benchmark models and datasets have not been curated to determine any biases that are present. As such, any existing biases in the system might have the potential to harm specific groups, when used in NLP downstream production tasks (Bender et al., 2021).

9 Acknowledgements

We would like to acknowledge funding from the ABSA Chair of Data Science, the Google Research scholar program, TensorFlow Award for Machine Learning Grant and the NVIDIA Corporation hardware Grant. Many thanks to all the anonymous RAIL reviewers for their valuable feedback.

References

Lasha Abzianidze, Johannes Bjerva, Kilian Evang, Hessel Haagsma, Rik van Noord, Pierre Ludmann, Duc-Duy Nguyen, and Johan Bos. 2017. The parallel meaning bank: Towards a multilingual corpus of translations annotated with compositional meaning representations. In *Proceedings of the 15th Conference of the European Chapter of the Association for Computational Linguistics: Volume 2, Short Papers*, pages 242–247.

David Adelani, Jesujoba Alabi, Angela Fan, Julia Kreutzer, Xiaoyu Shen, Machel Reid, Dana Ruiter, Dietrich Klakow, Peter Nabende, Ernie Chang, Tajuddeen Gwadabe, Freshia Sackey, Bonaventure F. P. Dossou, Chris Emezue, Colin Leong, Michael Beukman, Shamsuddeen Muhammad, Guyo Jarso, Oreen Yousuf, Andre Niyongabo Rubungo, Gilles Hacheme, Eric Peter Wairagala, Muhammad Umair Nasir, Benjamin Ajibade, Tunde Ajayi, Yvonne Gitau, Jade Abbott, Mohamed Ahmed, Millicent Ochieng, Anuoluwapo Aremu, Perez Ogayo, Jonathan Mukiibi, Fatoumata Ouoba Kabore, Godson Kalipe, Derguene Mbaye, Allahsera Auguste Tapo, Victoire Memdjokam Koagne, Edwin Munkoh-Buabeng, Valencia Wagner, Idris Abdulmumin, Ayodele Awokoya, Happy Buzaaba, Blessing Sibanda, Andiswa Bukula, and Sam Manthalu. 2022. A few thousand translations go a long way! leveraging pre-trained models for African news translation. In *Proceedings of the 2022 Conference of the North American Chapter of the Association for Computational Linguistics: Human Language Technologies*, pages 3053–3070, Seattle, United States. Association for Computational Linguistics.

Emily M. Bender, Timnit Gebru, Angelina McMillan-Major, and Shmargaret Shmitchell. 2021. On the dangers of stochastic parrots: Can language models be too big? In *Proceedings of the 2021 ACM Conference on Fairness, Accountability, and Transparency*, FAccT '21, pages 610–623, New York, NY, USA. Association for Computing Machinery.

Muhao Chen, Yingtao Tian, Kai-Wei Chang, Steven Skiena, and Carlo Zaniolo. 2018. Co-training embeddings of knowledge graphs and entity descriptions for cross-lingual entity alignment. *arXiv preprint arXiv: Arxiv-1806.06478*.

Anton A. Emelyanov and E. Artemova. 2019. Multilingual named entity recognition using pretrained embeddings, attention mechanism and ncrf. *BSNLP@ACL*.

Angela Fan, Shruti Bhosale, Holger Schwenk, Zhiyi Ma, Ahmed El-Kishky, Siddharth Goyal, Mandeep Baines, Onur Celebi, Guillaume Wenzek, Vishrav Chaudhary, et al. 2021. Beyond english-centric multilingual machine translation. *Journal of Machine Learning Research*, 22(107):1–48.

Hendrik J Groenewald and Liza du Plooy. 2010. Processing parallel text corpora for three south african language pairs in the autshumato project. *AfLaT 2010*, page 27.

Hendrik Johannes Groenewald and Wildrich Fourie. 2009. Introducing the autshumato integrated translation environment. In *Proceedings of the 13th Annual conference of the European Association for Machine Translation*.

Pratik Joshi, Sebastin Santy, Amar Budhiraja, Kalika Bali, and Monojit Choudhury. 2020. The state and fate of linguistic diversity and inclusion in the NLP world. In *Proceedings of the 58th Annual Meeting of the Association for Computational Linguistics*, pages 6282–6293, Online. Association for Computational Linguistics.

Xinyu Lu, Jipeng Qiang, Yun Li, Yunhao Yuan, and Yi Zhu. 2021. An unsupervised method for building sentence simplification corpora in multiple languages. *Conference On Empirical Methods In Natural Language Processing*.

Vukosi Marivate, Daniel Njini, Andani Madodonga, Richard Lastrucci, Isheanesu Dzingirai, and Jenalea Rajab. 2023a. The Vuk'uzenzele South African multilingual corpus.

Vukosi Marivate, Tshephisho Sefara, Vongani Chabalala, Keamogetswe Makhaya, Tumisho Mokgonyane, Rethabile Mokoena, and Abiodun Modupe. 2020. Investigating an approach for low resource language dataset creation, curation and classification: Setswana and sepedi. In *Proceedings of the first workshop on Resources for African Indigenous Languages*, pages 15–20.

Vukosi Marivate, Matimba Shingange, Richard Lastrucci, Isheanesu Dzingirai, and Jenalea Rajab. 2023b. The South African Gov-za multilingual corpus.

Louis Martin, Angela Fan, Eric Villemonte de la Clergerie, Antoine Bordes, and Benoît Sagot. 2022. Muss: Multilingual unsupervised sentence simplification by mining paraphrases. *International Conference On Language Resources And Evaluation*.

Laura Martinus and Jade Z Abbott. 2019. A focus on neural machine translation for african languages. *arXiv preprint arXiv:1906.05685*.

Cindy McKellar. (2020). Autshumato english-tshivenda parallel corpora, version 1.0, [multilingual text corpora: Aligned]. Retrieved From `https://hdl.handle.net/20.500.12185/569`.

Cindy McKellar. (2021). Autshumato english-isindebele parallel corpora, version 1.0, [multilingual text corpora: Aligned]. Retrieved From `https://hdl.handle.net/20.500.12185/572`.

Cindy McKellar. (2022)a. Autshumato english-isizulu parallel corpora, version 2.0, [multilingual text corpora: Aligned]. Retrieved From `https://hdl.handle.net/20.500.12185/575`.

Cindy McKellar. (2022)b. Autshumato english-sesotho parallel corpora, version 1.0, [multilingual text corpora: Aligned]. Retrieved From `https://hdl.handle.net/20.500.12185/577`.

Cindy McKellar. (2022)c. Autshumato english-setswana parallel corpora, version 2.0, [multilingual text corpora: Aligned]. Retrieved From https://hdl.handle.net/20.500.12185/578.

Cindy McKellar. (2022)d. Autshumato english-xitsonga parallel corpora, version 2.0, [multilingual text corpora: Aligned]. Retrieved From https://hdl.handle.net/20.500.12185/579.

Cindy A McKellar and Martin J Puttkammer. 2020. Dataset for comparable evaluation of machine translation between 11 south african languages. *Data Brief*, 29:105146.

Wilhelmina Nekoto, Vukosi Marivate, Tshinondiwa Matsila, Timi Fasubaa, Taiwo Fagbohungbe, Solomon Oluwole Akinola, Shamsuddeen Muhammad, Salomon Kabongo Kabenamualu, Salomey Osei, Freshia Sackey, et al. 2020. Participatory research for low-resourced machine translation: A case study in african languages. In *Findings of the Association for Computational Linguistics: EMNLP 2020*, pages 2144–2160.

Aasish Pappu, Roi Blanco, Yashar Mehdad, Amanda Stent, and Kapil Thadani. 2017. Lightweight multilingual entity extraction and linking. In *Proceedings of the Tenth ACM International Conference on Web Search and Data Mining*, pages 365–374.

Surangika Ranathunga and Nisansa de Silva. 2022. Some languages are more equal than others: Probing deeper into the linguistic disparity in the NLP world. In *Proceedings of the 2nd Conference of the Asia-Pacific Chapter of the Association for Computational Linguistics and the 12th International Joint Conference on Natural Language Processing (Volume 1: Long Papers)*, pages 823–848, Online only. Association for Computational Linguistics.

Holger Schwenk and Matthijs Douze. 2017. Learning joint multilingual sentence representations with neural machine translation. *ACL 2017*, page 157.

Holger Schwenk and Xian Li. 2018. A corpus for multilingual document classification in eight languages. *International Conference On Language Resources And Evaluation.*

Advaith Siddharthan. 2014. A survey of research on text simplification. *ITL-International Journal of Applied Linguistics*, 165(2):259–298.

Nomsa Skosana and Respect Mlambo. 2021. A brief study of the autshumato machine translation web service for south african languages. *Literator*, 42(1):7.

Simone Tedeschi, Valentino Maiorca, Niccolò Campolungo, Francesco Cecconi, and Roberto Navigli. 2021. WikiNEuRal: Combined neural and knowledge-based silver data creation for multilingual NER. In *Findings of the Association for Computational Linguistics: EMNLP 2021*, pages 2521–2533, Punta Cana, Dominican Republic. Association for Computational Linguistics.

A Appendix

A.1 Data Statistics

The data statistics for the datasets used for NMT bench-marking are provided in Tables 5, 6 and 7.

Table 5: Characteristics of the translation data for the Vuk'uzenzele (Vuk.) datasets

Translation Direction	Size #sents (#src / #trg tokens)
nbl→eng	136 (3.4k / 3.9k)
nso→eng	1715 (53.7k / 41.6k)
ssw→eng	1588 (29.9k / 37.6k)
sot→eng	260 (9.9k / 7.5k)
tsn→eng	1366 (49.8k / 31.7k)
tso→eng	1998 (58.9k/ 46.6k)
ven→eng	230 (9.1k / 7k)
xho→eng	1338 (25.8k / 31.5k)
zul→eng	1874 (34.1k / 43k)

Table 6: Characteristics of the translation data for the ZA-gov-multilingual (Gov.) datasets

Translation Direction	Size #sents (#src / #trg tokens)
nbl→eng	3513 (63.9k / 107k)
nso→eng	14742 (460.9k / 375k)
ssw→eng	15139 (291k/ 377.8k)
sot→eng	4995 (145.9k / 153.5k)
tsn→eng	14068 (493.1k / 362.2k)
tso→eng	15393 (466.4k / 381.2k)
ven→eng	3404 (68.2k / 96.6k)
xho→eng	15853 (318.2k / 389.5k)
zul→eng	15503 (327.5k / 384.1k)

Table 7: Characteristics of the translation data for the subsets of the available Autshumato datasets (Aut.)

Translation Direction	Size #sents (#src / #trg tokens)
nbl→eng	3513 (48.4k / 65k)
sot→eng	4995 (118.3k / 100.4k)
tsn→eng	14068 (335.1k / 274.7k)
tso→eng	15393 (193.7k/ 166k)
ven→eng	3404 (80.6k / 65.9k)
zul→eng	15503 (231.8k / 307.6k)

SpeechReporting Corpus: annotated corpora of West African traditional narratives

Katya Aplonova
LLACAN, CNRS
aplooon@gmail.com

Izabela Jordanoska
LACITO, CNRS
izabela.jordanoska@cnrs.fr

Timofey Arkhangelsky
Universität Hamburg
timarkh@gmail.com

Tatiana Nikitina
LACITO, CNRS
tavnik@gmail.com

Abstract

This paper describes the SpeechReporting Corpus, an online collection of corpora annotated for a range of discourse phenomena. The corpora contain folktales from 7 lesser-studied West African languages. Apart from its value for theoretical linguistics, especially for the study of reported speech, the database is an important resource for the preservation of intangible cultural heritage of minority languages and the development and testing of cross-linguistically applicable computational tools.

1 Introduction

Recent decades have seen an upsurge of interest in issues of language extinction, leading to increased efforts to describe and document the world's endangered languages. The major adverse effects of language endangerment are also associated with loss of different forms of traditional knowledge (Hale, 1992).

The SpeechReporting Corpus (Nikitina et al., 2022) explores the relationship between specific discourse practices that represent the nucleus of the transmission of traditional knowledge and the linguistic strategies associated with it, centering on one particular problem: discourse reporting in traditional oral storytelling in West Africa, the "oral continent par excellence" and the homeland of a rich and vibrant oral tradition (Scheub, 1985; Finnegan, 2007, inter alia).

The article is structured as follows: in Section 2 we discuss why the SpeechReporting database is particularly relevant for West Africa. Section 3 is dedicated to database composition. Our workflow and tools are described in Section 4, while Section 5 shows some basic principles of annotation of reported discourse. In Section 6, we show how the online interface of the corpus works. In Section 7, we illustrate how the corpus can be used for dissemination among linguistic communities in order to archive and help preserve intangible cultural heritage. Section 8 concludes the paper.

2 West African storytelling traditions

In traditional rural societies of West Africa, the acute feeling of loss is related to the diminishing role played by culturally significant discourse practices: even in communities that retain traditional social organization and economy, modern Western cultural practices seep into daily life with new forms of entertainment (television, radio broadcasts) and education (compulsory Western-style schooling). Under the pressure from these new practices, traditional forms of knowledge transmission — including techniques of storytelling and instruction — become unimportant, and may eventually go out of use.

In many local communities across Africa, storytelling is more than a favorite pastime. Viewed as a vital part of cultural heritage, it serves as a central medium for the transmission of cultural knowledge. Storytelling traditions have accumulated special linguistic techniques that respond to the needs of specific practices of textual production and performance. As storytelling traditions vanish with older generations of speakers, they take along with them an array of linguistic tools on which such specialized techniques relied (Nikitina, 2018).

While oral traditions of West Africa have received considerable attention from anthropologists (Finnegan, 1970, 2012), their linguistic aspects have not been subject to systematic investigation. Our knowledge of the special ways in which language is used in traditional genres is largely limited to observations of frequent use of special vocabulary and opening/closing formulae (Cosentino, 1980), singing (Innes, 1965; Burnim, 1976; Azuonye, 1999), and various forms of repetition (Finnegan, 1967, 1977). The goal of our database is to start filling this gap using an interdisciplinary approach combining rigorous analysis

Proceedings of the Fourth workshop on Resources for African Indigenous Languages (RAIL 2023), pages 26–31
May 6, 2023 ©2023 Association for Computational Linguistics

of primary data with meticulous attention to genre characteristics and culture-specific contexts of textual production.

3 Database composition

The SpeechReporting Corpus contains multiple sub-corpora of traditional folk stories, annotated for a number of discourse phenomena using the ELAN-CorpA software and tools (Chanard, 2015; Nikitina et al., 2019). It is updated regularly with newly available data, including data from new languages. The project currently involves 11 different languages, of which 7 are spoken in West Africa. All texts are transcribed, glossed, translated, and annotated. Table 1 lists the West African languages[1] in the database, their genetic affiliation and country where they are spoken.

Language	Affiliation	Place
Bandial	Atlantic	Senegal
Gizey	Chadic	Cameroon
Guro	Mande	Côte d'Ivoire
Kafire	Senufo	Côte d'Ivoire
Mwan	Mande	Côte d'Ivoire
Ut-Ma'in	Kainji	Nigeria
Wan	Mande	Côte d'Ivoire

Table 1: West African languages in the SpeechReporting database

In the project, we work with texts (both oral and written) and not with elicited data. This helps to avoid the influence of the working language, and speakers' potential judgment about 'proper language use'. For example, logophoric pronouns, repetitions and some interjections and ideophones are very hard to elicit, though they do occur frequently in narratives.

We also restricted the genre of the texts we work with. The corpus is annotated for reported discourse (see Section 6), and thus, we chose fairy tales as a main data source, since in most fairy tales the driving force of the narration is the communication among characters.

Despite trying to keep the genre consistent across languages, the data are still very diverse. For example, it includes archived transcriptions, data from the field, recordings of professional storytellers as well as of regular people, one or multiple participants. Table 2 contains information about the composition of the corpus.

Language	Data format	Tokens	Phrases	Texts
Bandial	text, audio, video	10,378	1260	28
Gizey	text, audio, video	5184	700	10
Guro	text, audio, video	7346	1129	2
Kafire	text, audio, video	14,921	2769	17
Mwan	text	24,949	1797	33
Ut-Ma'in	text	1159	246	7
Wan	text	48,195	5370	82

Table 2: Composition of the Discourse Reporting database (West African languages only)

In the table, 'Data format' refers to the modality of the data. For some languages, we have audio files, video files and corresponding written transcriptions, while for others, we only have the written transcriptions. While 'Tokens' refers to the number of tokens, 'Phrases' refers to the total number of intonational units into which the texts of that language are segmented. 'Texts' refers to the number of separate ELAN files per language, each corresponding to one narrative.

We transcribe texts using orthographies based on the International Phonetic Alphabet. The African languages in the database do not have a standardized orthography which is widely used by native speakers. Published materials are scarce and, in the majority of cases, were developed by the authors of the corpora and rely on the same or similar orthography.

4 Workflow and tools

The project unites multiple collaborators that work in different frameworks and use different tools for data documentation and analysis. As a result, we had two basic workflows. In one, segmentation and transcription are done in SayMore (Hatton, 2013) or ELAN (n.a., 2022; Sloetjes and Wittenburg, 2008). Segmented and transcribed texts are glossed in Toolbox or Flex and then imported to ELAN in order to add annotations of reported discourse. The other workflow allows researchers to use only one software product, ELAN-CorpA for segmentation, transcription, glossing and annotation of reported discourse.[2]

[1]In addition to describing strategies for reporting discourse employed in oral traditions of selected West African cultures, the project sets out to compare them to their functional counterparts from a geographically and historically unrelated area. Therefore, the database contains some languages spoken in Eurasia that will not be discussed in this article.

[2]ELAN-CorpA is a fork-version of ELAN, developed by Christian Chanard, check this link `https://llacan.cnrs.fr/res_ELAN-CorpA_en.php` for more information.

Annotated files are checked manually and by using ELAN Tools (Chanard, 2019), a collection of scripts that checks the consistency of labels and the structure of the ELAN files. The manual checking consists of, among other things, proofreading the free translations and looking out for irregularities in the glosses and the morphemic analysis. Double-checked files are uploaded to Tsakorpus.

Collaborators could contribute to the project in various ways. Since 2019, we have had 4 post-docs, 2 PhD students, 6 research assistants and 8 non-contractual academic visitors working on the corpus.

5 Annotation of reported discourse

Annotation of reported discourse consists of four levels: the function of the construction's elements; the construction's syntactic type; the semantic type of the discourse report; and the encoding of participants within the discourse report. They correspond to four additional ELAN tiers (in our template, `qt`, `rp`, `typ` and `par`, respectively). Figure 1 is an example of our annotation of a Gizey sentence in an ELAN file.

Explained below are the basic principles of annotation that are relevant to searching in the corpus interface.[3]

A reported speech construction consists of different elements; for example, in *John said: Hello!* the reported utterance (*Hello!*) is introduced by a clause describing the speech event (*John said*). In the Gizey example in Figure 1, "she says" is expressed by a Quotative, while "give millet; this red mare of mine..." is a Discourse report. The semantic type of the Discourse report is Command.[4]

Different syntactic types of reported discourse constructions are visually represented by different frames. The types are defined by the elements the construction consists of. The syntactic type in the Gizey example is Quotative + Discourse report.

The elements referring to participants in the current or reported speech event are annotated in the Participant tier. The Gizey example contains a reference to the Reported Speaker (RS).

In the Tsakorpus interface, these annotations are reflected by background colors, frames, and pop-up windows. This is illustrated in Figure 2 for a sentence in Bandial (also known as Jóola Eegima), where the reported segment is in green and the speech event is in red.

6 Searching in Tsakorpus

Equipping the annotated corpora with a web-based search interface makes them more accessible both to linguists and to language communities. We made our corpora available online with the help of the *Tsakorpus* platform.[5] The platform was mostly developed independently of the project. However, a number of features were added specifically to accommodate the needs of the SpeechReporting database.

Search queries in the online interface are formed by clicking on buttons and filling out text fields. A single-word query can include constraints on the word, its lemma, its part of speech and/or its glosses. All fields can handle Boolean functions (`,` for `AND`, `|` for `OR`, `~` for `NOT`). Word and lemma search can include regular expressions and provide instant suggestions when the user starts typing. Multi-word queries consist of several single-word queries with additional distance constraints.

When clicking "Search sentences", the user gets randomly ordered search hits, split into pages. The sound associated with a particular search hit, if any, can be played by clicking on that hit.

One limitation of Tsakorpus is that its basic search unit is a sentence (or any sentence-like segment of text). It is not possible to search for units that are either larger than a "sentence", or smaller than a "sentence" but larger than a word. ELAN segments (which normally represent intonational units) were reinterpreted as "sentences" in Tsakorpus. However, our discourse annotation often consists of multi-word spans that are either smaller than a sentence or transcend the segment sentence. In order to make them searchable, we add values of all discourse annotations that appear anywhere within a sentence as sentence-level metadata. This way, a query like "Quotative AND a word glossed as *say*" will return all sentences that contain both a Quotative span and a word glossed as "say", but they will not necessarily overlap. This option was added to Tsakorpus in the course of the project. Nevertheless, the exact spans inside sentences that have discourse annotations are highlighted with

[3]A detailed description of the annotation principles can be found on the project website `http://discoursereporting.huma-num.fr/annotation.pdf`

[4]The terminology used in the annotation of the syntactic and semantic elements in speech reporting comes from Spronck and Nikitina (2019).

[5]`http://discoursereporting.huma-num.fr/corpus/search`

Figure 1: Example of an annotated Gizey sentence in ELAN

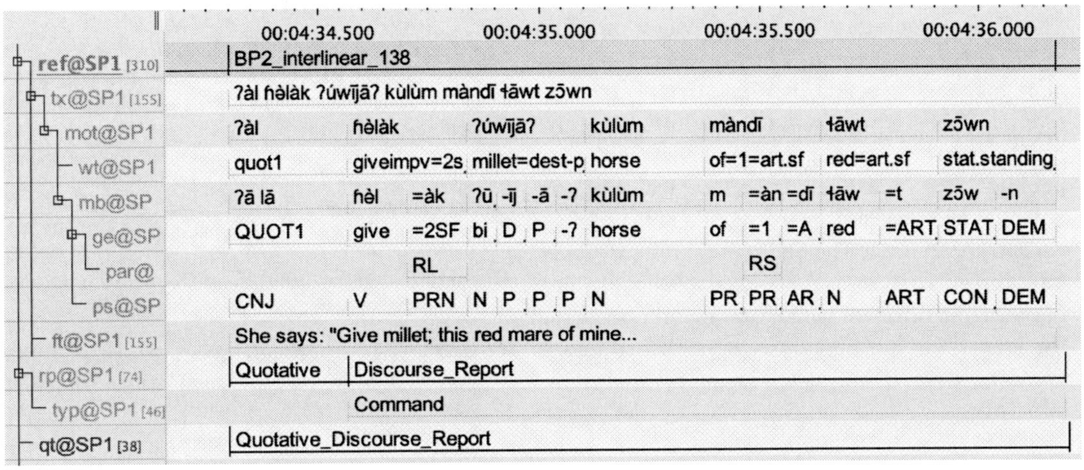

Figure 2: Example of search within Tsakorpus, a sentence in Bandial (Jóola Eegima)

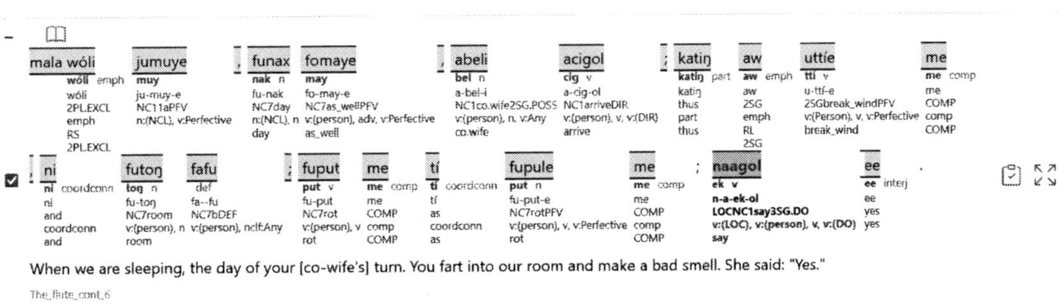

different colors in the search hits.

The online corpus contains all languages present in the Discourse reporting database. When searching in the corpora, the user can choose between selecting a specific language and searching in all language subcorpora at once. In the latter case, the search query must include annotation that is uniform across the subcorpora. This includes annotation of reported discourse (see Section 5) and part-of-speech tags in the UD format (de Marneffe et al., 2021).

Currently, the corpus interface is available in English and Russian. The French interface is under construction.

7 Dissemination

Target users of the SpeechReporting Corpus are linguists and anthropologists who are interested in traditional narratives.

Besides academic uses, this corpus is a valuable source of materials for language communities to keep their languages and linguistic traditions alive; first of all, by simply having online access to recorded narration sessions of some of their folktales. In addition, we make materials, such as storybooks, that the communities can use for educational purposes. Moreover, our project has received additional funding from the *Humanités Numériques et Science Ouverte* program of the Sorbonne Nouvelle in Paris for producing animated YouTube videos of the recorded folktales and spreading them among the linguistic communities and wider audiences.

Furthermore, the availability of open-access annotated linguistic data of minority African languages is important for the development of machine learning based technologies, which currently under-represent these languages.

8 Concluding remarks

The SpeechReporting Corpus provides meticulously annotated corpora of low-resourced indigenous languages spoken in West Africa. It also offers a digital representation of reported speech constructions on different levels of analysis (morphology, syntax and semantics), which opens a potential of a new understanding of a range of discursive phenomena. The SpeechReporting Corpus offers open access tools for comparable annotation of data from different languages. It contributes to the accessibility of previously unpublished traditional narratives in indigenous languages spoken in West Africa.

Limitations

One limitation of this corpus is the difficulty of comparing between the different languages. It is hard to identify typologically applicable categories based on limited amounts of data. For example, when deciding on which discourse categories to annotate, we had to make sure that we could use the same vocabulary for all the languages in our sample.

An additional limitation is the possible lack of consistency between the different subcorpora. The cross-checking of the data is done manually. This is a tedious task that is susceptible to human error, but it is necessary to improve the quality of individual data sets.

Furthermore, we have discovered that it is challenging to bring together a perfect team for a project that is both linguistic and technological in nature.

Another possible limitation is related to transparency. Considering possible future uses of our corpora, we have tried to make the annotations as transparent as possible and have documented them all on our website.

Interdisciplinarity is another challenge: the kind of data that is suitable for dissemination in the communities is slightly different from the kind of data that is of primary interest from the point of view of linguistic theory.

References

Chukwuma Azuonye. 1999. Igbo stories and storytelling. *Traditional Storytelling Today: An International Sourcebook*, pages 33–40.

Mellonee Victoria Burnim. 1976. *Songs in Mende Folktales*. Madison: University of Wisconsin.

Christian Chanard. 2015. ELAN-CorpA: Lexicon-aided annotation in ELAN. In *Corpus-based Studies of Lesser-described Languages*, pages 311–332. John Benjamins.

Christian Chanard. 2019. ELAN Tools: Python tools for ELAN. Online access: `https://llacan.cnrs.fr/res_manuels_en.php`, last accessed 13/02/2023.

Donald J Cosentino. 1980. Lele Gbomba and the style of Mende baroque. *African Arts*, 13(3):54–55.

Marie-Catherine de Marneffe, Christopher D. Manning, Joakim Nivre, and Daniel Zeman. 2021. Universal Dependencies. *Computational Linguistics*, 47(2):255–308.

Ruth Finnegan. 1967. *Limba stories and story-telling*. Oxford: Clarendon Press.

Ruth Finnegan. 1970. A note on oral tradition and historical evidence. *History and Theory*, 9(2):195–201.

Ruth Finnegan. 1977. Oral poetry: Its nature, significance and social context.

Ruth Finnegan. 2007. *The oral and beyond: doing things with words in Africa*. James Currey/University of Chicago Press.

Ruth Finnegan. 2012. *Oral literature in Africa*. Open Book Publishers.

Ken Hale. 1992. Endangered languages: On endangered languages and the safeguarding of diversity. *language*, 68(1):1–42.

John Hatton. 2013. Saymore: Language documentation productivity [Computer software].

Gordon Innes. 1965. The function of the song in Mende folktales. *Sierra Leone Language Review*, 4:54–63.

n.a. 2022. ELAN (Version 6.4) [Computer software].

Tatiana Nikitina. 2018. When linguists and speakers do not agree: The endangered grammar of verbal art in West Africa. *Journal of Linguistic Anthropology*, pages 197–220.

Tatiana Nikitina, Ekaterina Aplonova, Abbie Jordanoska, Izabela andHantgan-Sonko, Guillaume Guitang, Olga Kuznetsova, Elena Perekhvalskaya, and Lacina Silué. 2022. The speechreporting corpus: Discourse reporting in storytelling.

Tatiana Nikitina, Abbie Hantgan, and Christian Chanard. 2019. Reported speech annotation template for ELAN. (The SpeechReporting Corpus). Online access: `http://discoursereporting.huma-num.fr/annotation.pdf`, last accesed 16/03/2023.

Harold Scheub. 1985. A review of African oral traditions and literature. *African Studies Review*, 28(2-3):1–72.

Han Sloetjes and Peter Wittenburg. 2008. Annotation by category-ELAN and ISO DCR. In *6th international Conference on Language Resources and Evaluation (LREC 2008)*.

Stef Spronck and Tatiana Nikitina. 2019. Reported speech forms a dedicated syntactic domain. *Linguistic Typology*, 23:119–159.

A Corpus-Based List of Frequently Used Words in Sesotho

Johannes Sibeko
Nelson Mandela University
Port Elizabeth, South Africa
johannes.sibeko@mandela.ac.za

Orphée de Clercq
LT3, Ghent University
Ghent, Belgium
Orphee.DeClercq@UGent.be

Abstract

This article describes the development of a list of frequently used words in written Sesotho. The list has been created with the aim of incorporating it into frequency-based text readability metrics. The list was derived using a corpus-based approach. By leveraging three existing Sesotho corpora, frequency lists could be derived, which were subsequently merged and qualitatively analysed and fine-tuned by an experienced speaker of Sesotho. The main challenges in compiling the list included reconciling the spelling variations, the treatment of abbreviations, and the presence of unexpected words in the preliminary lists. The final list comprises 3037 entries and is made publicly available to the research community.

1 Introduction

South African learners struggle with reading comprehension even when reading in their home languages (Pretorius et al., 2020). As a result, they perform poorly on problems involving language (Van der Walt et al., 2008). This is especially pronounced in bilingual and multilingual learners since they develop literacy simultaneously in two languages (Cockcroft, 2016; Wilsenach and Schaefer, 2022). Such learners perform more poorly than monolingual learners who get in-depth exposure to one language (Cockcroft, 2016). This challenge of vocabulary and language demands is increased when South African learners with indigenous languages as their first languages move from the third to the fourth grade of education and where the language of instruction changes from indigenous languages to either English or Afrikaans (Sibanda and Baxen, 2016).

According to Stoffelsma (2019b,a), 78% of South African fourth graders were unsuccessful at extracting meaning from texts. Unfortunately, not being able to extract meaning from texts puts learners at risk of not being able to read as their lack of vocabulary affects their ability to read texts with desirable fluency (Pretorius and Stoffelsma, 2017; Stoffelsma, 2019a).

Sadly, learners' inability to read with the expected level of fluency and their inability to extract meaning from texts makes it difficult for teachers and assessors to choose reading passages. Reading interventions to assist learners with less-than-desired reading abilities are needed in most language classes. Unfortunately, teachers may not always be well-trained to teach reading and monitor reading interventions (Pretorius et al., 2020). Furthermore, teachers' levels of command may not always allow for successful interventions (Batinić et al., 2016). For higher pass rates, one might have to resort to using texts expected to be administered to learners with fewer years of schooling. This is particularly unfavourable for research on the development of reading metrics for South African indigenous languages.

Consistent estimations of readability levels are essential in educational contexts where instructors and examiners need to identify and assign texts to readers with specific levels of education. Such consistency in assigning readability estimations prevents instances where learners in higher grades are assigned texts that are easier to read than those that are assigned to learners in lower grades. Without readability metrics, authors, publishers, and readers may not always estimate readability levels accurately or consistently (Humphreys and Humphreys, 2013).

Unfortunately, as far as we are aware, there are no readability metrics for Sesotho. One solution to this may be the development of classical readability formulas. Classical readability metrics use mathematical formulas to estimate the level of education or the grade that a reader needs in order to read a specific text with ease (Gopal et al., 2021). These linear regression formulas are normally based on superficial text properties such as lengths of words,

Proceedings of the Fourth workshop on Resources for African Indigenous Languages (RAIL 2023), pages 32–41
May 6, 2023 ©2023 Association for Computational Linguistics

sentences, syllables, and frequency lists. Fortuitously, sentence and word lengths can easily be determined using universal preprocessing tools as they are language-independent. However, determining syllables and frequently used words requires specific language tools. As far as could be ascertained for this article, there are two syllabification systems for Sesotho, see Sibeko and Van Zaanen (2022b). As such, Sesotho syllable information can be extracted from texts. Unfortunately, there is no frequency-based list of the most used words to use in readability studies. Looking at existing readability formulas, one of the most well-known frequency lists is the one developed by Dale and Chall (1948). The strategy to compile this list was to directly present these words in reading to 4th-grade learners, a word made it to the list when it was known by at least 80 per cent of the children (Dale and Chall, 1948; Piu et al., 2020; Glazkova et al., 2021). Ideally, when devising a word list for Sesotho (or other indigenous languages) a similar technique should be used. Unfortunately, such a user-based approach may yield regressive results since the majority of learners in indigenous African language classes have low reading abilities and vocabulary knowledge (Stoffelsma, 2019a,b). In other words, the result of a user-based approach would be a list of reading entry-level words.

This article presents our efforts to create a list of the 3000 most frequently used words in written Sesotho using a corpus analysis approach. We position our work in research on adapting readability metrics (Section 2). We then present our methodology for creating the list (Section 3) and subsequently discuss the results (Section 4). We conclude our article by highlighting the strengths of the list and by formulating a set of suggestions for further improvements (Section 5).

2 Related Work

Digital language resources and human language technologies audits for South African languages indicate that all indigenous languages of South Africa are under-resourced (Grover et al., 2010, 2011; Barnard et al., 2014; Moors et al., 2018a,b). More specifically, Sibeko and Setaka (2022) reviewed the basic language resource kit for Sesotho and concluded that many necessary digital language resources are still lacking.

A few studies have assessed the readability of Sesotho texts using English readability metrics. For instance, Krige and Reid (2017) manually extracted textual properties used in classical readability metrics to investigate the readability of Sesotho health pamphlets. In another study, Reid et al. (2019) developed a Sesotho health literacy test. Unfortunately, the studies used English metrics without considering the differences between Sesotho and English textual properties. Therefore, the results from these studies may have misrepresented the context of Sesotho's written texts. Furthermore, due to the lack of resources, manual methods for extracting textual properties were used which is highly impractical to be used at a large scale and error-prone.

Multiple studies have explored the adaptation of classical readability metrics to lower-resourced languages. For Norwegian, Jakobsen and Skardal (2007) explored the adaptation of eight classical readability metrics, namely, the Automated Readability Index (ARI) (Smith and Senter, 1967), Coleman-Liau index (CLI) (Coleman and Liau, 1975), Flesch Reading Ease (FRE) (Flesch, 1974), Flesch-Kincaid Grade Level (FKGL) (Kincaid et al., 1975), Gunning Fog index (GFI) (Gunning, 1969), Lasbarhetsindex (LIX) (Anderson, 1983), Rate index (RIX) (Anderson, 1983), and Simple Measure of Gobbledygook (SMOG) (Mc Laughlin, 1969). Almost all those metrics were originally developed for English, except for LIX and RIX which were developed for Swedish. One of their most important findings was that syllable counts and complex words did not have the same effect on readability levels in Norwegian as they did in the English metrics. In the end, only the Swedish LIX and RIX metrics could successfully be adapted to the lower-resourced Norwegian.

The English FRE and FKGL formulas have also been adapted to Russian (Oborneva, 2006). In this process, the two text characteristics that are included in the formulas, i.e. average sentence and word length, were compared and the corresponding weights adapted (Glazkova et al., 2021). Similarly, the English FRE has been adapted to Dutch, by both Douma (Douma, 1960) and Brouwer (Brouwer, 1963), who each assigned slightly different weights in order to account for the differences in word and sentence length between English and Dutch. The popular FRE formula has also been adapted to French (Kandel and Moles, 1958; Henry, 1975), Czech (Bendová, 2021; Bendová and Cinková, 2021) and Italian (Franchina and Vacca, 1986).

A study by Van Oosten et al. (2010) revealed that the outcomes of classical formulas developed for English, Dutch and Swedish on Dutch data yield strong correlations, which is explained by the formulas' strong reliance on certain language-independent properties, such as average word or sentence length. However, failed attempts of adapting classical readability metrics using higher-resourced languages have also been reported. For instance, Sinha et al. (2012) reports an unsuccessful attempt at adapting the English FRE, GFI, FKGL and SMOG metrics into Hindi and Bangla. They concluded that new metrics which are based on Bangla and Hindi structural properties should be developed as the existing metrics yield out-of-bound results. New textual properties such as *Jukta-akshars* were then introduced in the resulting Hindi metrics. This implies that readability metrics can be adapted when there is comparability such as in the cases of English, Dutch and Swedish, which are all Germanic languages. However, new formulas may need to be developed when language structures are incomparable such as in the case of Hindi and English.

Moreover, certain popular classical formulas also comprise variables based on frequency lists. The most well-known formula in this respect is the Dale-Chall Reading Grade Score (Dale and Chall, 1948). Besides relying on average sentence length, this formula also counts how many words occur in the Dale-Chall word list. This list comprises 3,000 words which are known in reading by at least 80 per cent of fourth-grade children. An updated version of the list was published in 1995 (Chall and Dale, 1995).

The Dale-Chall formula or index is one of the most used metrics in health information (Palotti et al., 2016). Given that the formula was originally developed to assess reading material for children, it is recommended to adjust the formula, and especially the list of frequently used words when using it to measure readability for specific target audiences (Gauthier and Johnson, 2019). On the other hand, the list of common words has been criticised for failing to account for specialised meanings (Yan et al., 2006).

In this work, we wish to explore whether a similar list can be created for Sesotho. Ideally, we would like to also assess the word list with users such as school learners. Even so, before testing can begin, we need an initial list. We are also concerned that testing the list on school learners may be challenging due to the recently implemented gate-keeping procedures aimed at protecting vulnerable participants in the post-pandemic era. Nevertheless, we are exploring other user tests that could make our list applicable to other target audiences, such as adult readers, authors, and publishers.

Currently, there exist at least two lists of frequently used words in Sesotho, namely the MostCommonWords[1] and the Waston Chen[2] list. However, a few issues arise when consulting these lists. First of all, both lists have been (machine) translated from English into Sesotho, which means they are less representative of the Sesotho language. Moreover, for some of the translations in the Waston Chen list, Sepedi is being used (such as *kgauswi* instead of Sesotho *haufi* 'near'). Because of this translation from English into Sesotho both lists also contain various entries which are not single words but phrases. For instance, the Waston Chen list mentions *yuniti eno ya thuto* 'that unit of the lesson' for the English 'unit' entry. Similarly, the MostCommonWords list also mentions *a sebetsang a* 'that work' for the English entry 'active'. The lists also inconsistently interchange between two different orthographies, both the Lesotho Sesotho and the South African Sesotho orthography are being used. Finally, for both lists, it is difficult to find any background information on how the original lists were actually created.

We, therefore, believe that a more structured and purposed development of a frequency list is needed and opt for a corpus-based approach in this paper.

3 Methodology

We collected a total of three corpora which comprise original Sesotho text material, see Table 1 for some corpus statistics.

3.1 Corpus 1: Bible

We extracted text from the Sesotho (Southern Sotho) bible version SSO89 *Bibele* 'Bible'. The Bible texts were downloaded in SQL3lite format from `https://www.ph4.org/b4_index.php#google_vignette`. All texts were extracted using *bash* scripts. The Bible texts are divided into

[1]`https://3000mostcommonwords.com`

[2]`https://wastonchen.com/6417.html`

	# Tokens	# Sentences
Corpus 1	962 916	31 171
Corpus 2	4 614 565	216 854
Corpus 3	2 017 751	85 860
TOTAL	7 595 232	333 885

Table 1: The number of tokens and sentences present in the three Sesotho corpora used for this study.

three sections, namely, (i) bible books containing 66 rows of data, (ii) verses containing 31 171 rows of data and (iii) info containing 10 rows of data. For our corpus, we extracted verse texts, which were subsequently cleaned by removing book numbers, chapter titles and verse information. The texts were tokenized using *ucto* with default settings except for specific settings for displaying each sentence on a new line. In the end, the bible corpus contains around 1 million tokens.

3.2 Corpus 2: Autshumato

The Autshumato machine translation project developed a corpus of translation texts for South African indigenous languages. These texts were manually translated by professional translators from English into the other ten official languages of South Africa, namely, Afrikaans, IsiZulu, IsiXhosa, IsiNdebele, Siswati, Sesotho, Sepedi, Setswana, Xitsonga, and Tshivenḓa in no particular order of importance. The English-Sesotho texts can be publicly accessed on the South African Centre for Digital Language Resources (SADiLaR) online repository (Mckellar, 2023). The readme file indicates that this corpus may need further cleaning for future uses because it was specifically formatted for training machine translation systems. However, as we were only interested in the words used in the corpus, no further cleaning was necessary. For this article, the corpus was tokenised and sentence segmented using *ucto*.

In the end, the Autshumato corpus contained around 4.6 million tokens. Unfortunately, the original corpus contained scrambled texts, as such, we could not unequivocally ascertain all text types present in the Sesotho corpus. Even so, McKellar (2022) lists at least four text types, namely magazines, policies, newsletters, translation works and documents crawled from the government (`gov.za`) domain. We are therefore confident that the corpus comprises different genres.

3.3 Corpus 3: NCHLT

The National Centre for Human Language Technology (NCHLT) project aimed to develop speech and text data to enable HLT development for the 11 official languages of South Africa (Eiselen and Puttkamer, 2014; Badenhorst and De Wet, 2022). The text collection contains data crawled from the South African `gov.za` domain. Data for each language contains enough training and testing samples for tasks such as language identification (Duvenhage, 2019).

The text corpus contains three sets of data, namely, the source texts, lexica, and corpus [3] (Eiselen and Puttkamer, 2014). Instead of relying on the lexica, we decided to use the actual corpus data to have more control. Both raw and cleaned versions of the corpus are present, we used the cleaned version and again tokenized all text material with *ucto*. Basic settings were used with the sentence segmentation option. In the end, the NCHLT corpus comprises around 2 million tokens.

3.4 Towards a Common Word Frequency List

To derive the frequency list all words were first lowercased. Next, all frequencies were calculated per corpus. In order to have word frequencies which are independent of corpus size, these were normalized to frequencies per million words, which is the preferred standard measure also referred to as relative frequency.

Our primary objective was to end up with a list of 3000 unique words based on the three corpora. To this end, we merged the three lists and made sure to average the relative frequencies of duplicate entries. For example, the entry *'a'* appeared in all three lists, with a relative frequency of 54 073.57, 24 853.12 and 27 740.49, respectively. The resulting average relative frequency for this entry is 35 555.73.

After the list was derived automatically using corpus-based frequency measures it was also manually processed by a native speaker of Sesotho with much experience in Sesotho language teaching and writing research in order to end up with a clean list.

4 Results and discussion

As mentioned above the three frequency lists were merged and relative frequencies were calculated for duplicate entries. Afterwards, a qualitative analysis

[3]The corpus is available from `https://hdl.handle.net/20.500.12185/336`

was carried out on all entries, which is presented next.

4.1 Proper names

The Dale-Chall index considers names of people and organisations as familiar (Barry and Stevenson, 1975). Therefore, they do not need to be included in the list of frequently used words. As a result, we removed the names of people and organisations. People's names included biblical names like *Judase* 'Judas', typical Sesotho names like *Mmalerato* 'Mother of love', and names of public figures like *Madiba* 'the iconic Nelson Mandela'. Organisation names such as the South African Revenue Services abbreviated as SARS were also removed.

4.2 Spelling

According to Chokoe (2020), Sepedi and Setswana do not have rules governing the spelling of loan words. Similarly, loan words in Sesotho also vary in how they are spelt. For instance, the English word 'provinces' is written using four varying spellings in the corpora, that is, *diporofense*, *diporofensi*, *diporovense*, and *diprovense*. Inconsistencies like this can be expected when there is flexibility when forming loan words (Kosch, 2013). Although Sesotho words typically do not contain the letter 'v', it is used in loan words that originally contain 'v' letters such as *thelevishene* 'television'.

Taljard (2008) discusses three issues when deciding on the correct spelling. First, it would be easy to take the word that appears the most, however, a large enough corpus representing texts in that domain would be required. Second, the correct candidate word could be chosen based on their best conformity with the target language's standard spelling. In our previous example, this would entail eliminating options with the unusual 'v' letter. Unfortunately, when the language rules governing spelling are superficial, this method of choosing based on conformity is not necessarily the best solution (Taljard, 2008). In the end, all four spelling variations conform to the CV-syllable structure typically preferred in Bantu languages (Ditsele, 2014).

Among others, we noticed a trend of discord in the spelling of (i) *ne* and *ni*, as in the case of *metjhini*, and *metjhine*, (ii) *re* and *ri* as in the example of *rephaboliki* and *riphaboliki*, (iii) *pro* and *poro* as in *porofense* and *profense*, and (iv) *ka* and *kha* as in the case of *kabinete* and *khabinete*. We manually identified instances where spelling varied for one word and decided to retain different spelling variants if they were included in the 3000 most used words. However, these are considered variations and are thus kept in the list as two or more variants of the same entry. In the end, only 30 entries had such varied spellings.

4.3 Plural forms

We treated singular and plural as different entries in the list of frequently used words. For instance, the word *dikhemikhale* 'chemicals' appears in the lists of frequently used words while the singular form *khemikhale* 'chemical' does not. Most of the words starting with the letter b and the letter m in the lists are plurals. Given that we want to use our list to identify words that are frequently used, we assumed that the addition of the prefixes to the words changed how the word behaves and therefore should be acknowledged. However, we do acknowledge that the Dale-Chall list counts plurals together with singular forms (Barry and Stevenson, 1975). Identifying all singular and plural forms would result in a very long list where some infrequently used words are falsely identified as frequently used. Furthermore, such analyses would require a trusted lemmatiser. Although lemmatisers have been developed for South African languages (Eiselen and Puttkamer, 2014), the lemmatisers were evaluated on government texts and not on different types of Sesotho texts. As a result, we cannot ascertain their reliability and accuracy in other text genres.

4.4 Abbreviations

A few abbreviations and acronyms were also identified after merging the lists. During the qualitative analysis, it was decided to remove all abbreviations such as *jj* for *jwalojwalo* 'etcetera', *mohl* for *mohla* 'date', and others. Both the abbreviations and their full forms were present in our initial lists of frequently used words. In the end, only the full forms for *jj* and *mohl* were retained in the final list. Even so, we kept both the abbreviation of tv and the full word *thelevishene* 'television'. We decided to keep this abbreviation as it is common in Sesotho. In fact, both the abbreviation and the full word are frequently used Even so, they are retained as one entry with varied spellings (see section4.2 for our treatment of varied spellings).

Acronyms concatenate words into one. For instance, World Health Organisation is counted as one word when abbreviated as WHO (Funk, 1968). For consistency, we removed all instances of abbreviations and acronyms as per Dale-Chall's list which considers abbreviations as unfamiliar. We, however, kept two acronyms, namely, HIV and AIDS as they are globally used abbreviations. The translation of the latter '*eitsi*, was also retained in the final list as it also appeared within the top 3000 most frequently used words before manual editing. Both AIDS and *eitsi* are counted as one entry with varied spellings.

4.5 Unexpected words

A few instances of unexpected words were also identified in the merged list. For instance, letters such as n, d, l, c, r, and b were removed as they do not carry meaning. Instances of non-Sesotho terms were also present on the list. For instance, words such as 'services' and 'language' were identified and removed from the list. Unlike the other unexpected words, the English word 'sister' was not removed from the list. Although there are Sesotho equivalent words for a sister, a matron, a maiden and a nurse, the loan English word 'sister' is more common. In fact, the Sesotho equivalent, *mooki* did not appear in any of the three frequency lists.

4.6 Specific variations

We hope to adapt the English Dale-Chall metric into Sesotho. As a result, we also consider the composition of the Dale-Chall list used in the English metric[4]. The Dale-Chall index uses the formula below to compute estimated grade levels for the Dale-Chall index:

$$\text{Dale-Chall index} = 0.0496(\frac{\#words}{\#sentences}) + [11.8(\frac{\#difficultwords}{\#words}) * 0.1579] + 3.6365$$

Difficult words as used in the formula are those that do not appear in the list of frequently used words (Stocker, 1971). As evident from the formula, the identification of difficult words is only one textual property used in determining the readability of texts. Not all words and their variations are listed in the list of frequently used words. However, when computing the scores, specific variations are excluded from this list of difficult words. We focus on two such variations, namely verbs and adverbs.

According to Barry and Stevenson (1975), verbs that end in -s, -ed, -ing, and -ied are not counted as difficult words as they are simply varieties of basic verbs. The Sesotho verb structures do not have an -ing structure. Instead, the continuous tenses are indicated by progressive markers such as '*a, ya,* and *ntse*' which are stand-alone words and not suffixed to the verbs. The -ed and -ied structures are indicated by the use of *-wa* and *-uwa* which are suffixed to the verb. For instance, the word *qetwa/qetuwa* 'finished' is derived from *qeta* 'finish'. For the purpose of our list, we disregard these differences and instead count all verb forms as different items.

Finally, English adverbs that end in -ly are not counted as difficult words in the Dale-Chall list (Barry and Stevenson, 1975). Sesotho adverbs take a different type of structure. For instance, the adverb of manner 'lovingly', would be expressed as *ka lerato* as in 'with love'. As a result, distinctions between different adverbs are unimportant in Sesotho and thus for our list.

4.7 Final list

After all these manual steps, we end up with a list of 3000 unique entries. About one third of this list, 993 entries, are words which were frequent in all three corpora. Another third are words frequently appearing in both corpus 2 and 3, namely 975 entries. The final third consists of 723 unique words from corpus 1, 125 unique words from corpus 2, 109 unique words from corpus 3, 49 unique words from corpus 1 and 2 and 63 unique from corpus 1 and 3. Based on these numbers we do notice a difference between corpus 1 (the Bible) and the other two corpora (Autshumato and NCHLT). Further research incorporating this list into actual frequency-based readability metrics and with envisaged end-user will have to corroborate whether the list can be employed for readability purposes.

Please note that in order to allow for spelling variation of certain words (please refer back to Section 4.2 for more information on this) such variations were added to the list for 30 words. As a result, the total number of words included in the list amounts to 3037. The list is made available to the research community at the repository of the Language Resource Management Agency of SADiLaR `https://repo.sadilar.gov`.

5 Discussion and Conclusion

This article discussed the development of a list of frequently used words in Sesotho using a corpus-based approach. Three different corpora were employed to this end. Although possibly unconven-

[4] *see* https://github.com/words/dale-chall

tional the bible corpus has also been included in this investigation and the results seem to confirm that this corpus behaves somewhat differently. Nevertheless, we believe the inclusion of this corpus is fitting for Sesotho as new orthographies were introduced using bible translations (Makutoane, 2022). For instance, the South African Sesotho orthography was introduced through the 1960 bible translation. Initially, we also wished to incorporate texts from the Sesotho Wikipedia. However, upon closer inspection, it was found that the orthography used in the Wiki pages represents both Sesotho from South Africa and Sesotho from Lesotho depending on who did the translation and/or initial editing of the Wikipedia entry. Such inconsistencies in the orthography may result in misrepresented frequencies. Although some inconsistencies between the orthographies may be semi-automatically corrected, others need a case-by-case analysis.

The aim of designing objective methods for measuring text readability in Sesotho is to enable teachers and assessors, in general, to be able to choose educational texts consistently and fairly. In reality, it is difficult to find texts in an under-researched language such as Sesotho. Finding new texts for learners is not always easy for teachers. In the end, texts are re-used without being re-adjusted to learners' reading abilities. Even so, texts prepared by examiners and textbook compilers at national and provincial levels re-purpose literary texts such as novels and dramas together with magazine and newspaper articles. Some of the texts are even translated from online English texts. The extent to which these texts are suitably adapted to specific learners has not been investigated.

The presence of an empirically developed frequency list such as the one presented in this article allows for taking further steps towards developing classical readability metrics which use frequency lists. Although the texts used for our corpus analysis contain a vast amount of government texts, we believe the final list does not necessarily solely represent government texts, because the meanings of the words are taken out of context. For instance, words such as *leleme* 'tongue/language/gossiper', and *moputso* 'salary/wage/payment/reward/gain', which both appear on our list, are not only used in government texts. Furthermore, the frequency list from the bible corpus overlapped with more than a third of the frequency lists of the other two corpora. This is an indication that the words are not necessarily restricted to government texts and that the list may be relevant for use even in other contexts such as educational texts.

In future work, the frequency list will be further validated on a corpus of education texts (Sibeko and Van Zaanen, 2022a), and be incorporated into adaptations of several readability formulas requiring frequency word lists from English to Sesotho. Furthermore, the list will be tested on envisaged end-users such as learners, teachers and publishers for further validation.

Limitations

This creation of a list of frequently used words in Sesotho is limited by the corpora used in this article. As such, the variety of text genres represented in the corpora is limited.

Additionally, although the original English Dale-Chall list was designed with the participation of actual fourth graders, we have relied solely on existing resources. Regrettably, the COVID-19 pandemic national lockdown in South Africa has resulted in stricter restrictions being put in place, making it more challenging to access vulnerable participants such as school learners. As a result, obtaining permission to engage with these participants has become a time-consuming exercise. As a result, we were restricted to text-based resources. We hope to be able to carry out additional validation experiments with the envisaged end-users in future work.

Ethics Statement

All data used in this study was obtained from publicly available sources. No confidential or sensitive information was used. The study was cleared for ethics by North-West University with the ethics clearance number: NWU-00729-21-A7.

Acknowledgements

This article forms part of a doctoral project completed at North-West University. This article was completed under the supervision of Professor Orphée De Clercq during a research stay at Gent University. It is partly funded by the Global Minds Fund at Ghent University.

References

Jonathan Anderson. 1983. Lix and Rix: Variations on a little-known readability index. *Journal of Reading*, 26(6):490–496.

Jaco Badenhorst and Febe De Wet. 2022. NCHLT auxiliary speech data for ASR technology development in South Africa. *Data in Brief*, 41:107860.

Etienne Barnard, Marelie H Davel, Charl Van Heerden, Febe De Wet, and Jaco Badenhorst. 2014. The NCHLT corpus of the South African languages. In *Proceedings of the 4th International Workshop Spoken Language Technologies for Under-resourced Languages*, pages 194–200.

Jeanne Gardner Barry and Timothy E Stevenson. 1975. Using a computer to calculate the Dale-Chall formula. *Journal of Reading*, 19:218–222.

Dolores Batinić, Sandra Birzer, and Heike Zinsmeister. 2016. Creating an extensible, levelled study corpus of Russian. In *Proceedings of the 13th Conference on Natural Language Processing (KONVENS 2016)*, pages 37–43. Universität Bochum.

Kiára Bendová. 2021. Using a parallel corpus to adapt the Flesch Reading Ease formula to Czech. *Journal of linguistics*, 72(2):477–487.

Kiára Bendová and Silvie Cinková. 2021. Adaptation of classic readability metrics to Czech. In *Proceedings of the International Conference on Text, Speech, and Dialogue: 24th International Conference*, pages 159–171. Springer.

RHM Brouwer. 1963. Onderzoek naar de leesmoeilijkheden van nederlands proza (Research into reading difficulty in Dutch prose). *Pedagogische studiën*, 40:454–464.

Jeanne Sternlicht Chall and Edgar Dale. 1995. *Readability revisited: The new Dale-Chall readability formula*. Brookline Books.

Sekgaila Chokoe. 2020. Spell it the way you like: The inconsistencies that prevail in the spelling of Northern Sotho loanwords. *South African Journal of African Languages*, 40(1):130–138.

Kate Cockcroft. 2016. A comparison between verbal working memory and vocabulary in bilingual and monolingual South African school beginners: Implications for bilingual language assessment. *International Journal of Bilingual Education and Bilingualism*, 19(1):74–88.

Meri Coleman and Ta Lin Liau. 1975. A computer readability formula designed for machine scoring. *Journal of Applied Psychology*, 60(2):283.

Edgar Dale and Jeanne Sternlicht Chall. 1948. A formula for predicting readability: Instructions. *Educational research bulletin*, pages 37–54.

Thabo Ditsele. 2014. Why not use Sepitori to enrich the vocabularies of Setswana and Sepedi? *Southern African Linguistics and Applied Language Studies*, 32(2):215–228.

Hessel Douma. 1960. Readability of Dutch farm papers: a discussion and application of readability-formulas. *Wageningen: Afdeling Sociologie en Sociografie van de Landbouwhogeschool*, 17:433–470.

Bernardt Duvenhage. 2019. Short text language identification for under resourced languages. *arXiv preprint arXiv:1911.07555*.

Roald Eiselen and Martin J Puttkamer. 2014. Developing text resources for ten South African languages. In *Proceedings of the 9th International Conference on Language Resources and Evaluation*, pages 3698–3703.

Rudolph Flesch. 1974. *The art of readable writing*, 2nd edition. Harper, New York.

Valerio Franchina and Roberto Vacca. 1986. Adaptation of flesh readability index on a bilingual text written by the same author both in Italian and English languages. *Linguaggi*, 3:47–49.

Laverne Carl Funk. 1968. *The reading level of selected magazines as determined by the Dale-Chall readability formula*. Ph.D. thesis, University of Minnesota: Minnesota.

Martha Gauthier and Nathan Johnson. 2019. Identification and recommendations of readability tests for the evaluation of clinical outcome assessments. *Value in Health*, 22:s828.

Anna Glazkova, Yury Egorov, and Maksim Glazkov. 2021. A comparative study of feature types for age-based text classification. In *Analysis of Images, Social Networks and Texts: 9th International Conference, AIST 2020, Skolkovo, Moscow, Russia, October 15–16, 2020, Revised Selected Papers 9*, pages 120–134. Springer.

Revathi Gopal, Mahendran Maniam, Noor Alhusna Madzlan, Siti Shuhaida binti Shukor, and Kanmani Neelamegam. 2021. Readability formulas: An analysis into reading index of prose forms. *Studies in English Language and Education*, 8(3):972–985.

Aditi Sharma Grover, Gerhard B van Huyssteen, and Marthinus W Pretorius. 2010. The South African Human Language Technologies audit. In *Proceedings of the Seventh International Conference on Language Resources and Evaluation (LREC'10)*, pages 2847–2850.

Aditi Sharma Grover, Gerhard Beukes. van Huyssteen, and Marthinus W. Pretorius. 2011. The South African Human Language Technology audit. *Language resources and evaluation*, 45:271–288.

Robert Gunning. 1969. The fog index after twenty years. *Journal of Business Communication*, 6(2):3–13.

Georges Henry. 1975. *Comment Mesurer La Lisibilite (How to Measure Readability).* Labor, Brussels, Belgium.

Alexandra H Humphreys and Jere Thomas Humphreys. 2013. Reading difficulty levels of selected articles in the Journal of Research in Music Education and Journal of Historical Research in Music Education. *Music Education Research International*, 6.

Thomas Jakobsen and Thomas Skardal. 2007. Readability index. Report, Agder University.

Liliane Kandel and Abraham Moles. 1958. Application de l'indice de Flesch à la langue française (Application of Flesch index to the French language). *Cahiers Etudes De Radio-Télévision*, 19(1958):253–274.

Peter J Kincaid, Robert P Fishburne Jr, Richard L Rogers, and Brad S Chissom. 1975. Derivation of new readability formulas (Automated Readability index, Fog count and Flesch Reading Ease formula) for navy enlisted personnel. Report, Defense Technical Information Center.

Inge Kosch. 2013. An analysis of the oxford bilingual school dictionary: Northern Sotho and English (de schryver 2007). *Lexikos*, 23:611–627.

Daleen Krige and Marianne Reid. 2017. A pilot investigation into the readability of Sesotho health information pamphlets. *Communitas*, 22:113–123.

Tshokolo J Makutoane. 2022. 'The people divided by a common language': The orthography of Sesotho in Lesotho, South Africa, and the implications for bible translation. *HTS Teologiese Studies/Theological Studies*, 78(1):9.

Harry G Mc Laughlin. 1969. Smog grading-a new readability formula. *Journal of reading*, 12(8):639–646.

Cindy McKellar. 2022. *Autshumato Monolingual Sesotho Corpus*. South African Centre for Digital Language Resources. Available at: https://repo.sadilar.org/handle/20.500.12185/583 Accessed: 28 Jan 2023.

Cindy Mckellar. 2023. *Autshumato English-Sesotho Parallel Corpora*. Southern African Centre for Digital Language Resources. Available at: https://repo.sadilar.org/handle/20.500.12185/577 [Accessed: 6 Feb. 2023].

Carmen Moors, Illana Wilken, Karen Calteaux, and Tebogo Gumede. 2018a. Human Language Technology audit 2018: Analysing the development trends in resource availability in all South African languages. In *Proceedings of the Annual Conference of the South African Institute of Computer Scientists and Information Technologists*, pages 296–304.

Carmen Moors, Illana Wilken, Tebogo Gumede, and Karen Calteaux. 2018b. Human Language Technology audit 2017/18. Technical report, CSIR Meraka Institute.

Irina Vladimirovna Oborneva. 2006. *Avtomatizirovannaya otsenka slozhnosti uchebnykh tekstov na osnove statisticheskikh parametrov (Automated estimation of complexity of educational texts on the basis of statistical parameters).* Thesis, RAS Institut soderzhaniya i metodov obucheniya [RAS Institute of Content and Teaching Methods].

Joao Palotti, Lorraine Goeuriot, Guido Zuccon, and Allan Hanbury. 2016. Ranking health web pages with relevance and understandability. In *Proceedings of the 39th International ACM SIGIR conference on Research and Development in Information Retrieval*, pages 965–968.

Romana Kabir Piu, Kazi Rayed Hossain, Noor Hossain Sabab, and Rakib Bin Mannan Ar Rafi. 2020. *Hatred Message Identification using DistilBERT*. Ph.D. thesis, United International University.

Elizabeth Pretorius, Nompumelelo Mohohlwane, and Nicholas Spaull. 2020. Investigating the comprehension iceberg: Developing empirical benchmarks for early-grade reading in agglutinating African languages. *South African Journal of Childhood Education*, 10(1):1–14.

Elizabeth J Pretorius and Lieke Stoffelsma. 2017. How is their word knowledge growing? Exploring grade 3 vocabulary in South African township schools. *South African Journal of Childhood Education*, 7(1):1–13.

Marianne Reid, Mariatte Neil, and Edgar Janse Van Rensburg-Bonthuyzen. 2019. Development of a Sesotho health literacy test in a South African context. *African Journal of Primary Health Care and Family Medicine*, 11(1):1–13.

Jabulani Sibanda and Jean Baxen. 2016. Determining ESL learners' vocabulary needs from a textbook corpus: Challenges and prospects. *Southern African Linguistics and Applied Language Studies*, 34(1):57–70.

Johannes Sibeko and Mmasibidi Setaka. 2022. An overview of Sesotho BLARK content. *Journal of Digital Humanities Association of South Africa*, 4(2):1–11.

Johannes Sibeko and Menno Van Zaanen. 2022a. Final year high school examination texts of South African home and first additional language subjects. *Southern African Centre for Digital Language Resources*. Available at: https://repo.sadilar.org/handle/20.500.12185/568 [accessed: 29 dec. 2022].

Johannes Sibeko and Menno Van Zaanen. 2022b. Sesotho syllabification systems. *Southern African Centre for Digital Language Resources*. Available at: https://repo.sadilar.org/handle/20.500.12185/555 [accessed: 3 jan 2023].

Manjira Sinha, Sakshi Sharma, Tirthankar Dasgupta, and Anupam Basu. 2012. New readability measures for Bangla and Hindi texts. In *Proceedings of COLING 2012*, pages 1141–1151. Association for Computational Linguistics.

Edgar A Smith and R.J Senter. 1967. *Automated readability index*. University of Cincinnati, Ohio.

Leonard P Stocker. 1971. Increasing the precision of the Dale-Chall readability formula. *Reading Improvement*, 8(3):87.

Lieke Stoffelsma. 2019a. English vocabulary exposure in South African township schools: Pitfalls and opportunities. *Reading & Writing-Journal of the Reading Association of South Africa*, 10(1):1–10.

Lieke Stoffelsma. 2019b. From 'sheep' to 'amphibian': English vocabulary teaching strategies in South African township schools. *South African Journal of Childhood Education*, 9(1):1–10.

Elsabe Taljard. 2008. Terminology practice in a non-standardized environment: A case study. In *Proceedings of the XIII EURALEX International Congress (Barcelona, 15-19 July 2008)*, pages 1073–1080.

Marthie Van der Walt, Kobus Maree, and Suria Ellis. 2008. A mathematics vocabulary questionnaire for use in the intermediate phase. *South African Journal of Education*, 28(4):489–504.

Phillip Van Oosten, Dries Tanghe, and Véronique Hoste. 2010. Towards an improved methodology for automated readability prediction. In *Proceedings of the 7th Conference on International Language Resources and Evaluation (LREC 2010)*, pages 775–782. European Language Resources Association (ELRA).

Carien Wilsenach and Maxine Schaefer. 2022. Development and initial validation of productive vocabulary tests for isiZulu, Siswati and English in South Africa. *Language Testing*, pages 567—-592.

Xin Yan, Dawei Song, and Xue Li. 2006. Concept-based document readability in domain specific information retrieval. In *Proceedings of the 15th ACM international conference on Information and knowledge management*, pages 540–549.

Deep learning and low-resource languages: How much data is enough? A case study of three linguistically distinct South African languages

Roald Eiselen and **Tanja Gaustad**
Centre for Text Technology (CTexT)
North-West University
Potchefstroom, South Africa
roald.eiselen@nwu.ac.za, tanja.gaustad@nwu.ac.za

Abstract

In this paper we present a case study for three under-resourced linguistically distinct South African languages (Afrikaans, isiZulu, and Sesotho sa Leboa) to investigate the influence of data size and linguistic nature of a language on the performance of different embedding types. Our experimental setup consists of training embeddings on increasing amounts of data and then evaluating the impact of data size for the downstream task of part of speech tagging. We find that relatively little data can produce useful representations for this specific task for all three languages. Our analysis also shows that the influence of linguistic and orthographic differences between languages should not be underestimated: morphologically complex, conjunctively written languages (isiZulu in our case) need substantially more data to achieve good results, while disjunctively written languages require substantially less data. This is not only the case with regard to the data for training the embedding model, but also annotated training material for the task at hand. It is therefore imperative to know the characteristics of the language you are working on to make linguistically informed choices about the amount of data and the type of embeddings to use.

1 Introduction

Over the last decade vectorised word representations and the use of deep learning have become de facto standards in Natural Language Processing (NLP) (Alzubaidi et al., 2021; Khurana et al., 2023). There has also been a push to broaden the linguistic diversity in NLP research (Joshi et al., 2020). Both learning vectorised representations, a.k.a. embeddings, and deep learning are inherently data-driven procedures where models are trained from vast amounts of data to either represent language numerically or learn some downstream task. Including a bigger variety of languages than mainstream languages, such as English, Spanish, German, Japanese, etc., to achieve more linguistic diversity typically means studying low-resource or under-resourced languages.

This, however, leads to a dichotomy: High-performing deep learning models, like BERT, have been trained on billions of words. When developing models for languages other than English, lesser resourced languages (such as the South African languages) get left behind because there is very little available data. Also, evaluation of existing techniques is only partially applied to under-resourced languages and researchers typically assume that the generalisations achieved with training on a lot of data will mostly hold true with less data.

More recently there have been efforts to extend the usefulness of embeddings trained on well-resourced languages with languages that have substantially less data in so-called multi-lingual models, such as XLM-R (Conneau et al., 2020) and mBERT (Devlin et al., 2019). These models generate representations that are a combination of language specific information as well as information learned across all of the languages included in the model. Typically they are trained exclusively on web data like Common Crawl or Wikipedia, which have some inherent limitations (as discussed later in this paper), but also have limited availability for South African languages. For instance, isiNdebele has no Wikipedia data and is therefore not even present in Common Crawl. Consequently, most of the South African languages are not included in these multilingual models.

Doing NLP research on South African languages in this day and age then leads to the question of what the implications of working with very little data is on current standard techniques like embeddings and neural language models. Or in other words: how much data is needed for learning useful vector representations? The underlying assumption is that learning from less data will yield less representative and thus less useful models. It re-

Proceedings of the Fourth workshop on Resources for African Indigenous Languages (RAIL 2023), pages 42–53
May 6, 2023

mains to be seen, however, if this is truly the case. From a linguistic diversity point of view, it is also relevant to know how the embedding models vary from each other for structurally different languages and how the amount of available data influences the learned representations for typographically different languages.

In this paper, we present a case study attempting to answer these questions. Our setup consists of training embeddings for three linguistically distinct South African languages (Afrikaans, isiZulu, and Sesotho sa Leboa) to evaluate the impact of embeddings trained on increasing amounts of data for a part of speech (POS) tagging downstream task. The goal is to determine the influence of data size on the performance of different embedding types and to describe the effects observed for different languages. The results of our experiments show that even relatively little data can be useful in some scenarios and that morphologically complex and conjunctively written languages require substantially more data, both for training the embeddings and the downstream task, especially when using full/sub word representations.

2 Background

2.1 South African linguistic context

South Africa's eleven official languages include nine Niger-Congo-B (NCB) languages and two Germanic languages. The NCB languages (van der Velde et al., 2022) have a number of linguistic characteristics that make them substantially different from most Indo-European languages: all of them are tone languages; they use an elaborate system of noun classes with up to 21 classes; and their nominal and verbal morphology is highly agglutinative and very productive, which can result in a large vocabulary for those languages that follow the conjunctive writing system.

For historic reasons, the South African NCB languages adopted two different writing systems, either conjunctive or disjunctive, where a distinction is generally made between linguistic words and orthographic words. For conjunctively written languages one orthographic word (token) corresponds to one or more linguistic words, whereas for the disjunctively written languages several orthographic words can correspond to one linguistic word (Louwrens and Poulos, 2006). The four Nguni languages, isiNdebele, isiXhosa, isiZulu, and Siswati, are written conjunctively, while the three Sotho languages, Sesotho, Sesotho sa Leboa (also known as Sepedi), and Setswana, Tshivenḓa, a Venda language, as well as Xitsonga, a Tswa-Ronga language, are disjunctively written. This is a marked difference from the two Germanic languages present in South Africa, Afrikaans and English, where mostly a linguistic word and an orthographic word coincide.

The implication of these different writing systems is that multiple tokens in disjunctively written languages can correspond to a single token in the conjunctively written languages. This leads to sparse token frequency for the conjunctively written languages, while the opposite is true for the disjunctive languages. As an illustration, the parallel equivalents of a 50,000 word English corpus will have approximately 43,000 words for the conjunctively written languages, while the disjunctive languages will have approximately 60,000 tokens. This difference and its implications are discussed in more detail in Section 3.

One of the objectives of this paper is to investigate the influence of linguistic and orthographic differences in South African languages on using embedding models in NLP tasks, specifically POS tagging. To that purpose we have chosen one language from each family for our experiments: Afrikaans (Germanic), isiZulu (conjunctively written Nguni) and Sesotho sa Leboa (disjunctively written Sotho).

2.2 Embedding models

Since the introduction of the word2vec (Mikolov et al., 2013) and GloVe (Pennington et al., 2014) vectorised word representations, most (if not all) NLP tasks make use of learned vector representations, referred to as embeddings, to model the occurrences of words and their context. With these algorithms, embedding models are trained efficiently on large amounts of data and the learned representations, in combination with deep learning techniques, generally improve the results of downstream NLP tasks. In this paper we apply three embedding architectures, namely fastText (an extension of word2vec) and GloVe, two classical embeddings, and FLAIR embeddings, a character-based recurrent neural network.

GloVe embeddings (Pennington et al., 2014) learn representations of words using global co-occurrences to train a log-bilinear regression model. For each word in the vocabulary of the GloVe model a single n-dimensional vector is learned, while all unseen words generate the same vector representation. fastText embeddings (Bojanowski et al., 2017), an extension of word2vec (Mikolov et al., 2013), are based on local co-occurrences of words. In addition to the full word, the generation of the vector representations includes character n-grams, or "subwords", allowing these embeddings to also generate distinct representations for previously unseen words by combining the n-grams from the unseen word. fastText embeddings come in two variants, continuous bag-of-words (CBoW) and Skipgram models. Both GloVe and fastText learn a single vector representation for each word in the vocabulary. When retrieving this vector, the word will always receive the same vector, irrespective of the context in which the word appears.

In contrast, FLAIR embeddings (Akbik et al., 2018, 2019) learn representations for character sequences by training a long-short-term-memory (LSTM) recurrent neural network. This means that a distinct word occurring in different contexts can have a different vector representation depending on the character sequences (context) around the word. Furthermore, all character sequences receive a representation whether a sequence has been seen during training or not. This can help with the representation of rare or misspelled words as well as with individual morphemes or morphologically complex words. FLAIR allows for two variants, namely Forward and Backward depending on the direction in which the text is processed – either from the start (forward) or from the end (backward).

With the availability of these improved deep learning frameworks and an increased focus on linguistic diversity in the deep learning community, there has been a substantial rise in research on African languages. The focus of this work has been broad: From applications of embeddings and deep learning on individual languages and individual applications (Dlamini et al., 2021; Heyns and Barnard, 2020; Loubser and Puttkammer, 2020; Marivate et al., 2020; Ralethe, 2020), to investigations of multilingual embedding architectures for African languages (Alabi et al., 2022; Hanslo, 2021; Moeng et al., 2022) and transfer learning from well-resourced languages (Hedderich et al., 2020). The outcomes of these investigations have had mixed results, in some cases substantially improving technologies over previous best results, while other approaches show how the nature and quality of the data have a significant impact on the quality of the trained models. As far as we are aware, none of these studies have explicitly investigated the quality and nature of the embeddings when considering data size and morphosyntactic attributes of African languages.

3 Data

The major prerequisite for training embeddings and language models for any language is the availability of large amounts of text data. Although there have been several efforts to create such corpora for the South African languages (Eiselen and Puttkammer, 2014; Goldhahn et al., 2012; Marivate et al., 2020), there is still relatively little data available for most of them. The data collected for this study is a combination of various open data sets (mostly CC-BY and CC-NC licenses), as well as some data only available to the authors with copyright restrictions prohibiting the distribution of the full corpora. The data included in the training corpora for the isiZulu and Sesotho sa Leboa embeddings are primarily from the NCHLT Text Corpora (Eiselen and Puttkammer, 2014; Puttkammer et al., 2014c,d,e), Autshumato Corpora (McKellar, 2022a,b,c), Leipzig Corpus Collection (Goldhahn et al., 2012)[1], and Common Crawl corpus[2]. All of these sources are also used in the Afrikaans training corpus, along with additional data from publishers and private sources, i.e. the NWU/Lapa Corpus, NWU/Protea Boekhuis Corpus, and NWU/ATKV-Taalgenoot Corpus.

Although the data in both the Leipzig and Common Crawl corpora are language identified, an initial investigation showed that a substantial amount of the data is incorrectly attributed to one of the languages. This is primarily due to the fact that all three languages in this study have related languages that share similar orthographic features which leads to misclassification of the language data, specifically:

- Afrikaans ⇔ Dutch;
- isiZulu ⇔ isiNdebele, isiXhosa, and Siswati;
- Sesotho sa Leboa ⇔ Setswana and Sesotho.

Consequently, all of the data from the Leipzig and Common Crawl corpora were further cleaned with the NCHLT Language Identifier (Hocking,

[1] https://corpora.uni-leipzig.de/en
[2] https://commoncrawl.org

Language	Embeddings			POS tagging				
	Tokens	Vocab	Token:Vocab ratio	Train	Dev	Test	Orig. tags	Red. tags
Afrikaans	40,610,635[a]	311,719	0.0077	50,034	5,451	5,835	97	12
isiZulu	16,271,123	488,822	0.0300	39,768	4,376	4,955	97	17
Sesotho sa Leboa	8,909,133	80,919	0.0091	53,745	5,556	7,127	138	14

[a]Please note that this data was sampled from a larger 430 million token corpus.

Table 1: Summary of data available for training embeddings and POS tagging

2014; Puttkammer et al., 2018) at 80% confidence level. Since most of the data in the respective corpora originate from the web, all duplicates on paragraph level in the combined data are removed prior to training.

A summary of the data available for training embeddings is presented in Table 1. As was discussed in Section 2.1, there is a marked difference in the number of tokens in the vocabulary for each of the three languages for the same corpus sizes. One way of representing the combined effects of these morphosyntactic and writing system differences is by adding the token-vocabulary ratio to the reported token counts: a text in the conjunctively written, morphologically complex language of isiZulu typically displays a higher token-vocabulary ratio than a text in Sesotho sa Leboa, where a number of morphemes are written separately and therefore count as multiple tokens. In Afrikaans, where one token typically corresponds to one orthographic word, the token-vocabulary ratio is somewhere between the two extremes of the disjunctive and conjunctive languages. The vocabulary for Afrikaans is still more sparse than is typical in English since compounding is very common in Afrikaans and leads to a larger number of unique tokens, although it is not nearly as productive as the conjunctively written isiZulu.

The POS data used in this study is the NCHLT Annotated Corpora for Afrikaans and Sesotho sa Leboa (Puttkammer et al., 2014a,b), and the Linguistically enriched corpora for conjunctively written South African languages for isiZulu (Gaustad and Puttkammer, 2022; Puttkammer and Gaustad, 2021). Each annotated corpus consists of approximately 50,000 tokens for the training set, and a separate test set of approximately 5,000 tokens. Although the data is annotated on very fine-grained POS tag sets (typically consisting of 90+ tags), for this investigation we reduced the tag sets to between 12 and 17 tags by e.g. excluding class information and using only main POS classes. This makes the results between languages more comparable, but does not obscure the functional differences a conversion to UPOS[3] would. An overview of the POS data and tags is presented in Table 1.

4 Experimental Design

In order to determine the impact of different embedding architectures and morphosyntactic attributes on the usefulness of embeddings in low-resource environments, we perform a set of experiments to establish how these attributes in combination with data size affect the quality of a single downstream task, namely POS tagging.

The first step in the process is generating embeddings in each of the chosen architectures – fastText, GloVe, and FLAIR – with different data set sizes. For each language a random selection of paragraphs from the available corpus is made in iteratively larger sizes, starting with 10,000 paragraphs and doubling the amount of data randomly for each iteration. For isiZulu and Sesotho sa Leboa this process is repeated up to the full available corpus (292,600 and 838,000 paragraphs respectively), while for Afrikaans we only select data up to one increment above the largest of the other two languages (1,280,000 paragraphs).[4] Based on each data iteration, embeddings for all three architectures, including their different flavours, are trained.

To make the comparison of models as consequent as possible, the hyperparameters for each of the architectures are kept the same (typically the default settings, see Table 2) and no hyperparameter tuning is performed. Consequently, there may be certain hyperparameter selections for the different data set sizes and languages, that could lead to slight improvements in the results presented in this work, but different hyperparameters would make the comparison and resultant conclusions less generally applicable. Furthermore, this would also substantially increase the number of experiments that need to be trained (probably into the thousands) and cannot be ethically and environmentally

[3]https://universaldependencies.org/u/pos/

[4]See Table 3 in appendix for details.

Embedding	Embedding type	Hyperparameters
GloVe	Static word	Dimensions: 300 Epochs: 50 Min. occurences: 2 Window size: 20
fastText	Static word and subword	Dimensions: 300 Learning rate: 0.05 Epochs: 15 Min. occurences: 2 Minimum n: 3 Maximum n: 6
FLAIR	Contextual character	Dimensions: 2048 Learning rate: 10.0 Epochs: 15 Sequence length: 250 Layers: 1 Batch size: 64

Table 2: Hyperparameter settings for embedding training

justified due to additional power consumption. In total 110 embedding models are trained on an Intel i79700 CPU and four NVIDIA GeForce RTX 2060 6Gb GPUs, totalling 30 CPU hours and 252 GPU hours.

The quality of the embeddings trained on the different corpus sizes for the three languages is evaluated using a vanilla bidirectional LSTM-CRF POS tagger implemented as part of the FLAIR framework[5] (Akbik et al., 2019). A separate POS tagger is trained for each of the embedding models, on the same GPU hardware used to train the embeddings. The main reason for using the FLAIR framework is the fact that it has built-in support for all of the different embedding architectures, thus ensuring that the results of the respective taggers can reasonably be compared. As with the embedding models, the hyperparameters are kept to the default settings (hidden size: 256, learning rate: 0.1, drop out: 0.05, epochs: 40). It should also be noted that because the POS training sets are relatively small, fine-tuning of the embeddings during the POS tagger training is not carried out. All taggers are evaluated using the Accuracy metric, and compared to the NCHLT Web Services[6] POS taggers (Puttkammer et al., 2018) as a baseline for each language.

With such a large set of taggers (24 in total), the POS taggers were not trained multiple times with averaged scores. Doing so would once again substantially increase the required GPU hours (currently 82) required for the experiment, and cannot be justified, since the aim of the paper is not to create the best possible tagger, but rather to establish how the different embeddings influence the downstream results.

5 Results and discussion

We will now discuss the performance of the various embedding models with different data sizes for Afrikaans, isiZulu and Sesotho sa Leboa. A graphic representation of the performances on the POS tagging task can be found in Figures 1 (for Afrikaans), 2 (for isiZulu) and 3 (for Sesotho sa Leboa), with the full numerical results available in Table 3 in the appendix.

The first notable conclusion that can be drawn from inspecting the results is that even embeddings trained on very small corpora can benefit the quality of relatively simple downstream tasks, such as POS tagging, when compared to baseline systems. Specifically, the FLAIR contextual character embeddings produce downstream results that are surprisingly good, even for the conjunctively written isiZulu. It was expected that the character-based models would perform best with very small amounts of data, but the models trained on the smallest data sets actually perform comparably to the best results for any of the other embeddings. Conversely, although the FLAIR models perform best when trained with the largest data sets, there is not nearly the same level of improvement as there is for the other two architectures. One implication of these findings is that much smaller and faster models may perform well enough for certain purposes, if not necessarily attaining state-of-the-art results. This allows researchers and developers with limited hardware capacity to also benefit from using these types of embeddings.

As expected, GloVe embeddings consistently perform the worst of all the embedding types, especially so with the first couple of iterations of very small corpora, for two main reasons. Firstly, as these embeddings only generate representations for words in the vocabulary, all words in the tagging task that are not part of the vocabulary are represented by the same vector, and therefore do not have any distinctive representations. Secondly, since many words will only appear a small number of times in the training data, learning complex representations is difficult when a word is only seen in a small number of contexts. These problems are exacerbated for isiZulu where the conjunctive

[5] https://github.com/flairNLP/flair
[6] https://hlt.nwu.ac.za/

writing style causes a large number of distinctive co-occurrences for all words, especially less frequent words, and learning meaningful representations is almost impossible. For the disjunctively written Sesotho sa Leboa, however, the vocabulary is relatively representative even with a small corpus, and GloVe embeddings perform only slightly worse than the other embedding types.

The fastText models perform substantially better than the GloVe models with very small data sets, while still performing worse than the FLAIR embeddings. With the largest data sets, however, the fastText CBoW models perform either very similarly or better than the FLAIR models. Interestingly, with very small data sets the Skipgram models outperform the CBoW models for the first two or three data iterations, after which the CBoW models consistently perform better across all languages. It is not immediately obvious why this would be the case, but the fact that this occurs across all three languages definitively shows that with very small data sets Skipgrams are preferable over CBoW, whereas for any data set with more than 500,000 or a million tokens (corresponding to about 40,000 paragraphs in our data), the CBoW models generate better representations measured on the POS tagging task. This contradicts the initial findings of Mikolov et al. (2013), but is in line with the latest released fastText models[7] which have also switched to CBoW models by default, as opposed to previously released models (Bojanowski et al., 2017).

Our results also clearly show that the writing system of the language plays a major part in how much data is required to train embeddings that are useful to any degree. For conjunctively written languages, as the token-level morphological complexity of the language increases, so does the amount of data required to create meaningful representations. In the two extreme cases of isiZulu and Sesotho sa Leboa, even the embeddings from the largest available corpora for isiZulu perform substantially worse than the embeddings based on the smallest Sesotho sa Leboa corpus, with accuracies between 4.28% and 15.19% lower depending on the model. Afrikaans, which is slightly more morphologically complex on token level than Sesotho sa Leboa, but not nearly as complex as isiZulu, also performs somewhere between the two languages when considering the

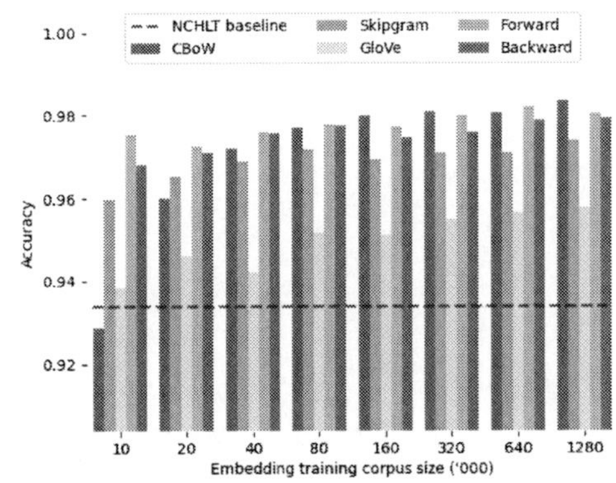

Figure 1: Accuracy of Afrikaans POS tagging using different embedding models with increasing data sizes

different data sizes and embeddings.

Apart from the general findings presented in the previous paragraphs, there are also certain language specific aspects of the results that warrant discussion. We include some broad linguistic error analysis for each of the languages to determine where the main focus of errors are for the best models for each language.[8]

For Afrikaans, the fastText CBoW model performs the worst of all models on the smallest data set, but shows the largest degree of improvement as the data size increases, to the point where it is the best performing of all models on the largest data set. Also, the Afrikaans FLAIR Forward model performs at almost an identical level to the fastText CBoW model, while the FLAIR Backward model is slightly worse. When considering the tag error differences between the embeddings trained on the smallest and largest corpora, it becomes clear that the main source of improvements for both fastText and GloVe embeddings is the size of the data. As more words are included in the vocabulary, the relative error rates for nouns, verbs, adjectives, and adverbs are reduced by between 35% and 45%. The relative error rate reductions for the FLAIR models are not as uniform across all open word classes. As an example, the FLAIR Forward model reduces the percentage of errors for adjective and verbs by 43% and 72% respectively, while increasing the number of errors for nouns or adverbs. The FLAIR Backward model shows improvements for adjectives (25%) and verbs (61%) as well, but also substantial improvements for nouns (64%) and adverbs (48%).

[7]https://fasttext.cc/docs/en/crawl-vectors.html

[8]Detailed information on the linguistic error analysis can be found in Tables 4, 5 and 6 in the appendix.

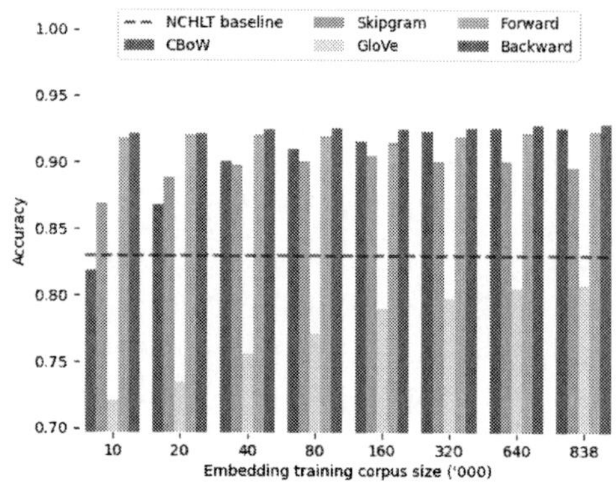

Figure 2: Accuracy of isiZulu POS tagging using different embedding models with increasing data sizes

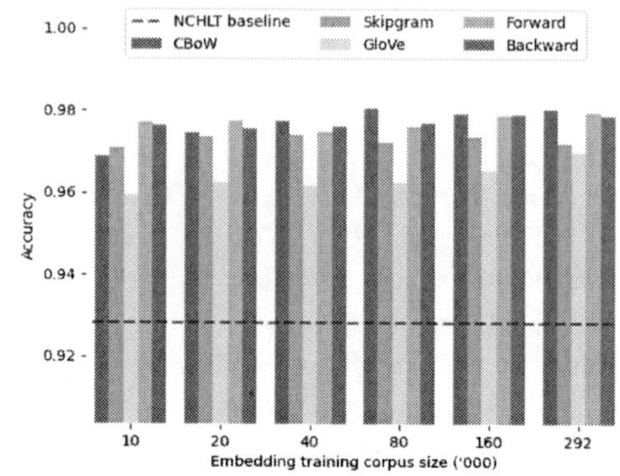

Figure 3: Accuracy of Sesotho sa Leboa POS tagging using different embedding models with increasing data sizes

In the case of isiZulu, the FLAIR Backward model performs best overall, although the FLAIR Forward performs comparably. This differentiation with Afrikaans is likely due to the fact that isiZulu uses prefixation more productively than suffixation, and processing data from the end of the text to the beginning leads to a slightly more informative model. The GloVe model for isiZulu is significantly worse than any of the other models trained in this investigation and is definitely a consequence of data sparsity during training as well as previously unseen words in the tagging task. This problem is less prevalent for the fastText models: Since the n-grams of previously unseen words can still generate a representation, and although not as informative to the task, these "subword" representations obviously have a substantial impact on the quality of the results. The CBoW and GloVe models show the largest error rate reductions across the major POS classes of between 17% and 77%, particularly for Possessives and Adverbs. The FLAIR models on the other hand do not show large improvements for any of the categories, and the improvements are counteracted by regressions in other classes, to which end the results remain relatively stable between the models trained on the smallest and largest corpora.

Even though the FLAIR embeddings perform best for isiZulu, there is very little improvement for these models as the size of the data increases. There are two possible, and related, reasons why this may be the case. Firstly, since most of the affixation in isiZulu is fairly regular, most of the morphological structure of the language may be encoded well with small amounts of data. This is supported by the fact that the most productive word classes (i.e. nouns, verbs, adverbs, possessives, and relatives) are tagged more accurately with a FLAIR model trained on the smallest amount of data, than for any of the other embedding models. The fastText CBoW model does perform similarly on these classes with the largest training set, and may possibly outperform the FLAIR models if more data is made available. The second possible reason is that the annotated POS training data is just too small for further improvements to be possible, and a substantially larger set is required to attain results comparable to those of Afrikaans or Sesotho sa Leboa.

All of the embedding models for Sesotho sa Leboa, with its disjunctive writing style, clearly already perform well with very small data sets. The improvements on the POS tagging task with larger data sets is also not nearly as large as for the other two languages. As with the other languages, the FLAIR models perform the best with very little data, while the fastText CBoW models generate the best overall results with more data. Surprisingly, the fastText Skipgram models do not show much improvement between the smallest and largest data sets, and there does not seem to be an easily identifiable reason for this result. As with both other languages, the GloVe embeddings generally show improvements with each iteration of larger data, and are likely to keep improving if more data were available to be included. For the GloVe and FLAIR models, the improvements in tag classes are much more moderate, between 8% and 46% for the noun, verb, concord, and adjective classes. Both of the

FLAIR models also regress on the adverb class. The fastText models do show more substantial improvements for some of the classes, but for the Skipgram model the error reduction in one class is counteracted by an increase in errors in another class. For example, the noun class errors are reduced by 40%, but the adjective and concordial classes increase their errors by more than 40%, resulting in Accuracies that are very similar to the model trained on the smallest data sets.

Generalizing our findings for the type of embeddings to use with little data, the takeaway is that FLAIR models will produce decent results, especially with very little data. With slightly more data, fastText CBoW embeddings will also perform adequately. GloVe, however, needs large amounts of data to reach enough generalization power to be applied successfully to a morpho-syntactic downstream task.

Our analysis also shows that the influence of linguistic and orthographic differences between languages should not be underestimated. A language such as isiZulu with a complex morphology and large vocabulary (and consequently more data sparseness) will need more data to train representative language models. But a better language model alone is not sufficient. More task related annotated data is also needed to substantially increase the POS accuracy – again an effect of trying to learn from sparse data. It is important to acknowledge the influence of data sparseness in both the learned representations and the actual task to be learned on the final tagging results.

6 Conclusion and Future Work

In this paper, we investigated how the amount of available training data and the linguistic attributes of a language influence the quality of learned embeddings. Our case study consisted of training three different embedding architectures on varying amounts of data, and evaluating the embeddings extrinsically on the downstream task of POS tagging for three linguistically distinct South African languages (Afrikaans, isiZulu and Sesotho sa Leboa).

Our results indicate that under certain conditions even relatively little data can produce useful representations for a specific task. We explicitly show that with very little data (approximately 300,000 tokens) FLAIR embeddings generate representations that perform comparably to any of the other architectures trained on the largest data sets, irrespective of the morphological complexity of the language. The FLAIR models do not generally show the same level of improvements as the other embedding types when larger data sets are available, and in some cases are out-preformed by the fastText CBoW embeddings with the largest available training sets.

The results further reinforce the knowledge that for morphologically complex, conjunctively written languages, substantially more data is needed to achieve good results, not only unannotated text for training the language model, but also annotated training material for the task at hand. Overall we conclude that it is imperative to know the characteristics of the language you are working on to make linguistically informed choices about the amount of data and the type of embeddings to use.

Although these results are encouraging for the relatively simple task of POS tagging, the same may not be true for other, more complex tasks, especially where semantic attributes are of interest. We do however expect that the shortcomings apparent in the fastText Skipgram and GloVe models will remain in under-resourced settings regardless of the task they are applied to. With this in mind there are two areas for future investigation. Firstly, these embedding models should be applied to different tasks that may require different linguistic attributes. Secondly, a comparable experimental design should be applied to transformer models, such as RoBERTa, and to fine-tuning multi-lingual language models (e.g. mBERT, XLM-R) to determine whether similar encouraging results are possible with these more complex architectures.

7 Limitations

There are several limitations of the research reported on in this submission, some of which are explicitly stated in the paper, and others that are expressed in this section as they do not fit well within the discussions of the paper.

The first major limitation of the work relates to the fact that the reported results for the downstream task are not averages of multiple runs, and that there was no hyperparameter tuning performed. Due to the nature of the investigation, i.e. not attempting to achieve state-of-the-art results, and the number of separate runs required to address this limitation, the authors do not expect the results to change such that the conclusions would be significantly affected. For these reasons and the ethical implications of performing unnecessary runs the authors decided not to perform these additional experiments.

Secondly, even though the submission reports on three linguistically distinct languages, care should still be taken when interpreting and applying these findings to other languages, especially where those languages differ significantly from those described in the paper, such as for instance Dravidian and Sino-Tibetan languages.

Lastly, the results of this submission specifically target the relatively simple POS tagging task, and further investigations on the findings of this paper in more complex NLP tasks is necessary to support these findings.

Acknowledgements

This work was made possible with the financial support of the National Centre for Human Language Technology, an initiative of the South African Department of Sports, Arts and Culture. The authors would also like to thank Martin Puttkammer for feedback during the writing and revision of this work.

References

Alan Akbik, Tanja Bergmann, Duncan Blythe, Kashif Rasul, Stefan Schweter, and Roland Vollgraf. 2019. FLAIR: An easy-to-use framework for state-of-the-art NLP. In *Proceedings of the 2019 Conference of the North American Chapter of the Association for Computational Linguistics (Demonstrations)*, pages 54–59, Minneapolis, Minnesota. Association for Computational Linguistics.

Alan Akbik, Duncan Blythe, and Roland Vollgraf. 2018. Contextual string embeddings for sequence labeling. In *Proceedings of the 27th International Conference on Computational Linguistics*, pages 1638–1649, Santa Fe, New Mexico, USA. Association for Computational Linguistics.

Jesujoba O. Alabi, David I. Adelani, Marius Mosbach, and Dietrich Klakow. 2022. Adapting pre-trained language models to African languages via multilingual adaptive fine-tuning. In *Proceedings of the 29th International Conference on Computational Linguistics*, pages 4336–4349, Gyeongju, Republic of Korea. International Committee on Computational Linguistics.

Laith Alzubaidi, Jinglan Zhang, Amjad J. Humaidi, Ayad Al-Dujaili, Ye Duan, Omran Al-Shamma, J. Santamaría, Mohammed A. Fadhel, Muthana Al-Amidie, and Laith Farhan. 2021. Review of deep learning: concepts, CNN architectures, challenges, applications, future directions. *Journal of Big Data*, 8(53).

Piotr Bojanowski, Edouard Grave, Armand Joulin, and Tomas Mikolov. 2017. Enriching word vectors with subword information. *Transactions of the Association for Computational Linguistics*, 5:135–146.

Alexis Conneau, Kartikay Khandelwal, Naman Goyal, Vishrav Chaudhary, Guillaume Wenzek, Francisco Guzmán, Edouard Grave, Myle Ott, Luke Zettlemoyer, and Veselin Stoyanov. 2020. Unsupervised cross-lingual representation learning at scale. In *Proceedings of the 58th Annual Meeting of the Association for Computational Linguistics*, pages 8440–8451, Online. Association for Computational Linguistics.

Jacob Devlin, Ming-Wei Chang, Kenton Lee, and Kristina Toutanova. 2019. BERT: Pre-training of deep bidirectional transformers for language understanding. In *Proceedings of the 2019 Conference of the North American Chapter of the Association for Computational Linguistics: Human Language Technologies, Volume 1 (Long and Short Papers)*, pages 4171–4186, Minneapolis, Minnesota. Association for Computational Linguistics.

Sibonelo Dlamini, Edgar Jembere, Anban Pillay, and Brett van Niekerk. 2021. isiZulu word embeddings. In *2021 Conference on Information Communications Technology and Society (ICTAS)*, pages 121–126. IEEE.

Roald Eiselen and Martin Puttkammer. 2014. Developing text resources for ten South African languages. In *Proceedings of the Ninth International Conference on Language Resources and Evaluation (LREC'14)*, pages 3698–3703, Reykjavik, Iceland. European Language Resources Association (ELRA).

Tanja Gaustad and Martin Puttkammer. 2022. Linguistically annotated dataset for four official South African languages with a conjunctive orthography: isiNdebele, isiXhosa, isiZulu, and Siswati. *Data in Brief*, 41.

Dirk Goldhahn, Thomas Eckart, and Uwe Quasthoff. 2012. Building large monolingual dictionaries at the Leipzig corpora collection: From 100 to 200 languages. In *Proceedings of the Eighth International Conference on Language Resources and Evaluation (LREC'12)*, pages 759–765, Istanbul, Turkey. European Language Resources Association (ELRA).

Ridewaan Hanslo. 2021. Evaluation of neural network transformer models for named-entity recognition on low-resourced languages. In *16th Conference on Computer Science and Intelligence Systems (FedCSIS)*, pages 115–119. IEEE.

Michael A. Hedderich, David Adelani, Dawei Zhu, Jesujoba Alabi, Udia Markus, and Dietrich Klakow. 2020. Transfer learning and distant supervision for multilingual transformer models: A study on African languages. In *Proceedings of the 2020 Conference on Empirical Methods in Natural Language Processing (EMNLP)*, pages 2580–2591, Online. Association for Computational Linguistics.

Nuette Heyns and Etienne Barnard. 2020. Optimising word embeddings for recognised multilingual speech. In *1st Southern African Conference for Artificial Intelligence Research*, pages 102–116. Southern African Conference for Artificial Intelligence Research.

Justin Hocking. 2014. Language identification for South African languages. In *Annual Pattern Recognition Association of South Africa and Robotics and Mechatronics International Conference (PRASA-RobMech)*. PRASA.

Pratik Joshi, Sebastin Santy, Amar Budhiraja, Kalika Bali, and Monojit Choudhury. 2020. The state and fate of linguistic diversity and inclusion in the NLP world. In *Proceedings of the 58th Annual Meeting of the Association for Computational Linguistics*, pages 6282–6293, Online. Association for Computational Linguistics.

Diksha Khurana, Aditya Koli, Kiran Khatter, and Sukhdev Singh. 2023. Natural language processing: state of the art, current trends and challenges. *Multimedia Tools and Applications*, 82:3713–3744.

Melinda Loubser and Martin Puttkammer. 2020. Viability of neural networks for core technologies for resource-scarce languages. *Information*, 11(1):41.

Louis Jacobus Louwrens and George Poulos. 2006. The status of the word in selected conventional writing systems - the case of disjunctive writing. *Southern African Linguistics and Applied Language Studies*, 24(3):389–401.

Vukosi Marivate, Tshephisho Sefara, Vongani Chabalala, Keamogetswe Makhaya, Tumisho Mokgonyane, Rethabile Mokoena, and Abiodun Modupe. 2020. Investigating an approach for low resource language dataset creation, curation and classification: Setswana and Sepedi. In *Proceedings of the first workshop on Resources for African Indigenous Languages (RAIL)*, pages 15–20, Marseille, France. European Language Resources Association (ELRA).

Cindy McKellar. 2022a. Autshumato monolingual Afrikaans corpus. `https://hdl.handle.net/20.500.12185/580`. South African Centre for Digital Language Resources (SADiLaR).

Cindy McKellar. 2022b. Autshumato monolingual isiZulu corpus. `https://hdl.handle.net/20.500.12185/581`. South African Centre for Digital Language Resources (SADiLaR).

Cindy McKellar. 2022c. Autshumato monolingual Sepedi corpus. `https://hdl.handle.net/20.500.12185/582`. South African Centre for Digital Language Resources (SADiLaR).

Tomas Mikolov, Ken Chen, Greg Corrado, and Jeffrey Dean. 2013. Efficient estimation of word representations in vector space. In *1st International Conference on Learning Representations ICLR 2013, Workshop Track Proceedings*, Scottsdale, Arizona, USA.

Tumi Moeng, Sheldon Reay, Aaron Daniels, and Jan Buys. 2022. Canonical and surface morphological segmentation for Nguni languages. In *Artificial Intelligence Research. Second Southern African Conference, SACAIR 2021*, pages 125–139, Durban, South Africa. Springer.

Jeffrey Pennington, Richard Socher, and Christopher Manning. 2014. GloVe: Global vectors for word representation. In *Proceedings of the 2014 Conference on Empirical Methods in Natural Language Processing (EMNLP)*, pages 1532–1543, Doha, Qatar. Association for Computational Linguistics.

Martin Puttkammer, Roald Eiselen, Justin Hocking, and Frederik Koen. 2018. NLP web services for resource-scarce languages. In *Proceedings of ACL 2018, System Demonstrations*, pages 43–49, Melbourne, Australia. Association for Computational Linguistics.

Martin Puttkammer and Tanja Gaustad. 2021. Linguistically enriched corpora for conjunctively written South African languages. `https://hdl.handle.net/20.500.12185/546`. South African Centre for Digital Language Resources (SADiLaR).

Martin Puttkammer, Martin Schlemmer, and Ruan Bekker. 2014a. NCHLT Afrikaans annotated text corpora. `https://hdl.handle.net/20.500.12185/296`. South African Centre for Digital Language Resources (SADiLaR).

Martin Puttkammer, Martin Schlemmer, and Ruan Bekker. 2014b. NCHLT Sepedi annotated text corpora. `https://hdl.handle.net/20.500.12185/325`. South African Centre for Digital Language Resources (SADiLaR).

Martin Puttkammer, Martin Schlemmer, Wikus Pienaar, and Ruan Bekker. 2014c. NCHLT Afrikaans text corpora. `https://hdl.handle.net/20.500.12185/293`. South African Centre for Digital Language Resources (SADiLaR).

Martin Puttkammer, Martin Schlemmer, Wikus Pienaar, and Ruan Bekker. 2014d. NCHLT isiZulu text corpora. `https://hdl.handle.net/20.500.12185/321`. South African Centre for Digital Language Resources (SADiLaR).

Martin Puttkammer, Martin Schlemmer, Wikus Pienaar, and Ruan Bekker. 2014e. NCHLT Sepedi text corpora. `https://hdl.handle.net/20.500.12185/330`. South African Centre for Digital Language Resources (SADiLaR).

Sello Ralethe. 2020. Adaptation of deep bidirectional transformers for Afrikaans language. In *Proceedings of the 12th Language Resources and Evaluation Conference*, pages 2475–2478, Marseille, France. European Language Resources Association.

Mark van der Velde, Koen Bostoen, Derek Nurse, and Gérard Philippson, editors. 2022. *The Bantu Languages*, 2nd edition. Routledge.

A Appendix

A.1 Full Results Table

	Paragraph count	Token Count	Vocabulary	Token:Vocab ratio	fastText CBoW	fastText Skipgram	GloVe	FLAIR Forward	FLAIR Backward
Afrikaans									
	10,000	316,704	13,152	0.0415	0.9287	0.9597	0.9385	0.9755	0.9680
	20,000	628,359	21,032	0.0335	0.9601	0.9652	0.9462	0.9726	0.9710
	40,000	1,253,597	33,657	0.0268	0.9719	0.9688	0.9424	0.9758	0.9757
	80,000	2,527,103	52,844	0.0209	0.9769	0.9717	0.9518	0.9777	0.9775
	160,000	5,067,551	82,314	0.0162	0.9798	0.9693	0.9513	0.9772	0.9746
	320,000	10,172,939	128,172	0.0126	0.9808	0.9710	0.9548	0.9798	0.9760
	640,000	20,303,831	199,335	0.0098	0.9806	0.9710	0.9566	0.9820	0.9787
	1,280,000	40,610,635	311,719	0.0077	0.9834	0.9738	0.9578	0.9803	0.9794
isiZulu									
	10,000	193,814	16,207	0.0836	0.8188	0.8694	0.7215	0.9181	0.9219
	20,000	394,523	29,120	0.0738	0.8686	0.8892	0.7354	0.9205	0.9217
	40,000	783,393	50,153	0.0640	0.9009	0.8977	0.7562	0.9209	0.9249
	80,000	1,561,536	50,914	0.0326	0.9100	0.9015	0.7711	0.9197	0.9255
	160,000	3,115,721	143,262	0.0460	0.9160	0.9051	0.7903	0.9154	0.9251
	320,000	6,232,015	240,454	0.0386	0.9233	0.9011	0.7980	0.9189	0.9261
	640,000	12,438,302	401,423	0.0323	0.9257	0.9015	0.8054	0.9227	0.9280
	838,000	16,271,123	488,822	0.0300	0.9261	0.8965	0.8075	0.9233	0.9290
Sesotho sa Leboa									
	10,000	302,923	10,464	0.0345	0.9689	0.9708	0.9594	0.9771	0.9763
	20,000	605,780	16,197	0.0267	0.9745	0.9736	0.9624	0.9773	0.9756
	40,000	1,214 472	25,243	0.0208	0.9774	0.9739	0.9616	0.9747	0.9761
	80,000	2,435,686	38,401	0.0158	0.9806	0.9721	0.9623	0.9760	0.9770
	160,000	4,878,117	58,097	0.0119	0.9792	0.9736	0.9655	0.9788	0.9791
	292,600	8,909,133	80,919	0.0091	0.9802	0.9719	0.9698	0.9794	0.9788

Table 3: Full results for Afrikaans, Sesotho sa Leboa and isiZulu on all types of embeddings with different input data sizes using a reduced POS tagset

A.2 POS Linguistic Analysis Tables

	# POS errors	N	ADJ	V	ADV	Other
fastText CBoW	in 10,000 paragr.	109	68	60	55	123
	in 1,280,000 paragr.	22	11	3	11	49
	% Improvement	79.82%	83.82%	95.00%	80.00%	60.16%
fastText Skipgram	in 10,000 paragr.	72	30	18	31	83
	in 1,280,000 paragr.	23	19	11	15	84
	% Improvement	68.06%	36.67%	38.89%	51.61%	-1.20%
GloVe	in 10,000 paragr.	104	59	37	35	123
	in 1,280,000 paragr.	66	36	31	19	92
	% Improvement	36.54%	38.98%	16.22%	45.71%	25.20%
FLAIR Forward	in 10,000 paragr.	22	23	25	15	58
	in 1,280,000 paragr.	25	13	7	20	50
	% Improvement	-13.64%	43.48%	72.00%	-33.33%	13.79%
FLAIR Backward	in 10,000 paragr.	53	24	13	31	65
	in 1,280,000 paragr.	19	18	5	16	61
	% Improvement	64.15%	25.00%	61.54%	48.39%	6.15%

Table 4: Linguistic error analysis for Afrikaans POS

	# POS errors	N	POSS	REL	ADV	V	ADJ	Other
fastText CBoW	in 10,000 paragr.	179	158	150	145	111	23	132
	in 838,000 paragr.	106	36	51	38	72	11	52
	% Improvement	40.78%	77.22%	66.00%	73.79%	35.14%	52.17%	60.61%
fastText Skipgram	in 10,000 paragr.	140	82	122	80	104	18	101
	in 838,000 paragr.	120	60	82	51	98	23	79
	% Improvement	14.29%	26.83%	32.79%	36.25%	5.77%	-27.78%	21.78%
GloVe	in 10,000 paragr.	272	217	284	222	229	29	127
	in 838,000 paragr.	184	179	196	132	146	20	97
	% Improvement	32.35%	17.51%	30.99%	40.54%	36.24%	31.03%	23.62%
FLAIR Forward	in 10,000 paragr.	113	33	56	35	86	15	68
	in 838,000 paragr.	102	41	49	36	80	12	60
	% Improvement	9.73%	-24.24%	12.50%	-2.86%	6.98%	20.00%	11.76%
FLAIR Backward	in 10,000 paragr.	123	26	47	29	83	11	68
	in 838,000 paragr.	93	37	45	35	60	9	73
	% Improvement	24.39%	-42.31%	4.26%	-20.69%	27.71%	18.18%	-7.35%

Table 5: Linguistic error analysis for isiZulu POS

	# POS errors	N	V	CONC	ADV	ADJ	Other
fastText CBoW	in 10,000 paragr.	48	31	17	13	10	90
	in 292,600 paragr.	12	25	17	12	4	63
	% Improvement	75.00%	19.35%	0.00%	7.69%	60.00%	30.00%
fastText Skipgram	in 10,000 paragr.	32	27	21	15	9	93
	in 292,600 paragr.	19	29	30	13	13	85
	% Improvement	40.63%	-7.41%	-42.86%	13.33%	-44.44%	8.60%
GloVe	in 10,000 paragr.	53	34	29	23	14	123
	in 292,600 paragr.	43	30	23	21	9	80
	% Improvement	18.87%	11.76%	20.69%	8.70%	35.71%	34.96%
FLAIR Forward	in 10,000 paragr.	23	20	17	12	6	81
	in 292,600 paragr.	19	16	13	13	6	71
	% Improvement	17.39%	20.00%	23.53%	-8.33%	0.00%	12.35%
FLAIR Backward	in 10,000 paragr.	25	30	21	12	15	57
	in 292,600 paragr.	21	25	17	14	8	59
	% Improvement	16.00%	16.67%	19.05%	-16.67%	46.67%	-3.51%

Table 6: Linguistic error analysis for Sesotho sa Leboa POS

IsiXhosa Intellectual Traditions Digital Archive: Digitizing isiXhosa texts from 1870-1914

Jonathan Schoots
LEAP
Stellenbosch University
jschoots@sun.ac.za

Amandla Ngwendu
Department of African languages and Literature
University of Cape Town
amandla.ngwendu@uct.ac.za

Jacques de Wet
Department of Sociology
University of Cape Town
jacques.dewet@uct.ac.za

Sanjin Muftic
Digital Library Services
University of Cape Town
sanjin.muftic@uct.ac.za

Abstract

This article offers an overview of the IsiXhosa Intellectual Traditions Digital Archive, which hosts digitized texts and images of early isiXhosa newspapers and books from 1870-1914. The archive offers new opportunities for a range of research across multiple fields, and responds to debates around the importance of African intellectual traditions and their indigenous language sources in generating African social sciences which is contextually relevant. We outline the content and context of these materials and offer qualitative and quantitative details with the aim of providing an overview for interested scholars and a reference for those using the archive.

1 Introduction

The IsiXhosa Intellectual Traditions Archive (IsiXIT)[1] is a collection of isiXhosa newspapers and books from the turn of the 20th Century, accessible online at `https://ibali.uct.ac.za/s/isixit/page/welcome`. This archive collects isiXhosa newspapers produced in the colonial period, covering 1870-1894 (with 1860-69 and 1895-1912 to be added in the future), as well as pioneering isiXhosa literature published in the early part of the 20th century. The archive allows users to browse images and to download MS Word text files[2] of early isiXhosa newspapers and books and collects metadata about each publication and its content.

There has been a great demand for deeper knowledge of African intellectual traditions, analyses, and histories. However, many key materials written in indigenous languages by African intellectuals have been inaccessible–available only as hard copies carefully preserved in archives, or as expensive and limited subscription services.

The IsiXhosa Intellectual Traditions Archive is in the process of creating a substantial digital and textual database of these early isiXhosa texts, in order to make this data freely available to researchers and the general public. Our aim is to both increase access to these important historical materials, and to advance research by making source materials 'research ready' and removing barriers to access, thereby allowing a wide community of researchers access.

The archive currently includes the newspaper *Isigidimi sama-Xosa*[3] (published from 1870 to 1888) and *Imvo Zabantsundu*[4] (published from 1884 onward) as well as the books *Zemk'inkomo Magwalandini*[5] first published in 1906 (Rubusana, 1911) and *Ityala Lamawele*[6] first published in 1914 (Mqhayi, 1931) . Other sources, including newspapers such as *Indaba* (1862-1865), and *Izwi Labantu* (1897-1909), as well as standalone works by early isiXhosa writers will be incorporated into the project over time. The entire archive can be easily browsed on our website (see above). We also make converted text files of these collections accessible for download using permanent DOI links (see footnotes above). These permanent links allow a stable way to access the files which will be maintain in perpetuity by UCT. Researchers can use these permanent DOIs to access and download the text files of the collection, and to view version changes over time. Researchers can also cite these collections to offer readers a permanent link to the data, thus supporting academic rigour.

[1]In addition to the authors, the archive has been created with the support of the following student research assistants: Zimingonaphakade Sigenu, Siphenkosi Hlangu, Sipile Nqiyama, Philisa Plamana, Sinovuyo Xhonga and Likhona Qazisa.

[2]We intent to expand download formats to include PDF and TXT formats in the future.

[3]Isigidimi sama-Xosa collection DOI: `https://doi.org/10.25375/uct.22332271`

[4]Imvo Zabantsundu collection DOI: `https://doi.org/10.25375/uct.22332268`

[5]Zemk'inkomo Magwalandini collection DOI: `https://doi.org/10.25375/uct.22332286`

[6]Ityala Lamawele collection DOI: `https://doi.org/10.25375/uct.22332277`

Proceedings of the Fourth workshop on Resources for African Indigenous Languages (RAIL 2023), pages 54–64

The newspapers and books in this collection represent the earliest written record of sustained intellectual and political debates by black South Africans. Produced in the eastern part of the Cape Colony (today's Eastern Cape), these texts capture the intellectual work of an emerging group of thinkers, activists, political leaders, and their wider public, as they developed new knowledge, oriented to understanding and engaging with colonialism and their changing social world from an African perspective. The isiXhosa newspapers were a central source of social, and increasingly political, reporting. They also make visible debates and dialogues of a wider public sphere through the printing of letters sent in from literate Africans from across present day South Africa, providing key insights on the development of African social and political discussion and theorizing. The archive also includes some of the earliest and most central isiXhosa book publications, published by leading figures of the African intellectual and political movement of the time. These publications offer one of the most systematic and complete records which reveal the development of African intellectual traditions in the face of colonialism.

2 IsiXhosa newspapers and books in historical context

The early isiXhosa newspaper press was a forerunner for African language newspaper publication on the continent. The first isiXhosa newspapers were published from 1837, and isiXhosa papers again took the lead in development as the first papers to be headed by African editors (Cagé and Rueda 2016; Switzer and Switzer 1979, see also Masilela 2009; McCracken 2015; Gilmour 2007). Isigidimi sama-Xosa had the first independent African editor, Elijah Makiwane, from 1876. The first black owned and run paper, Imvo Zabantsundu, appeared in 1884. These papers represent the first sustained platforms for African led journalism where an emerging class of isiXhosa speaking political leaders, activists, and intellectuals could share opinions, debate contemporary issues, and coordinate social and political activity. That they chose to write for a literate isiXhosa-speaking readership[7] is also significant. Contributors to this newspaper community increasingly "focused on conscientising educated Africans in order to mobilise support for social change" (De Wet, 2021). These newspapers published articles and editorials, reports written by correspondents across the eastern part of the Cape Colony, and letters written to the editor which represent the voices of a broad range of the newspaper's readership (Switzer and Switzer, 1979, 40–41, 45–46).

Isigidimi sama-Xosa (trans: The Xhosa Messenger) was founded in 1870 by James Steward of the Glasgow Missionary Society, and was published at Lovedale, the pre-eminent center of African missionary education in southern Africa at the time (Attwell, 2005). First published as the isiXhosa section of a dual language newspaper, it became an independent publication under the editorship of Elijah Makiwane from 1876 (Switzer and Switzer, 1979, 45–46). For 14 years, from its founding in 1870 until the founding of Imvo Zabantsundu in 1884, it was the leading site for African intellectuals of the eastern Cape colony to publish social, religious, and historical writings. It created a space of debate and analysis on a host of social issues by publishing letters written in from a wider community including some contributors from across present day South Africa (Odendaal, 2013). *Imvo Zabantsundu* (trans: Native Opinion) was the first African owned and run newspaper in South Africa. It was founded by John Tengo Jabavu in King William's Town with its first edition published in November 1884. Imvo Zabantsundu offered the first platform for African journalism, political and social commentary, and opinions which were free from any missionary control or censorship, and played a pivotal role in explicitly foregrounding African political interests. Imvo was primarily published in isiXhosa, but also included a translation of the editorial into English and at times published other English articles, letters, and advertisements (Switzer and Switzer 1979, 40–41, Moropa 2010; Mkhize 2018).

The IsiXIT collection also includes some of the earliest publications of isiXhosa literature - texts which emerged from leading intellectuals of the same community as newspaper contributors. These texts have gone on to be cultural touchstones of isiXhosa literature (Jordan, 1973). The books in this collection currently include Zemk'inkomo Magwalandini, a collection of praise poems and other writings, edited by Mpilo Walter Benson

[7]We refer throughout the paper to an isiXhosa speaking community instead of amaXhosa people because the community was comprised amaXhosa as well as amaMfengu, abaThembu as well as other participants and were united by the shared language format.

Rubusana one of the most important cultural and political leaders of the early 20th century (Jordan, 1984). The collection also includes Ityala Lamawele, the celebrated novel of Samuel Edward Krune Mqhayi, who is perhaps most remembered as the preeminent Xhosa poet and "African Shakespeare" (Mqhayi, 2009). The archive aims to host these and other writings of African intellectuals and social commentators whose writings significantly influenced African ideological and intellectual projects of the period.

3 Importance and possibilities of isiXhosa language historical archives

The immediate and practical goal of the IsiXIT archive is to make early isiXhosa texts authored by African intellectuals in the late 1800s and early 1900s available and "research-ready" for contemporary study. To the best of our knowledge there are no other open access digital archives for isiXhosa texts from the late 1800s and early 1900s that make OCRed texts available to users.[8] However, the added value of this archive lies in its contribution to emerging African social sciences. Inspired by the isiXhosa writings of the African intellectual S.E.K. Mqhayi, and by the work of the social scientist Neville Alexander on multilingualism and decolonising academia, we realised that if we are going to decolonise social sciences and contribute meaningfully to the making of an African sociology then we need to engage with these and other historical vernacular texts. This work requires grappling with the socially constructed meanings of African sociological concepts as they are conveyed through these texts and in relation to historical contexts.

Tracing socially constructed meanings of key isiXhosa sociological concepts at critical moments in the history of an indigenous sociolinguistic grouping is about mapping what Raymond Williams (1981:109) in his famous book "Keywords: A Vocabulary of Culture and Society" refers to as the "modulations of the word through history", which help us understand the term itself in relation to changing social conditions and lived experiences. We cannot generate African sociological theory without African concepts, because concepts are the building blocks of theory. This scholarship, which relies on texts in indigenous languages, is grounded in African ontologies and what Mafeje (2000) calls endogeneity.

Up until recently, the challenge has been accessing and collecting these early isiXhosa writings and then converting image files of newspapers found in various library archives into a text format that is more easily researchable. The value of the IsiXIT digital archive gained considerable urgency after the devastating fire at the University of Cape Town in 2021 that damaged multiple buildings and destroyed many primary African collections, which were housed in the African Studies library.

IsiXhosa speakers have also alerted us to another advantage of drawing on the IsiXIT archive to explain the meanings of African sociological concepts and incorporate African languages in the evolution of social sciences on the continent (and elsewhere). It is a matter of identity affirmation. One of the authors of this paper recalls how one of his isiXhosa-speaking students articulated the ability of the archive and associated research to change her view of Sociology in relation to identity. She said that when she first studied Sociology she could not find herself in the discipline; she saw it as something foreign. In time and after working on the IsiXIT Digital Archive and reading the research outputs, her view changed: The archive helped her locate herself in the discipline and began to see Sociology as "something that is ours". This insightful observation reminds us of the value of the IsiXIT Digital Archive as a source for decolonising our curricula. When Sociology and other social sciences are no longer foreign, and students can identify with them, and academia as a whole, then we are likely to see new contextually relevant innovative research that pushes the frontiers of knowledge both locally and globally.

To-date, numerous studies and research outputs have drawn on the textual data from the IsiXIT archive. These include, for example, studies on the socially constructed meanings of "Imfundo" (De Wet, 2021), "Impucuko" (Sigenu, 2021), and "Umsebenzi" (Qazisa, 2022), examinations of IsiXhosa tradition and culture as presented in African newspapers (Majokweni, 2022), and the role of African intellectuals, social networks, and newspaper discourse in shaping the innovation seen in emergence of African nationalism (Schoots, 2021).

[8] There is a growing effort by libraries, universities, and private companies to make digital scans of African newspapers available through paid (or limited but growing free) services. This project advances what is available by making OCRed texts available, for free, with an interactive website that facilitates rich navigation, searching and browsing.

4 Description of archival materials

4.1 Qualitative description of the materials

Newspapers: Both newspapers in this collection include a variety of published content, including leading newspaper articles, shorter articles and reports written by a staff of newspaper correspondents, letters written by the general public, and a range of announcements, advertisements, and government proclamations. Figure 1 shows a sample front page of one edition of each newspaper in the collection. To offer a taste of each newspaper's own specific style and ethos we now outline some of the content published in both Imvo Zabantsundu and Isigidimi sama-Xosa.

Isigidimi Sama-Xosa.
IMVO ZABANTSUNDU
NATIVE OPINION
H. S. WAUGH & CO.
QUEEN'S TOWN

Figure 1: Front pages of Isigidimi (left) and Imvo (right)

Imvo Zabantsundu published a great number of announcements and advertising containing a wealth of information. Such announcements relayed important messages from local chiefs, alerted its audience to new consumer goods such as medications (traditional and Western) or wedding attire, and announced newly-opening shops, church services, and deaths, among many other topics. Adverts in the paper cover a wide range of places and companies, ranging from shipping or land transportation companies to companies selling clothing or new medications for animals. Announcements too reflect a wide range of topics, from updates about influential and famous people which reveal details and activities of their lives, announcements of open job positions, or the latest telegrams. All these adverts and information sought to help the readers stay informed in their everyday lives. At times these adverts specifically were directed to abantu abantsundu (Black/African people), showing the overall intended audience and sense of collective identity fostered by this newspaper. This advertising thus offers a window which extends beyond the regular publication of writing and ideas, showing the advertised image of the lifestyle, consumption patterns, and gender norms and expectations which were received by the readers.

Isigidimi sama-Xosa is particularly notable in the way that it tells stories. Through these narratives we learn details of events specific to that period, which reveal the ways people understood what was happening around them. The missionary foundation of Isigidimi is revealed in the frequency of church and Bible stories. Articles cover topics about churches and priests, including what they preached about. They also talk about the different chiefs and what they achieved, as well as discuss the wars of the period and the effects they had on the black people of the time. The paper also offers insights into the Lovedale Missionary school (where the paper was also printed) and offers rich information about the education of the time, including details about the students, such as the number of students of different races that study there. Articles also speak about quotidian topics like farming and the harvesting of crops.

Isigidimi sama-Xosa also includes a range of letters and adverts which give broader insight into debates around important social issues of the day (such as questions of drinking and temperance, or debates around cultural and religious practice), as well as offer reflections on the professions of the letter-writers (notably teachers). Announcements in the paper give information into important meetings and emerging organizations of the time, court cases, the opening of university, and available bursary, among other topics. Adverts reveal what is available at the market and even their prices, and show the sale of land, or medication.

In summary, these papers offer a revealing window into the events of the period. They make visible the ideas of both African intellectuals and a letter writing public in the eastern part of the Cape Colony and richly reveal a picture of daily life of the time through adverts and announcements.

Books: Zemk'inkomo Magwalandini (1906) was written by Mpilo Walter Benson Rubusana. Literally translated the title of this book would be "The Cows have Gone, you Cowards!" In this book the author reprimands isiXhosa-speaking people for allowing their heritage to be lost. The text also argues for a hybrid combination of a re-imagined isiXhosa culture and sense of self that appropriates

Newspaper Title	Date Range	Publication	Pages per edition	Total Editions	Total Pages	Total Words
Isigidimi sama-Xosa	Oct 1870 - Dec 1888	Monthly	8	202	1543	1,619,386
Imvo Zabantsundu	Nov 1884 - Dec 1894	Weekly	4	518	2065	5,473,187
Total				**720**	**3608**	**7,092,573**

Table 1: Details of digitized newspapers

Book Title	Author (Year)	Total Pages	Total Words
Zemk'inkomo Magwalandini	Rubusana (1906)	583	62,568
Ityala Lamawele	Mqhayi (1914)	204	31,228
Total		**787**	**93,796**

Table 2: Details of digitized books

Paper	IsiXhosa Section	English Section	Xhosa / Eng (%)
Isig	1,600,272	19,114	98.8/1.2
Imvo	3,986,546	1,486,641	72.8/27.2

Table 3: Language composition of newspapers

(and integrates) aspects of English and isiXhosa culture.

The book is a compilation of works by a number of authors edited by Rubusana. Substantial selections include religious poetry. There are also three famous sections by William Wellington Gqoba; two of which are entitled Ingxoxo Enkulu Yom-Ginwa nom-Kristu (Big Discussion between the "Pagan" and the Christian) and the third is called Ingxoxo Enkulu Ngemfundo (Big Discussion on Education).

Ityala Lamawele (1914) was authored by Samuel Edward Krune Mqhayi and includes fiction, history and poetry. The title means "the lawsuit of the twins", which is taken from the story narrated in the first half of the book. The plot is inspired by the biblical story about twins in Genesis Chapter 38. Mqhayi uses different aspects of the story to present a picture of the operation of customary law among isiXhosa-speaking people, in particular, its democratic character, as well as their social life during the reign of King Hintsa. The second part of the book is a historical account of the relations between the amaXhosa, the amaMfengu and the colonialists. The remainder of the book focuses on the political manoeuvring by the English in fuelling tensions between various isiXhosa-speaking groupings up to the 1917 sinking of the troopship the SS Mendi (there were 607 black South African troops on board, all of whom perished). The book ends with short biographies of the new leaders of the "reaction to conquest".

4.2 Overview by the numbers

The collection represents a significant contribution to making isiXhosa historical text available. Notably, the collection already includes over 7 million words in newspapers alone and an additional almost 100,000 words of book materials. This sizable collection is thus useful for large scale isiXhosa computational text analysis. The collection also has considerable time coverage: the newspaper collection currently spans 25 years from 1870 to 1894, covering an especially important period of the formation of new social, political, religious, and other institutions. The two books also reflect some of the most famous early 20th Century isiXhosa literature. We intend to extend this collection as we continue to grow the archive.

Table 1 and 2 report the key statistics of the archive's current collection of newspapers and books. Table 3 shows an estimate of the total isiXhosa language section words and English language section words. This is assessed at the paragraph level, and reflects whole blocks of English or isiXhosa text, not the use of single words. This analysis shows that Isigidimi sama-Xosa is published almost entirely in isiXhosa. The approximately 1% of English text comes from the very few letters, advertisements, or government announcements printed in English. Imvo has a far more substantial, although still minor, English language section, on average covering about 27% of the printed content. This included the editorial translated to English as well as other letters, articles, or adverts.

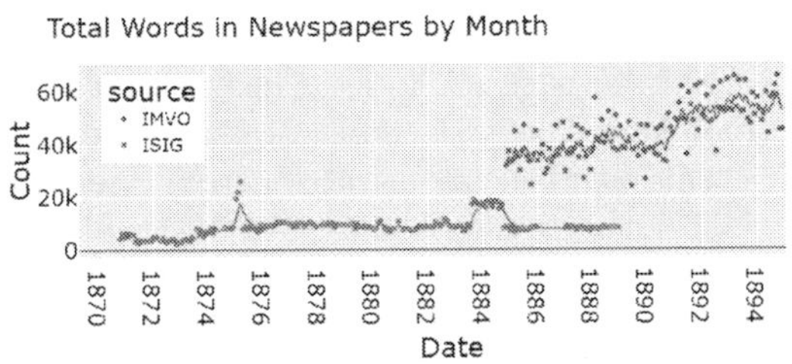

Figure 2: Count of all words in Isigidimi and Imvo

Figure 2 shows the total count of all words (isiXhosa and English) for both papers over the period, grouped by month. Isigidimi is shown in orange and Imvo is shown in blue. The dots represent the count of words, and the line represents a smoothed moving average. While both publications have approximately the same number of words per edition, this monthly grouping shows that the total volume of Imvo was far higher than Isigidimi due to its weekly publication. This also shows that, while Isigidimi published monthly for most of its lifespan, the paper was published twice monthly between July 1883 and September 1884.

Editions missing from the collection: While we have aimed to have as complete an archive as possible, at times some editions are no longer available in hard copy at South African institutions. Most notably, the collection is missing the entirety of the year 1886 editions of Isigidimi, which we have been unable to locate in hardcopy original. A small number of other individual editions are missing due to the inability to access hard copy scans. However, these missing editions are sporadic and limited.

5 Overview of the digitizing process

The goal of our digitizing process has been to create materials which are easily accessible and offer a high quality replica in both image and digital text formats. We start with high quality scanning undertaken by the National Library of South Africa of original hard copy documents, producing a high resolution .tiff image of no less than 400 dpi. From this image we undertake Optical Character Recognition (OCR) using ABBYY FineReader 15. We use ABBYY's built in language model for both English and isiXhosa during this scanning process. These scans then go through a two stage checking, correction, and quality assurance process by our team of isiXhosa language experts. The first stage involves working to correct any character errors in the OCR process. Each page is read over by one of our team of first language isiXhosa speakers. They pay particular attention to areas where the ABBYY program itself has highlighted uncertainty, but also check the entire text correcting errors. This results in the completion of the first quality assurance stage. The text is then output as a .docx file with the aim of preserving the layout of the original image. A second stage of correction and quality assurance is then undertaken on these documents, ensuring that the layout and formatting of the document is readable and reflects the original, while also seeking to catch any other outstanding problems. With the completion of this second quality assurance stage, the documents are completed. We then undertake an additional audit of around 20% of these final documents to ensure that we are producing high quality output and to catch any systematic errors in the process.[9] These documents are uploaded to our hosting site with additional metadata created for each newspaper edition. They are also hosted as complete collections for download on our repository hosted on UCT's Zivahub which is accessible via the website and via permanent DOIs (see footnote 3-6). Metadata for each newspaper edition and each book includes the available information on the title, date issued, volume and edition numbers, editor or author, publisher, media type (newspaper or book), extent or number of pages, and available formats of the files. More details on this hosting are outlined in the following section.

6 Showcasing the archive with Omeka S and IIIF on Ibali: UCT Digital Collections

In 2021, the Digital Library Services (DLS) department at the University of Cape Town Libraries launched a university-wide showcasing platform for the university's digital collections, here: `https://ibali.uct.ac.za`. The site is called Ibali: UCT Digital Collections (isiXhosa for 'story') and it runs on a set of semantic web technologies called Omeka S and IIIF. Ibali is part of the Libraries' drive to nurture an Open Access space where digital collections can be created, curated, published

[9]We currently rely on human correction by isiXhosa experts rather than an automated approach. Because we correct all OCR with human correction we do not calculate the OCR error rate. We do not currently include automated spell checking due to limited tools as the orthography of turn of the 20th century isiXhosa is different from present day isiXhosa. However, we recognize that automatic error detection and statistics would be valuable for the project and hope to explore automated checking and reporting approaches in the future.

and showcased. It is a highly collaborative and flexible, future-thinking online repository space. Since its launch a number of diverse collections have already been showcased on Ibali - including a library of open access resources focusing on climate change, an archive of an active theatrical research project and the IsiXhosa Intellectual Traditions under Colonialism collection.

The main architecture of Ibali is the open source software Omeka S[10]. Omeka S is a web publishing platform for GLAMs (Galleries | Libraries | Archives | Museums), designed to create relationships between objects in collections as well as describe them through linked open data resources on the internet. The 'S' in Omeka S stands for 'semantic', as in connecting to the semantic web, where data in web pages is structured and tagged. Its primary focus is on organising elements of a collection such that the links in between items and the greater elements of the internet are strengthened, allowing for much more relevant searches and deeper explorations. It relies heavily on metadata and allows creators of websites great flexibility to set up metadata templates to consistently describe their items. These templates are constructed out of internationally recognized metadata standards (Dublin Core, schema.org) as well as customised ontologies. It makes Omeka S a piece of software that is both heavily customizable, while at the same time being rigorous and interoperable with metadata.[11]

Creating a collection showcase site such as one for IsiXIT is done in partnership with Digital Library Services. Initially, we engaged in a collection/site interview where key aspects of the collection are identified together with desired characteristics of the site. It was identified that the ability to engage with the newspapers visually while having the ability to download the working files was key to create an interesting collection website. The process of building the site onto Ibali was split into three steps: 1) Prepping the Metadata Entries 2) Packaging Data and Metadata for Upload and 3) Website Design. Steps 1 and 2 would be repeatable to accommodate batches of completed newspaper editions.

The prep for the metadata entries required looking at the appropriate metadata fields to create a template that would align itself with the publication of the items of the collection (predominantly newspapers). We were able to select metadata properties from the ontology standards of Dublin Core and Schema.org to include entries for vol number, issue number, editor, language, etc. As Omeka S allows for the capturing of items which are not just media, we looked at creating items for the people who were instrumental in the publishing of the newspapers such as John Tengo Jabavu. With Omeka S functioning as a database, we could also work on linking every single issue of a newspaper to its edition, thus allowing users to quickly jump back and forth between a single issue and its edition. This allowed us to organise and keep track of the different newspaper editions, so that the database queries underneath Omeka S could return user queries based on their search. All of this metadata was mapped to a spreadsheet so that the team could populate the entries with new batches of newspaper editions.

Another column within the spreadsheet contained the names of the transcribed WORD files relevant to that issue (which would be preloaded onto the server). Using the CSV Import module of Omeka S, the columns in the spreadsheet would be mapped to the different metadata fields, and each row would be considered a new item. Omeka S then created items for each of the issues, with the metadata linking the word transcript files. Together with the included OCR module, it also looked at the imported Word Documents and extracted the text so that a full text internal search could be made on the site.

Once these items are uploaded, Omeka S automatically creates website pages for each item. The look and feel of these pages is dependent on the look and feel of the site. In Omeka S this is managed through Themes, with many of them being available freely online. They are also heavily customizable with some programming experience in a combination of CSS, HTML and PHP. Within the Omeka S site creation tool it is also possible to create stand alone pages which can highlight certain aspects, or to create landing pages for the collection. The theme can then be customised to present a particular look and feel to the site, and we worked together on finding design choices that would make navigation easy as well as present the newspapers and their media in an interesting way.

A couple of Omeka S modules also enhanced the process, such as the ability to quickly create an index list of items based on shared metadata. With

[10]Visit `https://omeka.org/s/` for a tour of Omeka S.

[11]Omeka S also has a large community developing additional open source modules and themes which add extra functionality to the main software architecture.

this module we created an index tree for each year that would allow users to quickly jump to an issue in a particular month of a particular year. Another important consideration was allowing multiple languages to be presented on the page, as is the case with having website text in IsiXhosa as well as English.

6.1 Facilitating both exhibition and analysis: combining Omeka S exhibition with Figshare repository

Our overall aim to make materials easy to access for both researchers and a general public leads to two goals: 1. Exhibiting and creating user friendly access to the materials and 2. making the underlying data easily and permanently available to the research community.

We use Omeka S for exhibition and broad access. This offers us a location for a public facing exhibition of these materials on a platform that facilitates intuitive and visually appealing exploration as well as metadata presentation and a robust faceting search for processed articles.

We use UCT's digital repository Zivahub, hosted on the Figshare repository system, to make the whole collection easily accessible for download for scholars who will use these materials offline for both quantitative analysis (such as linguists or computational social scientists) and qualitative analysis (such as historians or Media studies scholars). Zivahub offers a permanent record of the available files, including DOIs which will always reference the materials, and a permanently accessible version history. This allows researchers to both access and reference the materials in a format that will always be accessible to the scholarly community. ZivaHub will ensure that our dataset will always be available no matter what versions or formats of the data we share. This will assist the project in making the data FAIR (Findable, Accessible, Interoperable and Reusable).

7 Example of article search with keywords

We are also developing extended search functionality in this archive which is currently offered on the 'Article Search' tab of the site. By using the power of Omeka S and combining it with work done to catalogue, label, and extract information of the articles of the newspaper, we are able to offer a powerful search feature which allows users to explore the papers in new ways. This search is already available for both Isigidimi and Imvo for the year of 1885[12], and we intend to expand this detailed metadata in the future to encompass more of the collection.

This search functionality allows the user to search for keywords together with a set of five additional labels which capture the type and content of each newspaper item. This includes capturing the 'type' of article (advert, letter, editorials, etc) and sub-types (or topics such as education, law services, politics, or marriages). These two columns were formatted as a controlled vocabulary, meaning that the entries came from a limited pool of options. Additional search labels also include author, location, and language (isiXhosa or English) of the newspaper item when available.

The 'type' and 'subtype' labels were developed through human qualitative analysis and coding of newspaper articles by project researchers and research assistants. The 'type' category was developed to capture different newspaper item type categories such as articles, letters, adverts, announcements, etc. The 'sub-type' category was created to capture the primary topic or content of the item. The controlled vocabulary of each of these sets were created, tested, and revised through a pilot coding of four editions. The two coders both covered all editions and met to define a list together with the supervisor. This was then used to code the full dataset. Regular meetings were held during the full coding process to ensure common coding practices and inter-coder reliability, and to assess if additional labels needed to be added to the sets. Finally, the labels were checked and cleaned by a supervising researcher, using text analysis approaches to remove spelling errors, standardize formats of names and places, and clean and merge subcategories as necessary to create a standardized and computer readable label set.[13]

We use this coding together with the tools of Omeka S to offer a search page which allows researchers to select from these identified labels, thus

[12] 1885 was selected as it is the first full year that both Isigidimi and Imvo were published (after Imvo's founding in Nov 1884)

[13] We hope in the future to incorporate automation into this label generation process to more quickly label additional texts. We are exploring using the human coded labels as training data for a supervised machine learning approach to label recommendation. As isiXhosa language NLP tools advance we will also explore Named Entity recognition and topic identification approaches among others, which can further enrich the search functionality.

facilitating the cross search of articles by any combination of article type, subtype, author and location while also searching for any keywords in the text. This then returns links which take the user to the text of the specific articles and links to the display of that newspaper.

To offer an example of the utility of this search: a user might search widely, perhaps for all use of the term *'umsebenzi'* (work), seeing how newspaper contributors use this concept. The user might also use a much more focused search, perhaps looking only at editorials which mention "Sprigg" (the Prime minister of the Cape), or letters which discuss "*Rulumente*" (parliament). A search might combine labels, searching for all announcements and advertisements which come from King Williams Town or Ngqamakwe. Searching by combining language and labels attached to articles offers an exciting opportunity to quickly move through the newspaper collection in a new and nonlinear way, and enables easy research and exploration of specific topics as well as content, people, or places. This search capacity is thus an exciting and powerful extension of the archive which supports research. Although generating this newspaper item level information is time consuming, we are currently seeking ways to expand this level of search to all newspapers in the archive.

8 Possibilities for research using the archives

The isiXhosa materials held in this archive have great potential to open up exciting new avenues for research across a number of disciplines, including Sociology, Political Science, History, Literature and Languages, Linguistics, Media studies, Data Science and many more. Possible examples of research are wide ranging. We imagine that these sources may be useful for questions which range across topics such as: discovering specific historical details, following the writings of individuals or small groups, studies of advertising, analysis of the linguistic structure of historical isiXhosa, the development of isiXhosa intellectual concepts and analysis, or building computational tools for the analysis of isiXhosa text, to name just a few examples. Such wide ranging research possibilities will inevitably be undertaken from a diverse range of disciplinary and methodological perspectives.

For this reason we have aimed to produce materials in a format which allows a broad range of engagement. For example, historical analysis might prioritise the exact replica of the image to preserve the maximal detail of the source, while computational text analysis approaches might be happy to strip the material to represent only the text of the corpus. We have aimed to host the material in a format which seeks a middle ground by making the digitized and OCRed newspaper pages available for download in a .docx format.[14] This format preserves the layout of the original newspaper page, allowing qualitative readers to use word searching techniques while still experiencing the layout and style of the original paper. For researchers who are interested in only the textual corpus, the text can be extracted from these documents to support corpus linguistics or other computational text analysis methods. We also allow users to view the image scans on the website in a lower resolution JPG format which facilitates a "reading room" experience, allowing researchers browse and peruse the newspapers as they please. However, we do not offer access to image download, as the high resolution original images remain the property of National Libraries South Africa. To maximise access to the materials in the future we will explore making other download formats available including .pdf and .txt versions which might be suitable for different research needs such as preserving the visual architecture of the newspaper (pdf) or accessing the text only corpus (txt).

9 Conclusion

This paper has outlined the scope, content, and context of the materials collected in the IsiXhosa Intellectual Traditions Archive. We intend this to serve as a reference for scholars already utilizing the archive and as an overview for scholars interested in new research possibilities created by the archive. We believe this archive offers resources which may advance research in a wide range of fields, and we hope to continue to expand our coverage in the future to incorporate all major isiXhosa newspapers and books from 1860-1914.

Limitations

This paper outlines an archival collection with the intention of detailing useful information for a range of research fields. However, the focus of the infor-

[14]Although MS Word .docx is a proprietary format, most people have access to a version of the software. However, we are looking into using other open formats in the future.

mation has been shaped by the specific perspective created by our own limited disciplinary lens, grounded in the fields of Sociology and African Languages and Literature. For this reason, while we seek to provide adequate information for a broad audience, we may not provide the information or metrics most desirable to researchers in other fields. In addition, the information we provide now is a static snapshot of an evolving archive which we hope will expand. The information provided here will always provide a useful overview, but the specific details will continue to evolve as the archive grows.

Ethics Statement

We provide access to digitized versions of isiXhosa texts which are all in the public domain. We do so for free with the intent to make materials available for both researchers and the general public. It is thus our aim to expand access to historically difficult to access materials, in a language which has faced a lack of research resources. Our hope is that this gives more access to historically marginalized researchers and publics. This project is not subject to ethics review as there are no living subjects discussed in these materials. The authors have acquired permission from quoted participants to use these quotes and conversations.

Human coders and language editors who have worked on this archive are all employed as members of the project. All coders and editors are first language isiXhosa speakers and are either students or researchers.

Acknowledgements

This article was written with partial supported from the National Research Foundation of South Africa, grant number 138493.

References

David Attwell. 2005. The Transculturation of Enlightenment. The Journal of Tiyo Soga. *D Atwell, Rewriting modernity. Studies in black South African literary history (Pietermaritzburg, KwaZulu-Natal University Press, 2005)*, pages 40–41.

Julia Cagé and Valeria Rueda. 2016. The long-term effects of the printing press in sub-saharan africa. *American Economic Journal: Applied Economics*, 8(3):69–99.

Jacques P. De Wet. 2021. Social construction of the meanings of imfundo by African intellectuals in the Cape Colony at the turn of the twentieth century. *Canadian Journal of African Studies / Revue canadienne des études africaines*, pages 1–23.

Rachael Gilmour. 2007. Missionaries, Colonialism and Language in Nineteenth-Century South Africa. *History Compass*, 5(6):1761–1777.

Archibald Currie Jordan. 1973. *Towards an African Literature: The Emergence of Literary Form in Xhosa*. University of California Press, Berkeley.

Pallo Jordan. 1984. Zemk'inkomo magwalandini. The life and times of WB Rubusana (1858-1936). *Sechaba*, 4.

Archie Mafeje. 2000. Africanity: a combative ontology. *CODESRIA Bulletin*, pages 66–71.

Anelisa Majokweni. 2022. *We are the voice of our people: IsiXhosa tradition and culture as presented in African newspapers: 1874-1890*. Honours Thesis, Department of History, Stellenbosch University, Stellenbosch.

Ntongela Masilela. 2009. The Vernacular Press and African Literature. *Unpublished paper*, pages 1–13.

Donal P. McCracken. 2015. The imperial British newspaper, with special reference to South Africa, India and the 'Irish model'. *Critical Arts: A South-North Journal of Cultural & Media Studies*, 29(1):5–25. Publisher: Routledge.

Khwezi Mkhize. 2018. 'To See Us As We See Ourselves': John Tengo Jabavu and the Politics of the Black Periodical. *Journal of Southern African Studies*, 44(3):413–430.

Koliswa Moropa. 2010. African voices in *Imvo Zabantsundu* : Literary pieces from the past. *South African Journal of African Languages*, 30(2):135–144.

Samuel E. K. Mqhayi. 2009. *Abantu Besizwe: Historical and biographical writings 1902-1944 SEK Mqhayi*. Wits University Press, Johannesburg.

Samuel Edward Krune Mqhayi. 1931. *Ityala Lama-Wele*. Lovedale Press, Lovedale, South Africa.

André Odendaal. 2013. *The founders: The origins of the ANC and the struggle for democracy in South Africa*. The University Press of Kentucky, Kentucky.

Likhona Qazisa. 2022. *Socially Constructed Meanings of Umsebenzi and Associated Terms*. Honours Thesis, Department of Sociology, University of Cape Town, Cape Town.

Walter Benson Rubusana. 1911. *Zemk'iinkomo Magwalandini*. Selwood Printing Works, Frome.

Leo Jonathan Schoots. 2021. *Novelty, Networks, and the Rise of African Nationalism: African Intermediary Intelligentsia and the Making of Political Innovation in Colonial South Africa (1860-1890)*. Ph.D., The University of Chicago, United States – Illinois.

Zimingonaphakade Sigenu. 2021. *Socially Constructed Meanings of Impucuko in a Comparative Historical Analysis*. Master's Thesis, Department of Sociology, University of Cape Town, Cape Town.

Les Switzer and Donna Switzer. 1979. *The Black press in South Africa and Lesotho: a descriptive bibliographic guide to African, Coloured, and Indian newspapers, newsletters, and magazines, 1836-1976*. Boston: Hall.

Analyzing political formation through historical isiXhosa text analysis: Using frequency analysis to examine emerging African Nationalism in South Africa

Jonathan Schoots
LEAP
Stellenbosch University
jschoots@sun.ac.za

Abstract

This paper showcases new research avenues made possible by applying computational methods to historical isiXhosa text. I outline a method for isiXhosa computational text analysis which adapts word frequency analysis to be applied to isiXhosa texts focusing on root words. The paper showcases the value of the approach in a study of emerging political identities in early African nationalism, examining a novel dataset of isiXhosa newspapers from 1874 to 1890. The analysis shows how a shared identity of 'Blackness' (*Abantsundu* and *Abamnyama*) dynamically emerged, and follows the impact of leading intellectuals as well as African voter mobilization in shaping communal political discourse.

1 Introduction

The growing wave of digitization of African text sources and the creation of new digital African language archives creates exciting new possibilities for researchers. Materials which were once difficult to access, available only in hard copy in archives, are already more widely accessible than ever before, often in digital text format. As the pace and scope of digitization grows, such access will only increase. The availability of these materials comes alongside an academic and public demand for more knowledge about African intellectual histories and knowledge traditions. Questions and sources fit hand in hand in this exciting new opening for research. How can researchers who are interested in substantive and 'humanistic' (historical, cultural, literary, etc) questions, especially in African language contexts, seize the opportunities created by these sources?

This paper draws on a novel digital archive of historical isiXhosa text and showcases some possibilities that digital archives and computational text analysis can offer humanistic and social science scholars working in African languages. The study examines political identity formation in the period of emerging African nationalism in South Africa by looking at isiXhosa newspapers from 1874-1890. I use computational text analysis methods to explore the collective development of a shared language of political identity in the emerging 'proto-nationalist' movement in what is today the Eastern Cape of South Africa.

The paper has two goals. First, to outline the method used. I draw on frequency analysis over time, an approach which can overcome the current limitations in the Natural Language Processing (NLP) tools for isiXhosa, and remains accessible to qualitative and humanistic scholars because it operationalizes a research approach which is conceptually straightforward to non-experts in Natural Language Processing (NLP). IsiXhosa, like many other under-resourced languages, faces a lack of NLP tools which are available for English and other highly resourced languages. IsiXhosa is an agglutinative language, and the structure of isiXhosa morphology and grammar means that many NLP tools cannot be imported from other languages. In particular, tools for the accurate parsing of the subunits of compound words–including stemming or lemmatizing, parts of speech tagging, and stopword removal–cannot be imported. These 'preprocessing' steps often form the necessary basis for other more advanced NLP techniques (cf. word embeddings or topic models), which themselves are not built to deal with the range of variations created by the prefix, infix and suffix structure of agglutinative languages. Such tools are being developed by isiXhosa computational linguists (Mzamo et al., 2015; Puttkammer and Toit, 2021), but are not yet sufficiently advanced to be used for social science or humanities inquiry.

This paper engages this problem by drawing on the established method of frequency analysis (Baron et al., 2009) and highlighting its utility for analysis of isiXhosa and other agglutinative lan-

Proceedings of the Fourth workshop on Resources for African Indigenous Languages (RAIL 2023), pages 65–75
May 6, 2023 ©2023 Association for Computational Linguistics

guages. Very little work has used computational text analysis on isiXhosa texts for social science or humanities research. This paper shows that by adapting a frequency analysis to the structure of isiXhosa grammar, it is possible to advance in new ways. I show that this approach can be tailored to resolve the problem of agglutinative grammar by focusing on root words. This can effectively bypass the need for NLP pre-processing tools, and thus can be applied to isiXhosa texts using currently available tools. A frequency analysis approach has added advantages for social science and humanistic scholars. It is analytically clear (simply counting the number of word occurrences) where more advanced approaches can remain an opaque 'black box' to non-experts. It is also relatively technically simple and thus has a lower technical barrier to entry. Nonetheless it creates new opportunities to analyze isiXhosa texts which have not been possible using the dominant close textual analysis approach. These features commend it to scholars interested in new social and humanistic answers.

The second goal is to showcase the analytical capacity of this approach through a specific example: an analysis of collective political concept formation in the early period of African Nationalism in South Africa. Here I examine the shifting ideas of collective identity in isiXhosa newspaper publications which shaped the debates of the nascent 'proto-nationalist' movement. I follow a 16-year period as this emerging movement developed from a series of social and political debates among African intellectuals into an increasingly interlocked set of political organizations mobilizing Africans to protect African political interests. To do so, I draw on a novel dataset of digitized isiXhosa newspapers, following *Isigidimi sama-Xosa* and *Imvo Zabantsundu*, which gave voice to the first ideas and organizations of early African nationalism.

This analysis reveals a diverse emerging ideological landscape with a surprising amount of flux in the conceptual language of the African political community. I show how different notions of Ethnicity, Nationhood, and Race ebbed and flowed as the focal conceptions of the political self. I then focus on isiXhosa speakers' own language of 'Blackness'—-*Ntsundu* and -*Mnyama*—demonstrating how frequency analysis reveals surprising new aspects of political development within this important proto-nationalist community.

2 Creating the digital text dataset

This paper draws on a novel dataset of digitized isiXhosa newspapers and books created by myself and a team of researchers at the University of Cape Town. To create this dataset, we scanned hard-copies of these newspapers held at The National Library of South Africa, and at Corry Library of Rhodes University. We then performed Optical Character Recognition to produce a digitized version of the newspaper. Every page of digitized text was checked by a team of first language isiXhosa speaking researchers to correct any errors. This produced a high-quality digital replica of the original newspapers. More information about this project, along with downloadable texts are available at `https://ibali.uct.ac.za/s/isixit/`.[1]

This analysis focuses on all available editions of *Isigidimi sama-Xosa* and *Imvo Zabantsundu* from 1874-1890. Details of these papers are reported in Table 1.[2] Some hard copies are missing from the archival record. Most notably, the whole year of *Isigidimi* 1886 is no longer available in hard copy. A small number of other individual editions are missing due to the inability to access hard copy scans. These missing editions seem sporadic and random and are not expected to introduce any systematic bias into the analysis.

This analysis focuses only on isiXhosa text. Since some articles written in *Imvo Zabantsundu* are in English, I identified and removed all English text to produce an isiXhosa only corpus.[3] Isigidimi and Imvo are comprised of 98.8% and 72.8% isiXhosa words respectively.

3 Methods of computational text analysis

3.1 The opportunities of 'distant' reading

This paper draws on computational text analysis techniques to examine the dynamics of emerging African political thought in ways that have not previously been possible, showing the shifting empha-

[1]The data is also permanently available for access and download from a repository, Isigidimi: `https://doi.org/10.25375/uct.22332271` and Imvo: `https://doi.org/10.25375/uct.22332268`

[2]Included is the type-to-token ratio (TTR), a ratio of the number of unique words to the number of total words. This captures lexical diversity in the text. When considered for individual editions of both papers, this ratio remains very stable throughout the period ($Imvo: 0.608 \pm 0.036, Isig: 0.554 \pm 0.052$).

[3]This is done by identifying and excluding all paragraphs containing >50% English words using the English word list from the NLTK package nltk.corpus.words.

Newspaper Title	Date Range	Total Editions	Total Pages	Publication Frequency	Pgs per Edition	Total Words	Type to Token Ratio
Isigidimi sama-Xosa	Jan 1874 - Nov 1888	168	1,352	Monthly	8	1,403,237	0.156
Imvo Zabantsundu	Nov 1884 - Dec 1890	314	1,259	Weekly	4	2,081,047	0.125

Table 1: Details of digitized newspaper dataset used in this analysis

sis of a community over time as they created the foundations of a new political framework.

Recent scholarship has emphasized the importance of turning to African intellectuals and knowledge systems, an area which has historically been marginalized. Scholars of South Africa have increasingly highlighted the importance of African intellectuals who preceded the formation of the famous African National Congress (ANC) and who laid a foundation for new and creative African responses to colonialism and apartheid (Attwell, 2005; Mkhize, 2008, 2018; Mangcu, 2014; Masilela, 2013, 2014; Ndletyana, 2008; Nyamende, 2000; Odendaal, 2013; Schoots, 2020, 2021). Such scholarship has largely focused on individual intellectuals or intellectual lineages, primarily drawing on close textual analysis and biography to illuminate the larger currents of emerging African intellectual thought. This scholarship is immensely valuable in deeply examining the experiences, thoughts, and innovation of prominent African intellectuals as responded to colonialism, however this individualized approach makes it difficult to see the dynamics of a larger intellectual community.

This paper seeks to contribute a new perspective on this important tradition of research by drawing on computational text analysis. Using these tools I seek to explore two elements of intellectual transformation which are harder to see though the dominant methodological paradigm of close reading and individual biography.

First, this study emphasizes the *language use of a shared community of African writers*, and thus captures a much wider audience than close reading methods do. The African language newspapers still limit our view to African journalists and the contributions of literate African letter writers. Yet here we are able to see the shifting conceptual trends of a community much wider than the traditional focus on a few key intellectuals. This wider community was collectively instrumental in early protonationalist politics, and by looking at this collective dialogue we avoid the possibility of generalizing any idiosyncratic emphases of individual leaders.

Second, this analysis *foregrounds dynamic change over time by emphasizing frequency and chronology*. Close reading methods must flatten time to some extent, as they synthesize the different writings of a person to form a fuller picture of their ideas. The analyses presented here loses this synthetic depth, yet clearly highlight larger trends in shifting attention and the influence of critical events and punctuated moments in reorienting attention and discourse. For these reasons, this paper offers a set of methods which go hand-in-hand with close reading approaches. The findings offered here only make sense when contextualized by the deeper dynamics revealed in close studies, yet this analysis is able to reveal dynamics which are surprising and unexpected by such close analyses.

3.2 Analysing collective concept formation with frequency analysis

To undertake this communal and temporal analysis of ideas, this paper adapts the the method of historical text frequency analysis (Jucker et al., 1999; Baron et al., 2009), highlighting how it is useful for isiXhosa. Frequency analysis consists simply of counting the number of words of a text. Using search pattern matching (here I use regular expressions) it is possible to define a 'root word' pattern to search and count. This approach is simple and powerful when applied to agglutinative languages like isiXhosa and can bypass the need for NLP tools which are not yet sufficiently developed for isiXhosa.

Due to the variations from prefixes, infixes and suffixes of isiXhosa agglutinative grammar, it is not possible to use words as tokens because the variation in word spelling masks the use of common terms or concepts. Stemming or lematizing and parts of speech (PoS) tagging are NLP approaches used to solve this challenge in well-resourced languages. However, these tools are still being developed for isiXhosa (although advances are being made (Mzamo et al., 2015; Puttkammer and Toit, 2021)) and other under-resourced languages. This paper applies one approach which can bypass the need for these NLP tools. This is useful for isiXhosa and might also be applied to other under-resourced agglutinative languages. Despite the lack of more advanced NLP tools, I show that the approach can offer a significant new perspective, showing patterns which have been hidden in close textual analysis.

Studying frequency over time involves grouping texts into time periods, counting the frequency of selected root words in each period, and plotting these over time. In the analysis showcased below, frequency analysis offers a conceptually intuitive and technically simple way to quantify how much 'attention' is paid to different concepts over time.

Technically, I use the python coding language to group texts and count the number of occurrences of root words using regular expressions (detailed below). I use the pandas package to organize data and the plotly package to plot results. I normalize the frequency counts by reporting frequency as a percentage of all words used. This accounts for differences in the total volume of the text.[4] For this analysis I group each newspaper into months. For *Isigidimi*, which published monthly for most of its life, each month mostly represents one edition. For *Imvo*, which published weekly, each month groups mostly 4 editions.

3.3 Focusing on key root words

The key value of using frequency analysis for isiXhosa is the ability to define and examine root words over time. In practice a root word must be carefully and clearly defined and then counted for each grouped period. This comes with some limitations: first, the set of words analyzed is defined by the researcher, who must identify concepts which may be important or meaningful. It thus requires a sufficient qualitative, hermeneutic, and historical knowledge of the texts and their contexts, as well as sufficient language competence. Thus, this method may be best used by humanities or social science scholars who likely already require such competencies. The second limitation is that the approach does not scale well, and is most fit to explore on the order of 10s to perhaps 100s of words. The approach must thus be guided by the researchers existing contextual knowledge and expectations and thus benefits from the support of qualitative and historical analysis which can guide the researcher's intuition.

Analysis of root words in this analysis took the following steps: 1. define the relevant focal concepts and terms, identifying the root word(s) which capture the usage of this term. This includes defining inclusions and exclusions in the search pattern to correctly select only relevant words. I used regular expression matching which offer powerful tools for pattern identification. 2. Check the words and frequencies identified by this pattern to ensure that the defined pattern collects only the desired word set. To achieve this, I output a list of the frequency counts of all unique words identified by the pattern in the whole corpus[5]. This makes it easy to check if words which do not match the concept are being included. An iterative process of defining and checking the search pattern ensures accuracy and confidence that the analysis reveals only the frequency of the desired words. A simple example: If *uhlanga* ('nation/race') is the desired concept/term, 'hlang' is the core root. It is desirable to capture many variations of this term (e.g. *yohlanga*, *bebehlanga*, etc) but other words such as *umhlanga* ('reed') or *-hlangana* ('gathering') should be excluded. The regular expression `"(?<!m)hlanga\b"` more clearly defines the desired word set than `".*hlang.*"`. Once defined these roots can be used in the approach outlined in the section above.

This approach has been developed for a specific analysis of isiXhosa texts. However, it may also be useful for other underresourced agglutinative languages which also use root words with modifications. A limitation of this paper is that this analysis has not tested the approach on any language other than isiXhosa. The grammatical similarities between isiXhosa and other Southern Africa and Bantu languages, and the structure of agglutinative

[4] I also check for correlation between this frequency percentage and total words as well as the type-to-token ratio at the level of newspaper edition. For the two focal words analysed below (-Ntsundu and -Mnyama) there is no statistically significant correlation between frequency percentage and total words. There is no statistically significant correlation between TTR and frequency percentage, except for a very low correlation magnitude between TTR and Mnyama in Imvo ($r(311)=0.11$, $p=.0476$) and for TTR and Ntsundu in Isigidimi ($r(163)=.24$, $p=.002$). These non-significant or low magnitude correlations suggest that changes in total text volume and lexical diversity (shown by the TTR) are not driving the changes seen in the analysis.

[5] I use a python dict, incrementing the count of each unique word matched by the pattern.

languages in general, theoretically suggest the possible extension. However, the author has not tested the extent and limitations of applications to other languages.

4 Case study: The shifting language of emerging political community

The paper turns to exemplify the utility of this approach by looking at emerging ideas of African nationalism in isiXhosa newspaper texts. The first recorded accounts of African nationalism and Pan-Africanism in South Africa began in isiXhosa intellectual communities. First appearing in print from the 1860s (Soga, 1983), these ideas developed in the 1870s in contexts like the *Isigidimi* newspaper as well as other social venues where communities of missionary educated African intellectuals developed an increasingly critical analysis of colonization and the government's legislation on Africans. In the 1880s these ideas were turned into political action: a range of the new African political organizations emerged and flourished, experimenting with various political forms and projects which laid the ground for African nationalism across Southern Africa (Odendaal, 2013, see for more).

The two papers studied here: *Isigidimi sama-Xosa*and *Imvo Zabantsundu* were central to this emerging movement. These were the first African language newspapers with an African head editor, and they both offered a mouth-piece to early African political and social organizations (Switzer and Switzer, 1979, 40–41, 45–46).

The frequency analysis approach outlined here offers a 'distant reading' perspective (see Moretti, 2013; Jänicke et al., 2015; Bode, 2017) of the early African language press, and makes visible how a community of African writers were involved in a collective process of shaping the foundations of emerging African nationalism. These texts show an unexpected fluidity of many concepts of identity that have since become fixed and taken for granted, and show how political identity was being dynamically and communally shaped in the period.

Figure 1 demonstrates this conceptual flux by looking at the *Isigidimi* newspaper, examining the changing frequency of three of the most central concepts of proto-nationalist political identity: Nationhood, Ethnicity, and Race.

Figure 1 plots the frequency of several different root words which mark different concepts of group identity (note that 1886 is missing data).

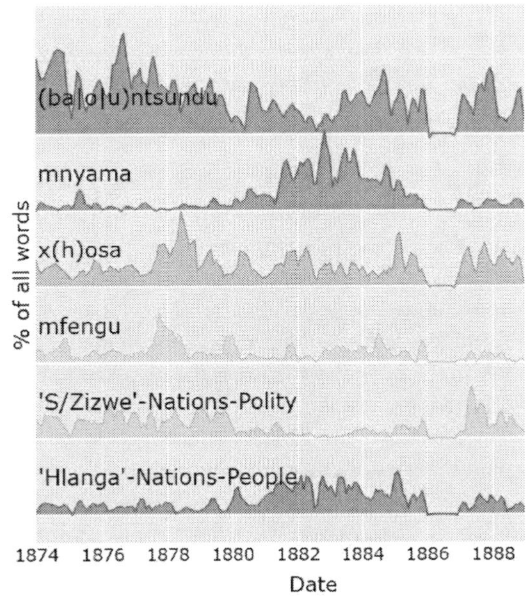

Figure 1: Frequency of identity words in Isigidimi

The first thing to note is that multiple isiXhosa terms cover what are considered in English to be unified concepts. Two root words for race are shown: *-Ntsundu*, meaning 'Dark Brown' (henceforth 'Brown') and *-Mnyama*, meaning Black. Both terms mark community based on skin colour. Yet their changing frequency reveals a great degree of conceptual transformation over the period. Ntsundu identity begins as the most frequent of all the identities plotted in Figure 2, yet falls away almost entirely by 1883, being replaced by a surge of usage of Mnyama. Yet from 1883 onward, Ntsundu returns, used alongside Mnyama for a time, and then spiking back to prominence in 1887.

This flux in 'racial' language is not unique. Ethnicity and Nationhood, two additional concepts central to emerging African nationalism, both show significant shifts in emphasis in this time period. *Xhosa* and *Mfengu*, the most politically central ethnic identities of this community, also shift in focus. Ethnic identification peaks in focus around 1877, and while both diminish, *Xhosa* identification remains more frequent than *Mfengu* identification. The figure also shows competing conceptions of Nationhood shifting through the period. The language of *Isizwe/Izizwe* (sg./pl.) ('Nation/Tribe/Kingdom') and *Uhlanga* ('Nation/People/Lineage/Race') compete for centre stage as the leading imagination of collective nationhood over the period. Both terms imply the community as a shared nation or people, but *Isizwe* has the connotations of a polity—a territory or kingdom, where *Uhlanga* has the connotations of a people—a lineage. *Uhlanga* supersedes *Isizwe* as the focal concept in 1880, yet *Isizwe* returns strongly albeit briefly in 1887.

The shifting use of language offers a perspective on early political identification which might surprise even experts in this time period. The significant shift in frequency shows isiXhosa speaking communities collectively working with and transforming a range of conceptions of communal identity in their own languages as they worked to build a growing consciousness of their shared identity. These observations directly counteract some dominant theories of emerging nationalism. For example, here we see that the ideas Africanness, Blackness, or Nationhood were not simply an import from European nationalism, not merely a 'derivative discourse' (Chatterjee, 1986) or a 'colonization of consciousness' (Comaroff and Comaroff, 1991, 1997). Instead, these isiXhosa texts point to a real wrestle, even an internal conflict, over how African/Black/National identity should be defined within the proto-nationalist movement - a debate happening on isiXhosa, not European, terms.

5 Changing conceptions of Race in early African nationalism

To explore these shifting concepts of identity more deeply, I now focus in on the root terms *-Ntsundu*, and *-Mnyama* which offered two contrasting and competing conceptions of what today might be termed 'Black' or 'African'.

Figure 2 shows how the usage of words containing the root terms -Ntsundu and -Mnyama changed across 16 years of the emerging proto-nationalist movement.[6] Each dot here shows the percentage frequency of usage in one month of Isigidimi (orange) or Imvo (blue) with the line representing a moving weighted average. In the beginning of the period, Ntsundu identity was dominant, and its usage reached a local peak around 1877 when it began to decline. Mnyama usage remained infrequent until 1881 when it began to rapidly rise to prominence and peaked between 1883 and 1884, its peak beginning when Ntsundu reached its lowest usage late in 1882. Yet from 1884 Mnyama began to rapidly recede and Ntsundu usage dominated

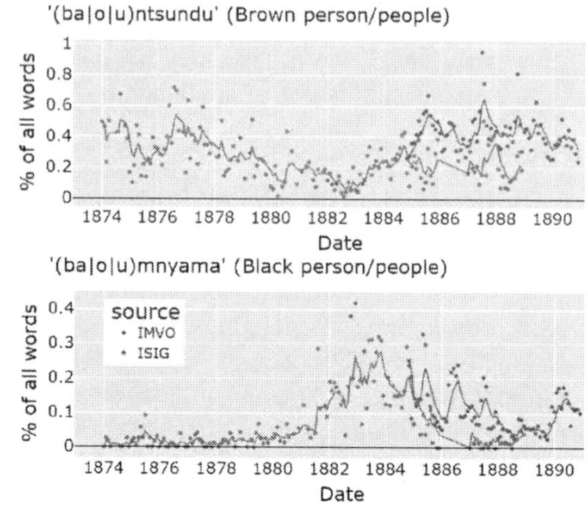

Figure 2: Frequency of Ntsundu and Mnyama

the final period, being used more frequently in the newly founded Imvo Zabantsundu paper than in Isigidimi.

These findings are surprising in light of both the historical analysis to date and present-day language usage. The expectation from the literature or from present day usage is that these terms for 'blackness' might be either equivalent and substitutable, or that Mnyama usage might be the dominant and more frequent expression of racial identity.

A brief explanation of these terms offers useful context. Some scholars, such as Ncedile Saule (2017), have argued that *Abantsundu* was the Xhosa people's own language and conception of skin colour or race ('dark brown') before colonial conceptions of Black and White (see Mzileni, 2019, 86 footnote 5). The term was also translated by missionaries and African writers to the colonial term 'native', showing that in addition to a pre-colonial resonance, the term was also connected to colonial conceptions of difference-yet ones not racially marked.[7] Mnyama more explicitly invokes a binary paring in a way Ntsundu does not: of both white-black (*mhlophe-mnyama*) and light-darkness (*ubukhanya-ubumnyama*). In this way, Mynama might more explicitly invoke the racial binaries of the colonial experience. The term might implicitly foreground a binary opposition with (*abamhlophe* ('white people') in a way that is not implicit in Abantsundu. Mnyama language may thus have more directly addressed the racial distinctions that colonists made between 'Black' and 'White'.

This discussion only begins to scratch at a se-

[6]This analysis focuses on these terms as they are used in relation to people (in both singular and plural) by including the prefixes -ba, -o, or -u in the search.

[7]Consider that 'native' was a global colonial term not simply connected to 'blackness' (cf. the US or New Zealand).

ries of new questions which the analysis presented in Figure 2 raises: what were the different meanings of these terms? Why were they used in such clear contrast where today they might be taken as synonyms? This paper will examine only the significant moments of linguistic shift. I leave for future analysis investigation into the rich historical and linguistic connotations of these two terms.

6 Editors, elites, and identity language

One key insight into the shaping of this discursive space becomes visible when we switch perspectives from newspapers to newspaper editors. Figure 3 now presents the four different editors who headed these papers over the period. In purple is James Stewart, the missionary editor who oversaw Isigidimi until 1876. In green is Elijah Makiwane, the first African newspaper editor who headed Isigidimi until 1881. In orange we see John Tengu Jabavu, in both his role as editor of Isigidimi from 1881 to 1884 and his shift to his own paper Imvo Zabantsundu, which he founded when he left Isigidimi in late 1884. Finally, William Wellington Gqoba, shown in blue, was the editor of Isigidimi from late 1884 until his death in 1888, and Isigidimi closed soon after his passing.

Looking at editorship, we see that Ntsundu was used frequently under the missionary leadership of Stewart. It was also resonant to an isiXhosa editor, spiking when Makiwane, the first African editor, took over. Yet the usage slowly declined under Makiwane's editorship. Figure 3 also shows that Mnyama identity was not used frequently under the editorship of either Stewart or Makiwane, and that Mnyama language did not rise to substitute Ntsundu language during its slow decline. Instead, we see the clearly visible impact that J.T. Jabavu had on promoting Mnyama identity. From the beginning of his tenure as the editor of Isigidimi, we see a sharp increase in the usage of Mnyama. This makes it clear that Jabavu played a large role in promoting a shared *Abamnyama* identity for the emerging proto-nationalist movement.

The historical context of Jabavu helps to contextualize this promotion of Mnyama identity. Jabavu was a key leader in the emergence of organized African political activity, but also had particularly deep exposure to colonial society. As editor of Isigidimi and later Imvo Zabantsundu, Jabavu mobilized a 'progressive' political strategy that looked to the African future instead of to the African

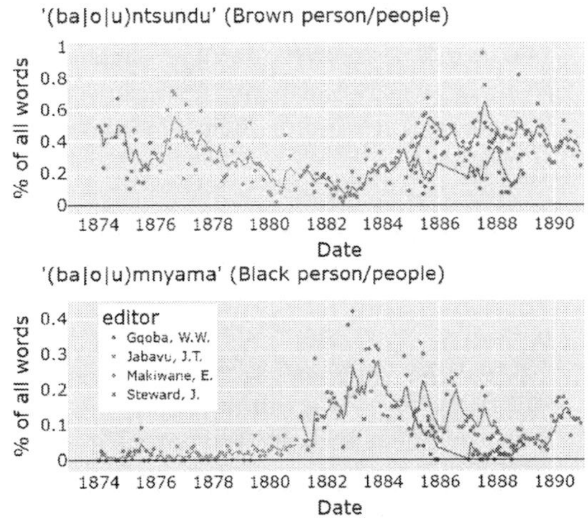

Figure 3: Editors and Ntsundu and Mnyama

past. Other leading Xhosa intellectuals of the period had promoted an African and Xhosa identity which deepened and renewed ties to Xhosa culture, history, and identity (Soga, 1983; Wauchope, 2008; Gqoba, 2015; Mqhayi, 2009). Jabavu instead sought African advancement through the mobilizing of Africans to participate more directly in colonial institutions, especially the Cape Parliament. He believed that to win gains for African people it was necessary to directly assert and defend African rights within the colonial political and legal system.

This history helps to contextualize the powerful shift of race language seen emerging under Jabavu's editorship. Mnyama language in this context appears to lean into colonial conceptions of African identity on the basis of Black vs White. Such an identification is useful when it is in direct dialogue with colonial institutions and authorities, highlighting and challenging colonial racism. Jabavu's early emphasis of Mnyama identity thus appears to be a "Black consciousness of Blackness" (Mbembe, 2017, 30), forged by a man who had been embedded in relationships with whites who viewed him as Black, and who sought to mobilize around racial identity to both challenge the racial inequalities which he confronted, and to build a new political movement pursuing Black modernity.

This editorial influence shows the powerful role that African intellectual and political elites, like Jabavu, had in shaping the discourse and dialogue of emerging proto-nationalist politics. Yet it does not tell the whole story. While it is clear that Jabavu set out to forge a collective sense of shared *Abamnyama* identity when he took over Isigidimi, *this focus on Mnyama language did not stick.* To understand why Mnyama language receded, we must again switch perspective to make visible another driving influence of the period: African voter mobilization and electoral participation in the Cape Parliament.

7 The impact of African franchise on shared identity

Figure 4 overlays key events in the history of African voter mobilization over the changes of word frequency. As I will show, mobilizing the African community to vote and opposing African disenfranchisement had a significant impact on the language of early Proto-nationalism.

The establishment of "Responsible Government" in the Cape in 1872 shifted power from a colonially appointed Governor to an elected Parliament. At this time the Cape Colony followed the British model of voter limitations based on class: there was no racial limitation, but voters had to qualify by holding property (land) or earning above a yearly income threshold. While few missionary educated Africans qualified to vote, proto-nationalist organizations saw an opportunity to mobilize more rural Xhosa people who were eligible due to their communal land tenure. Following voter-mobilization drives, by 1886 African voters made up 47 percent of all voters in 5 key Eastern Cape districts, the heartland of the proto-nationalist movement. In these districts, African voters could decisively swing the vote to send their chosen candidate to the Cape Parliament (Walshe, 1969; Odendaal, 2013, 96 for voter breakdown). In 1887 new laws (Parliamentary Voters Registration Act) were proposed which directly threatened African electoral participation. These laws, among other changes, would remove tribal land holdings as a basis to meet the property qualification to vote (see Odendaal 2013, 144, Walshe 1969, 587). The proto-nationalist community immediately responded and political activity reached a new peak across the eastern Cape with new connections forged between rural and urban African political communities (Odendaal, 2013). Although the bill passed in September 1887, political defeat only heightened the organizing efforts of the proto-nationalist movement which strongly mobilized and participated in the 1889 election.

This brief history offers the context to understand the significant shifts seen in figure 4. The vertical dotted blue lines show new elections to the Cape Parliament in 1879, 1884 and 1889. We see

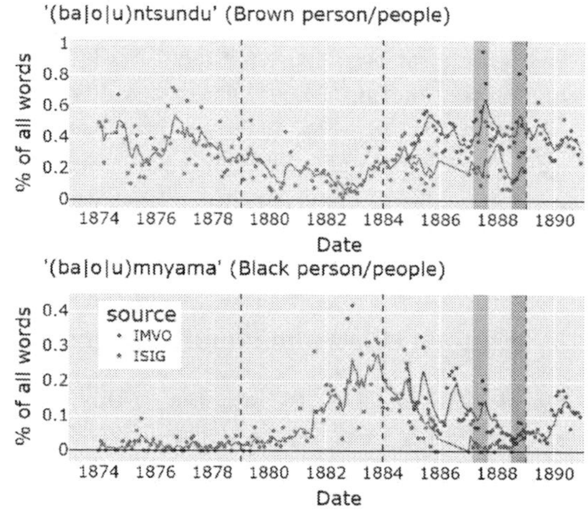

Figure 4: Elections and Ntsundu and Mnyama

no particular impact on Ntsundu and Mnyama language in 1879, when there was no effort by African leaders to mobilize Africans to vote. Yet, we see a significant impact on language use by the election of 1884. In the lead up to this election the Xhosa intellectual community, especially Jabavu, were deeply engaged in discussing the election, although registration numbers were not yet high enough for African's to swing the vote.

Two key shifts are visible: first, under Jabavu's editorship, discussion of Mnyama identity peaks in the run-up to the 1884 election. It is also at this moment that Ntsundu language reaches its inflection point: shifting from its lowest point at the end of 1882, and beginning to rise from 1883, right in the lead up period to the election. Ntsundu comes close to catching Mnyama language just before the election. Mnyama language peaks at approximately 0.275% of all words and Ntsundu language reaches approximately 0.225%. Second, we see the contrasting influence of elites and the wider community. Jabavu, who was very active in the 1884 election, appears to have pushed his focus on Mnyama identity to new heights to mobilize Africans during the election period. Yet the return of Ntsundu language may point to the wide communal resonance of the term which was activated in light of the election.

This wider social resonance of Ntsundu identity is made clear in 1887 and 1888. We see the highest spike in the frequency of Ntsundu language in 1887 during the Parliamentary discussion of the proposed disenfranchisement laws (red-shaded area). In Imvo the spike happens alongside the parliamentary debate period and in Isigidimi the spike happens directly after the law was passed. We also see the impact of the 1889 election, with the 6-month lead up to the elections shaded blue. In this election campaigning period we see a spike in both papers in the use of Ntsundu identity.

This emphasis of Ntsundu identity fits a larger pattern. After the election of 1884, Ntsundu continued to rise and Mnyama usage swiftly declined. In the face of voter disenfranchisement, Ntsundu usage surges to nearly 1% of all words in one month, where Mnyama has a small rise which only reaches 0.2%. The lead up to the 1889 elections (blue shaded area) might even suggest a suppression of Mnyama language, reaching its lowest point in Imvo and remaining low throughout 1889.

These changes in language show a clear relationship to African voter mobilization and elections. This suggests that the language of shared 'Blackness' was not determined by intellectual elites alone. Instead Ntsundu identity appears to have had a significant resonance within the larger community that Mnyama did not have. Remember that it was largely African voters with rural or tribal land holdings who could register to vote, and it was these voters who were threatened with the loss of their voting rights. This suggests that Mnyama and Ntsundu language might have been meaningful for different reasons to different communities. Mnyama identity language seems to more explicitly foregrounded Black/White racism, and it may thus have resonated more with figures like Jabavu and other missionary educated or urban Xhosa who were daily in contact with white colonists and facing racism through the language of Black and White. However, it may be that Ntsundu language was indeed a conception which held deeper resonances for the broader proto-nationalist rural community, drawn from an older isiXhosa epistemological framework which existed before colonialism. Evidence from newspapers also shows that African organizations which had started in the 1880s were already using Ntsundu language far more than Mnyama language, and also amplified this identity in election periods.

This analysis also suggests that Jabavu was sensitive and responsive to this wider community resonance. Notably, although he had promoted Mnyama identity during his time at Isigidimi, the 1884 election may have shown Jabavu that this identity was not the one with the most resonance. When he chose the name for his new newspaper Jabavu himself turned to Ntsundu identity: Imvo Zaba***ntsundu***. Overall, this analysis shows the impact that leaders like Jabavu could have on political discourse and identity. Yet it also shows that the larger community had a powerful and, for this period, defining impact on the language of political discussion. These findings show that isiXhosa speakers were engaged in debates about identity on isiXhosa epistemological terms, and reveals how individuals, events, and collective political engagement all shaped and reshaped core ideas of political self-hood in early African nationalism.

8 Conclusion

This paper outlines an application of text frequency analysis over time which focuses on root words and offers an accessible method to study isiXhosa texts. This method has particular advantages because it by-passes the need for other complex Natural Language Processing tools which are limited for isiXhosa. For this reason, the approach might also be useful for other under-resourced agglutinative languages. The approach is also useful for humanities and social science scholars as it is technically simple, yet requires sufficient contextual knowledge of the examined texts.

I showcase the utility of this approach through an analysis of shared political identity formation in early African Nationalism. Using the outlined methods, I visualize shifts in the usage of key identity terms. I have focused on competing isiXhosa conceptions of shared 'Blackness', -Ntsundu and -Mnyama. The paper has examined how individual leaders (like J.T. Jabavu), historical events (such as African voter mobilization and disenfranchisement), and the wider community (such as rural Xhosa voters) all played an influential role in shaping collective identity discourse. This case shows the opportunities created by applying computational text analysis methods to isiXhosa, as the study is able to reveal communal shifts in the identity language of early African nationalism which have remained invisible to close textual analysis or historical approaches to these materials. These approaches thus support and augment existing qualitative methods. This offers new opportunities to study isiXhosa and other African language materials, and new perspectives on important humanities and social science questions.

Limitations

The paper presents a method which is developed on isiXhosa texts, which the paper suggests might be useful for under resourced agglutinative languages, including African and other global languages. As highlighted in the main text, a key limitation is the application to only isiXhosa text analysis. It may be the case that grammatical features of other languages are not compatible with the approach. This limitation may be mitigated in some ways: isiXhosa shares many grammatical features of the larger group of Bantu languages including a common class system and thus the method outlined here is likely extendable. Agglutinative languages in general share a structure of root words modified by prefixes and suffixes which this method is designed to utilize. However, the author has not tested the extent and limitations of applications to other languages.

The analysis presented here is also limited: the case study is partial and cannot fully make visible the depths and limits of the historical and qualitative analysis which was used alongside the quantitative analysis due to space limitations. This limitation means the case study is best taken as an exemplar of possible research rather than a fully demonstrated historical claim. The author of this paper is not a first language isiXhosa speaker. Qualitative research which supports the argument has combine reading of sections of isiXhosa newspaper text which use the key words discussed, and has been supplemented with broader readings of primary literature in translation and secondary literature written in English.

Ethics Statement

This research has drawn on isiXhosa historical text which is in the public domain and has been digitized and made publicly available.

Human coders and language editors who worked on the digitized text analyzed here are all employed as members of the larger archival research project. All coders and editors are first language isiXhosa speakers who are students or researchers.

The method outlined in this paper may be of particular use to under resourced languages. The approach does not use cutting edge tools, but rather outlines how accessible methodological approaches can be used to by-pass more complicated NLP steps which may not be available for under resourced languages. For this reason, the author believes that this research has limited potential to cause harm. Instead it may have potential to enhance computational research in under resourced languages, fostering more equal access to computational text research methods

Acknowledgements

This article was written with partial supported from the National Research Foundation of South Africa, grant number 138493.

References

David Attwell. 2005. *Rewriting Modernity: Studies in Black South African Literary History*. KwaZulu-Natal University Press, Pietermaritzburg.

Alistair Baron, Paul Rayson, and Dawn Archer. 2009. Word frequency and key word statistics in corpus linguistics. *Anglistik*, 20(1):41–67.

Katherine Bode. 2017. The Equivalence of "Close" and "Distant" Reading; or, Toward a New Object for Data-Rich Literary History. *Modern Language Quarterly*, 78(1):77–106.

Partha Chatterjee. 1986. *Nationalist Thought and the Colonial World: A Derivative Discourse?* Zed Books.

Jean Comaroff and John L. Comaroff. 1991. *Of revelation and revolution, volume 1: Christianity, colonialism, and consciousness in South Africa*, volume 1. University of Chicago Press.

John L. Comaroff and Jean Comaroff. 1997. *Of revelation and revolution, volume 2: The dialectics of modernity on a South African frontier*, volume 2. University of Chicago Press.

William Wellington Gqoba. 2015. *Isizwe esinembali: Xhosa histories and poetry (1873-1888)*. University of KwaZulu-Natal Press, KwaZulu-Natal.

Andreas H Jucker, Franz Lebsanft, and Gerd Fritz. 1999. Historical dialogue analysis. *Historical Dialogue Analysis*, pages 1–486.

S Jänicke, G Franzini, M F Cheema, and G Scheuermann. 2015. On Close and Distant Reading in Digital Humanities: A Survey and Future Challenges. *Eurographics Conference on Visualization (EuroVis)*, page 21.

Xolela Mangcu. 2014. *Biko : a life*. I.B. Tauris, London.

Ntongela Masilela. 2013. *An Outline of the New African Movement in South Africa*. Africa World Press, New Jersey.

Ntongela Masilela. 2014. *The Historical Figures of the New African Movement*. Africa World Press, New Jersey.

Achille Mbembe. 2017. *Critique of Black Reason*. Duke University Press.

Khwezi Mkhize. 2008. Carrying the Cross: Isaac William(s) Wauchope's Ingcamango Ebunzimeni. Master's thesis, University of the Witwatersrand.

Khwezi Mkhize. 2018. 'To See Us As We See Ourselves': John Tengo Jabavu and the Politics of the Black Periodical. *Journal of Southern African Studies*, 44(3):413–430.

Franco Moretti. 2013. *Distant Reading*. Verso Books.

Samuel E. K. Mqhayi. 2009. *Abantu Besizwe: Historical and biographical writings 1902-1944 SEK Mqhayi*. Wits University Press, Johannesburg.

Lulamile Mzamo, Albert Helberg, and Sonja Bosch. 2015. Introducing xgl-a lexicalised probabilistic graphical lemmatiser for isixhosa. In *2015 Pattern Recognition Association of South Africa and Robotics and Mechatronics International Conference (PRASA-RobMech)*, pages 142–147. IEEE.

Pedro Mzileni. 2019. (Re)imagining Mandela's Leadership esiXhoseni. *International Journal of Critical Diversity Studies*. Publisher: Pluto Journals.

M. Ndletyana, editor. 2008. *African intellectuals in 19th and early 20th century South Africa*. HSRC Press, Cape Town.

Abner Nyamende. 2000. *The Life and Works of Isaac William(s) Wauchope*. PhD Thesis, University of Cape Town, Cape Town.

André Odendaal. 2013. *The founders: The origins of the ANC and the struggle for democracy in South Africa*. The University Press of Kentucky, Kentucky.

Martin Puttkammer and Jakobus S. Du Toit. 2021. Canonical Segmentation and Syntactic Morpheme Tagging of Four Resource- scarce Nguni Languages. *Journal of the Digital Humanities Association of Southern Africa*, 3(03).

Ncedile Saule. 2017. King Hintsa memorial lecture. Public lecture.

Jonathan Schoots. 2020. S.E.K. Mqhayi and African social analysis: African sociological thought in colonial South Africa. *Social Dynamics*, 46(3):493–514.

Leo Jonathan Schoots. 2021. *Novelty, Networks, and the Rise of African Nationalism: African Intermediary Intelligentsia and the Making of Political Innovation in Colonial South Africa (1860-1890)*. Ph.D., The University of Chicago, United States – Illinois.

Tiyo Soga. 1983. *The journal and selected writings of the Reverend Tiyo Soga*. The Graham's Town series 7. A.A. Balkema, Cape Town.

Les Switzer and Donna Switzer. 1979. *The Black press in South Africa and Lesotho: a descriptive bibliographic guide to African, Coloured, and Indian newspapers, newsletters, and magazines, 1836-1976*. Boston: Hall.

A. P. Walshe. 1969. The Origins of African Political Consciousness in South Africa. *The Journal of Modern African Studies*, 7(4):583–610.

Isaac Williams Wauchope. 2008. *Isaac Williams Wauchope: selected writings 1874-1916*. Van Riebeeck Society, Cape Town.

Evaluating the Sesotho rule-based syllabification system on Sepedi and Setswana words

Johannes Sibeko
Nelson Mandela University
Linguistics and Applied Linguistics
Port Elizabeth, South Africa
johannes.sibeko@mandela.ac.za

Mmasibidi Setaka
South African Centre
for Digital Language Resources
Potchefstroom, South Africa
mmasibidi.setaka@nwu.ac.za

Abstract

The purpose of this article is to demonstrate that the recently developed automated rule-based syllabification system for Sesotho can be used broadly across the officially recognised South African Sotho-Tswana language group encompassing Sepedi, Sesotho and Setswana. We evaluate the automatic syllabification system on 400 words comprising 100 most frequently used words and 100 least-used words in Sepedi and Setswana as evident in the Autshumato corpus publicly available online. It is found that the Sesotho rule-based syllabification system can be used to correctly identify vowel-only syllables, consonant-vowel syllables and consonant-only syllables in Sepedi and Setswana. Among other findings, it has been demonstrated that words with diacritics as in the case of Sepedi are correctly broken down into syllables. We make two main recommendations. First, the rules for syllabification should be updated so that Sepedi diacritics are accommodated. Second, the syllabification system should be updated so that it reflects the broader Sotho-Tswana language group instead of being limited to Sesotho. Further research is needed to ascertain whether the complex consonant [ɲ] behaves similarly in all three officially recognised Sotho-Tswana languages and evaluate the need for a specific rule for the [ɲ] nasal consonant.

1 Introduction

This article presents an evaluation of the Sesotho rule-based syllabification system for use in Sepedi and Setswana written texts. The Republic of South Africa recognises eleven official languages, namely, Afrikaans, English, isiNdebele, isiXhosa, isiZulu, SiSwati, Sepedi, Sesotho, Setswana, Tshivenda, and Xitsonga (Republic of South Africa, 1996). Of these eleven languages, Afrikaans and English are often identified as Germanic languages (Zulu et al., 2008). Even so, some argue that Afrikaans is an African language as it is spoken in Africa even though it is a variant of Dutch (Willemse, 2018; Staphorst, 2022). IsiNdebele, isiXhosa, isiZulu and isiSwati are classified under the Nguni language group. Sepedi [also referred to as Northern Sotho (Rakgogo and Zungu, 2021)], Sesotho [also referred to as Southern Sotho (Demuth, 2007)], and Setswana [sometimes referred to as Western Sotho (Mojela, 2016)] are grouped under the Sotho-Tswana language group. These Sotho-Tswana languages have many variations within themselves. Even so, they are mutually intelligible in that the speakers of these languages can understand each other without difficulty (Makalela, 2009). The national language bodies, under the auspices of the Pan South African Language Board (PanSALB) have dictated three different orthographies for these languages. PanSALB develops rules and standards for spelling and orthography for the proper functioning of all official languages[1].

According to the 2011 census[2], there were at least 4 618 577 Sepedi first language speakers, 3 849 562 Sesotho first language speakers and 4 067 248 Setswana first language speakers in South Africa alone (Lehohla, 2011). Sesotho is also an official language in Lesotho and Zimbabwe. Setswana is also one of the official languages of Botswana. The South African Human Language Technologies surveys indicate that there is a paucity of research in syllabification systems for the indigenous languages of South Africa (Grover et al., 2010, 2011; Barnard et al., 2014; Moors et al., 2018a,b). As far as we are aware, Sesotho is presently the only South African indigenous language to have a publicly accessible rule-based syllabification system. Even so, according to Sibeko and Setaka (2022), there are two systems for syllabification in Sesotho. The machine learning TEX-based pattern-

[1] see mandates for South African language boards accessible at https://static.pmg.org.za/PanSALB_APP_2122_compressed_reviewed_08032021_final.pdf

[2] South Africa's 2022 census results have not been released

Proceedings of the Fourth workshop on Resources for African Indigenous Languages (RAIL 2023), pages 76–85
May 6, 2023 ©2023 Association for Computational Linguistics

ing system relies on gold-standard corpora with exemplified syllable annotations. The Sesotho TEX-based syllabification system used a gold standard list of words and their syllables[3]. Unfortunately, we are not aware of similar lists for Sepedi and Setswana. As such, we cannot evaluate this machine learning system in this article.

This article aims to demonstrate the applicability of the Sesotho rule-based system in identifying syllables in the wider South African Sotho-Tswana language group. We provide a very brief background to orthographies of South African languages and expected syllable types in Sepedi and Setswana in section 2. We then describe our method of data collection in section 3. Finally, we discuss our findings in section 4 and end with a discussion in section 5.

2 Background

2.1 Orthographies

Written languages have systematic rules for spelling words (Matlosa, 2017). Rules for writing in African languages were introduced by religious missionaries. As a result, most orthographies of African languages are modelled after European orthographies (Mahlangu, 2015). Two major writing systems are used in South African languages. First, the Sotho-Tswana language group together with Tshivenda and Xitsonga use disjunctive writing systems, while the Nguni language group composing isiZulu, isiXhosa, isiNdebele, and SiSwati, use a conjunctive writing system (Prinsloo, 2011). The writing systems are illustrated below:

(a) Bana ba ya matha. - Sesotho

Children they are running. - English

(b) Abantwana bayagijima. - Isizulu

The+children they+are+running. - English

As exemplified above, languages such as Sotho-Tswana languages with disjunctive writing systems isolate words while languages with conjunctive writing systems [for example, isiZulu] combine some parts of speech such the present tense and the plural subject marker in the word *bayagijima*. Nonetheless, Sotho-Tswana languages are easy to compare as they follow the same phonemic orthography where seven phonemic representations are mutually common [ɑ, e, i, o, u, ɛ, and ɔ] (Dickens, 1978; Matlosa, 2017).

[3] The Sesotho syllable information annotated wordlist can be freely accessed at `https://repo.sadilar.org/handle/20.500.12185/556`

Sesotho has two recognised orthographies, namely, (i) the South African Sesotho (SAS) orthography and (ii) the Lesotho Sesotho (LS) orthography. One of the main differences between SAS and LS orthographies is the use of diacritics in LS orthography. For instance, see examples (c) and (d) below:

(c) Tshepiso. - SAS orthography

Promise. - English

(d) Tšepiso. - LS orthography

Promise. - English

In the example above, the LS orthography uses the accented š letter while the SAS orthography uses the '*sh*' digraph. Differences between SAS and LS orthographies are discussed thoroughly in studies such as Demuth (2007) and Matlosa (2017). The rule-based syllabification system evaluated in this article uses the SAS orthography (Sibeko and van Zaanen, 2022a).

According to Suyanto et al. (2021), rule-based systems perform better for low-resourced languages with limited to no gold standard corpora. This was also demonstrated in the case of Sesotho where the rule-based system outperformed the TEX-based patterning system (Sibeko and van Zaanen, 2022a). Rule-based systems are based on sets of rules carefully designed by language experts. According to Sibeko (2022), when the designed list of rules is properly implemented, syllable boundaries can be identified in any Sesotho word.

The Sesotho rule-based system for syllabification uses rules for vowel-only syllables (v-syllables), consonant-only syllables (c-syllables), and consonant-vowel syllables (cv-syllables). According to Sibeko (2022) and Guma (1982) these are the only syllable types in Sesotho. Sibeko and Van Zaanen's (2022b) rule-based syllabification system takes one word per line as input and then outputs the syllabified version. The syllable boundaries are indicated by spaces.

The rule-based syllabification system recognises only 26 letters of the alphabet [abcdefghijklmnopqrstuvwxyz]. The rules for syllabification identify three main syllable types together with sixteen subtypes. These types, subtypes, and examples are presented in table 1. Interestingly, the Sesotho rule-based syllabification system used in this article demonstrated exceptional accuracy by achieving a rate of 99.6% (Sibeko and van Zaanen, 2022a,b).

The sounds w and y are considered semivowels

Type	Sub-types	Input	Syllabified	English
V	word-initial vowel	*oma*	*o-ma*	dry
	consecutive vowels	*boena*	*bo-e-na*	brotherhood
	word-final vowel	*lemao*	*le-ma-o*	needle
CV	one consonant - one vowel	*nama*	*na-ma*	meat
	one consonant - semi-vowel- one vowel	*lwetse*	*lwe-tse*	september
	two consonants - one vowel	*tlola*	*tlo-la*	skip
	two consonants - semi-vowel- one vowel	*shwashwi*	*shwa-shwi*	gossiper
	three consonants - one vowel	*tlhapa*	*tlha-pa*	insult
	three consonants - semi-vowel- one vowel	*tshweu*	*tshwe-u*	white
C	nasal consonant n, m - non-nasal consonant	*ntja*	*n-tja*	dog
	nasal consonant n, m - nasal consonant	*mmoho*	*m-mo-ho*	together
	nasal consonant n - complex nasal consonant	*nngwe*	*n-ngwe*	one
	complex nasal consonant ŋ - vowel	*ngola*	*ngo-la*	write
	complex nasal consonant ŋ- non-nasal consonant	*hanghang*	*ha-ng-ha-ng*	immediately
	word-ending complex nasal consonant ŋ	*mang*	*ma-ng*	who
	consecutive lateral consonants l	*lla*	*l-la*	cry

Table 1: Syllabification rules and examples.

when they occur at the onset of a syllable. However, some studies, such as Nkolola-Wakumelo et al.'s (2012) analysis of Setswana and Sesotho syllables, use the term "glides" instead.

2.2 Sepedi syllables

According to Wilsenach (2019), Sotho-Tswana languages have similar syllable structures. That is, Sepedi words can also be broken down into v-syllables, cv-syllables and c-syllables. The v-syllables are formed using only one vowel either at the beginning, middle or end of a word, or by monosyllabic words formed only of a vowel. The cv-syllable structure can contain between one and four onsets. The four onsets can be composed of three consonants (ccc) as in words like *tlhekišo* [tlhe-ki-šo], and a semi-vowel (w) resulting in the four onsets and a vowel syllable (cccwv) as in words like *tlhwekišo* [tlhwe-ki-šo].

The c-syllables can be formed m, n, l, r, ɲ, and ŋ syllabic consonants (Chokoe, 2020). First, c-syllables are formed when two identical syllabic consonants occur in succession within a single word, for instance in words like *ba-l-li* 'criers', and *wa-r-ra* 'brother' (Chokoe, 2020). Second, when nasal consonants precede any other consonant, for instance in words like *n-tšha* 'draw', and *m-phsa* 'new'. Third, the ŋ c-syllable is formed when the ŋ complex nasal takes the word-final position such as in words like *n-tlo-ng-* (Makaure, 2021; Chokoe, 2020).

2.3 Setswana syllables

There are also three syllable structures in Setswana Otlogetswe (2017). First, Setswana uses the open cv-syllable structure where cv-syllables can contain between one (cv) and four (cccwv) onset consonants (Sebina, 2014). Second, v-syllables can be formed using one vowel either at the word-initial, word-medial or word-final positions such in words like *a-lo-la, lo-e-to, bo-e-* 'make, trip, return'. Vowel-only monosyllabic words are also used in Setswana, for instance in words like *ao* 'to/of'. Third, like Sepedi, c-syllables can be formed by the m, n, l, r, and ŋ syllabic consonants. The simple syllabic consonants can appear at the word-initial position such as in words like *m-ma* 'mom', and word-medial positions such as in words like *bo-r-re* 'fathers' (Otlogetswe and Ramaeba, 2022). The ŋ nasal consonant can also appear at the word-final position such as in words like *fi-sa-ng-* 'hot'. While other syllabic consonants behave similarly to those in Sesotho, the current Sesotho syllabification system does not account for the representation of the r c-syllable in its rules.

3 Methodology

The South African Centre for Digital Language Resources hosts a publicly available online repository at `repo.sadilar.org`. For this article, we collected two Autshumato 6 corpora, that is, the Sepedi (McKellar, 2022a) and Setswana (McKel-

word	syllables	word	syllable	word	syllable	word	syllable
go	go	bo	bo	tla	tla	feta	fe ta
ya	ya	mmušo	m mu šo	na	na	barutwana	ba ru twa na
le	le	rena	re na	tšeo	tše o	mokgwa	mo kgwa
ka	ka	yona	yo na	swanetše	swa ne tše	karolo	ka ro lo
a	a	kudu	ku du	wo	wo	leo	le o
e	e	swanetšego	swa ne tše go	pele	pe le	fela	fe la
ba	ba	godimo	go di mo	bona	bo na	maemo	ma e mo
tša	tša	gagwe	ga gwe	gona	go na	kgopelo	kgo pe lo
o	o	nngwe	n ngwe	gomme	go m me	moo	mo o
di	di	mongwe	mo ngwe	gago	ga go	dingwe	di ngwe
ye	ye	gape	ga pe	be	be	bjo	bjo
se	se	fao	fa o	ao	a o	ngwaga	ngwa ga
ke	ke	ngwala	ngwa la	bjalo	bja lo	ntle	n tle
wa	wa	tshedimošo	tshe di mo šo	batho	ba tho	lebaka	le ba ka
tše	tše	motho	mo tho	dira	di ra	tee	te e
gore	go re	bala	ba la	yo	yo	šomiša	šo mi ša
ga	ga	morago	mo ra go	lego	le go	mešomo	me šo mo
sa	sa	tšwa	tšwa	bao	ba o	nago	na go
la	la	ile	i le	moka	mo ka	latelago	la te la go
ge	ge	mabapi	ma ba pi	seo	se o	maleba	ma le ba
goba	go ba	mošomo	mo šo mo	borwa	bo rwa	tšona	tšo na
re	re	gare	ga re	afrika	a fri ka	lenaneo	le na ne o
mo	mo	naga	na ga	setšhaba	se tšha ba	ditirelo	di ti re lo
bja	bja	mme	m me	bohlokwa	bo hlo kwa	taolo	ta o lo
yeo	ye o	molao	mo la o	nako	na ko	šoma	šo ma

Table 2: Lists of frequently used words and syllabified counterparts in Sepedi

lar, 2022b) Autshumato monolingual corpora. The Sepedi corpus contained a total of 3 458 067 words while the Setswana corpus contained a total of 5 219 070 words.

We used *bash* to extract four frequency lists. One, a list of one hundred most frequently used words in Sepedi. Two, the hundred most frequently used words in Setswana. Three, the hundred most infrequently used words in Sepedi. Four, the hundred least frequently used words in the Setswana corpus.

We then extracted the syllabification information from all four lists using Sibeko and Van Zaanen's (2022b) rule-based syllabification system that was also downloaded from SADiLaR's repository[4].

4 Results

This section presents the results of the syllabification process. Both the 100 most used words and the 100 least used words from the Autshumato corpora for Sepedi and Setswana are presented. Stop words were not considered for any of the four lists.

4.1 Sepedi

4.1.1 Frequently used words

The hundred most frequently used Sepedi words ranged between 229 028 times [for the word *go*] and 3 387 times [for the word *šoma*]. The list of original words and their syllables are presented in table 2. The v-syllable, cv-syllable, and c-syllable types can be observed from the list. Note that we use the dash (-) to indicate syllable boundaries while the syllabification system only uses spaces.

The v-syllables structure was observed for monosyllabic vowel-only words such as a, e, ɛ, ɔ and o. Furthermore, we observed v-syllables at the word-initial position in words such as *ile* [i-le-] 'went', the word-medial position in words such as *taolo* [ta-o-lo-] 'control', and the word-final position in words such as *tee* [te-e-] 'only'. We did not observe any erroneous identification of v-syllables.

At least four cv-syllable types are present on the list. First, the one-consonant-one-vowel structure was observed in words such as *kudu* [ku-du-] 'a lot' which was correctly broken into two syllables. Second, the cwv syllable structure was evident in words such as *bohlokwa* [bo-hlo-kwa-] 'important' which was broken into three syllables. Third, the ccv structure was evident in words such as *tšeo* [tše-o-] 'those'. Fourth, the ccwv structure was evident in words such as *ngwaga* [ngwa-ga-] 'year' which was broken into two syllables. Fifth, the cccv structure was observed in words such as *setšhaba* [se-tšha-ba-] 'nation' which was broken into three syllables. Unfortunately, there were no instances of cccwv syllable structures on the list.

[4] *see* https://repo.sadilar.org/handle/20.500.12185/556 for the Sesotho syllabification systems

word	syllables	word	syllable	word	syllables
ac	a c	abakase	a ba ka se	abalanago	a ba la na go
aar	a a r	abakeng	a ba ke ng	abelanang	a be la na ng
acr	a cr	abalobi	a ba lo bi	abelanego	a be la ne go
adi	a di	abapile	a ba pi le	abitafiti	a bi ta fi ti
abby	a bby	abelala	a be la la	addictive	a ddi cti ve
abel	a be l	abelano	a be la no	adiolotši	a di o lo tši
abis	a bi s	abeleng	a be le ng	advantage	a dva n ta ge
abiy	a bi y	abetswe	a be tswe	abonagala	a bo na ga la
aesa	a e sa	abganya	a bga nya	aaaahhhhhh	a a a a hhhhhh
aces	a ce s	abidjan	a bi dja n	abagantšhe	a ba ga n tšhe
acsa	a csa	abiwego	a bi we go	abaganwego	a ba ga nwe go
acts	a cts	abišana	a bi ša na	ablefetile	a ble fe ti le
adha	a dha	abokato	a bo ka to	aerospeisi	a e ro spe i si
adiš	a di š	aerobic	a e ro bi c	acceptable	a cce pta ble
aakar	a a ka r	adalats	a da la ts	accredited	a ccre di te d
abdel	a bde l	adilego	a di le go	adimišanwa	a di mi ša nwa
abedi	a be di	abattoir	a ba tto i r	abaganywago	a ba ga nywa go
abego	a be go	abdicate	a bdi ca te	abahlankedi	a ba hla n ke di
abeke	a be ke	adminiša	a dmi ni ša	adopthilwego	a do pthi lwe go
abjwe	a bjwe	abelanye	a be la nye	aaohegnoboae	a a o he gno bo a e
abona	a bo na	aeration	a e ra ti o n	accessibility	a cce ssi bi li ty
abubi	a bu bi	aeskrimi	a e skri mi	accommodation	a cco m mo da ti o n
abuja	a bu ja	aethiops	a e thi o ps	actinomycetes	a cti no myce te s
accom	a cco m	abrahams	a bra ha m s	adumeletšwego	a du me le tšwe go
adira	a di ra	accounts	a cco u n ts	adoption	a do pti o n
adult	a du lt	acidosis	a ci do si s	advocate	a dvo ca te
aeemo	a e e mo	adimišwa	a di mi šwa	abortion	a bo rti o n
abacus	a ba cu s	adimišwe	a di mi šwe	abaganago	a ba ga na go
acacia	a ca ci a	admirale	a dmi ra le	abaganeng	a ba ga ne ng
acdasa	a cda sa	aemiše	a e mi še	abagantše	a ba ga n tše
achmat	a chma t	aeneng	a e ne ng	abulela	a bu le la
acquah	a cqu a h				
aakpaorleatsštwikai			a a kpa o rle a tsštwi ka i		
abeahlalošetšamapho			a be a hla lo še tša ma pho		
abonagopotologafaoabegoa			a bo na go po to lo ga fa o a be go a		
adiraboipiletšobjakagare			a di ra bo i pi le tšo bja ka ga re		
abonakebonabaobafetelwago			a bo na ke bo na ba o ba fe te lwa go		
abelwagokelenaneoedirwemenyetlayagoyagoile			a be lwa go ke le na ne o e di rwe me nye tla ya go ya go i le		

Table 3: Lists of least used words and syllabified counterparts in Sepedi

Furthermore, our list of frequently used words was limited in that it did not reflect all possible consonant-only syllable types. Even so, we were able to investigate the behaviour of the syllabic m and n nasal consonants. For instance, we find words such as *mmušo* [m-mu-šo-] 'government' and *nngwe* [n-ngwe-] 'one' which were correctly broken into syllables.

4.1.2 Least used words

We also surveyed the hundred least-used words from the Sepedi corpus. Each of the words appeared no more than once in the corpus. The original words and the derived syllables are listed in table 3.

Our Sepedi list of most infrequently used words contained instances of untranslated English words. Some of the English words were left as references for newly coined Sepedi words. We did not clean the list, instead, we fed it into the syllabification system to see how the system would handle all the different unexpected words.

Fortunately, rule-based syllabification systems are best for unseen words (Adsett et al., 2009). Being able to handle unseen words allows the syllabification system to identify syllable boundaries in unexpected words such as concatenations like *abelwagokelenaneoedirwemenyetlayagoyagoile* and in words from a different language such as the English word 'Abrahams' [a-bra-ha-ms].

Three v-syllable structures were observed. First, the word-initial v-syllable structure was observed in words such as *abjwe* [a-bjwe-] 'shared' which was broken down into two syllables. Second, the word-final v-syllable structure was observed in the word *aaohegnoboae*[5] which was broken into eight syllables [a-a-o-he-gno-bo-a-e-]. Finally, the word-

[5]note that this is another instance of a non-Sepedi word. It was used here due to the absence of a proper Sepedi word with the word-final v-syllable

word	syllables	word	syllable	word	syllable	word	syllable
a	a	tswa	tswa	letsatsi	le tsa tsi	re	re
wa	wa	fela	fe la	madi	ma di	rona	ro na
ba	ba	ga	ga	maemo	ma e mo	sa	sa
baagi	ba a gi	gago	ga go	metsi	me tsi	se	se
baithuti	ba i thu ti	gagwe	ga gwe	mme	m me	sengwe	se ngwe
bana	ba na	gape	ga pe	mmogo	m mo go	seno	se no
batho	ba tho	go	go	mo	mo	teng	te ng
batla	ba tla	godimo	go di mo	mongwe	mo ngwe	thata	tha ta
bile	bi le	gore	go re	morago	mo ra go	thusa	thu sa
bo	bo	haba	ha ba	motho	mo tho	tiro	ti ro
bona	bo na	jaaka	ja a ka	na	na	tla	tla
bone	bo ne	jalo	ja lo	nako	na ko	tlaa	tla a
borwa	bo rwa	jo	jo	nang	na ng	tlase	tla se
ya	ya	jwa	jwa	ne	ne	tsa	tsa
di	di	ka	ka	neng	ne ng	tse	tse
dilo	di lo	karolo	ka ro lo	ngwaga	ngwa ga	tsela	tse la
dingwe	di ngwe	ke	ke	nna	n na	tshedimosetso	tshe di mo se tso
dintlha	di n tlha	kgona	kgo na	nne	n ne	tshwanetse	tshwa ne tse
dira	di ra	kgotsa	kgo tsa	nngwe	n ngwe	tsotlhe	tso tlhe
dirisa	di ri sa	kwa	kwa	ntlha	n tlha	farologaneng	fa ro lo ga ne ng
ditirelo	di ti re lo	kwala	kwa la	ntse	n tse	aforika	a fo ri ka
ditiro	di ti ro	la	la	o	o	botlhokwa	bo tlho kwa
e	e	latelang	la te la ng	pele	pe le	yo	yo
eno	e no	le	le	puo	pu o	yona	yo na
fa	fa	leng	le ng	puso	pu so	yone	yo ne

Table 4: Lists of frequently used words and syllabified counterparts in Setswana

medial v-syllable structure was observed in words such as *aemiše* [a-e-mi-še-] 'he stops' which was broken into four syllables.

Five cv-syllable structures were identified from the word list. First, the one-consonant-one-vowel structure was observed in words such as *abulela* 'he opened' which was broken into four syllables [a-bu-le-la-]. Second, the cwv structure was evident in words such as *adimišwe* 'lend' which was broken into four syllables [a-di-mi-šwe-]. Third, the ccv structure was observed in words such as *abagantše* 'divided' which was broken into five syllables [a-ba-ga-n-tše-]. Fourth, we observed the ccwv structure in words like *adumeletšwego* [a-dume-le-tšwe-go-] 'approved' which was broken into six syllables. Finally, we observed the cccv structure in words such as *abagantšhe* [a-ba-ga-n-tšhe-] 'separate' which was broken into five syllables. There were no instances of the cccwv structure in the current word list.

Only two c-syllable structures were observed from the list of one hundred least frequently used words. First, the n syllabic nasal structure was observed in words such as *abagantše* discussed above. Second, the ŋ complex syllabic nasal structure was observed in words such as *abaganeng* [a-ba-ga-ne-ng-] where it is in the word-final position.

Although there were no instances of the syllabic nasal m, there is an interesting behaviour of the consonant m in words such as *adminiša* [a-dmi-ni-ša-] 'administer' and *admirale* [a-dmi-ra-le-] 'admiral' which are respectively broken down into four syllables. This structure of the *dmi* syllable is unexpected in the Sepedi language and it is enabled only by naturalised loaned words. One would expect a vowel between the letters d and m as in *adiminiša* [a-di-mi-ni-ša-] and *adimirale* [a-di-mi-ra-le-].

Nonetheless, Sotho-Tswana languages do not have strict rules for spelling loaned words. As a result, the 'dmi' syllable does not break spelling rules as it is a ccv syllable which falls under the cv-syllable structure generally preferred in Bantu languages (Ditsele, 2014). What is important here is that the syllable boundaries are correctly identified.

4.2 Setswana

4.2.1 Frequently used words

The one hundred most frequently used Setswana words ranged between 334 188 times [for the word *go*] and 4 688 times [for the word *yona*].

Vowel-only monosyllabic words such as a, e, and o were frequently used in the corpus. Furthermore, we observed v-syllable structures in word-initial positions in words such as *eno* [e-no-] 'that one', in word-final positions such as in words like *puo* [pu-o-] 'speech', and in word-medial position in words such as *'jaaka'* [ja-a-ka-] 'like'. Overall, no

word	syllables	word	syllable	word	syllable
aaa	a a a	acae	a ca e	abiweka	a bi we ka
aabb	a a bb	accelerated	a cce le ra te d	abolition	a bo li ti o n
aaferika	a a fe ri ka	accidental	a cci de n ta l	abolokiwang	a bo lo ki wa ng
aaforika	a a fo ri ka	accom	a cco m	abone	a bo ne
aakantse	a a ka n tse	accountancy	a cco u n ta n cy	aboratoring	a bo ra to ri ng
aakaretsang	a a ka re tsa ng	accra	a ccra	abosesebalolang	a bo se se ba lo la ng
aamebitlwa	a a me bi tlwa	accuweather	a ccu we a the r	about	a bo u t
aamogetse	a a mo ge tse	acdasa	a cda sa	absorbers	a bso rbe rs
aasa	a a sa	ace	a ce	absorption	a bso rpti o n
aau	a a u	acesulfame	a ce su lfa me	abueng	a bu e ng
abakhase	a ba kha se	achievable	a chi e va ble	abuiwa	a bu i wa
abalanang	a ba la na ng	acln	a cln	abuja	a bu ja
abapisa	a ba pi sa	actions	a cti o n s	abula	a bu la
abaram	a ba ra m	actives	a cti ve s	abuse	a bu se
abasa	a ba sa	activities	a cti vi ti e s	abutiago	a bu ti a go
abasetsana	a ba se tsa na	actt	a ctt	abutilelapa	a bu ti le la pa
abat	a ba t	actuarial	a ctu a ri a l	acacia	a ca ci a
abbotsford	a bbo tsfo rd	actuary	a ctu a ry	adhanom	a dha no m
abbott	a bbo tt	acumda	a cu m da	adikarabo	a di ka ra bo
abdalla	a bda l la	acwa	a cwa	adikolo	a di ko lo
abdel	a bde l	acwy	a cwy	adileng	a di le ng
abderrahmane	a bde rra hma ne	acyclovir	a cyclo vi r	adimaneng	a di ma ne ng
abeetsweng	a be e tswe ng	adalats	a da la ts	adimanwe	a di ma nwe
abel	a be l	adama	a da ma	adimelwang	a di me lwa ng
abelanweng	a be la nwe ng	adapotara	a da po ta ra	adimeng	a di me ng
abelweng	a be lwe ng	adb	a db	adimetsweng	a di me tswe ng
abengditirelo	a be ng di ti re lo	adc	a dc	adiminsanang	a di mi n sa na ng
aberbargoed	a be rba rgo e d	added	a dde d	adimisane	a di mi sa ne
abgn	a bgn	address	a ddre ss	adimisaneng	a di mi sa ne ng
abillweng	a bi l lwe ng	adelaide	a de la i de	adimisanwang	a di mi sa nwa ng
abining	a bi ni ng	adenoviuses	a de no vi u se s	adimiswang	a di mi swa ng
abiotiki	a bi o ti ki	adequate	a de qu a te	adimiwe	a di mi we
abis	a bi s	adha	a dha	adimlweng	a di m lwe ng
adingwe	a di ngwe				

Table 5: List of least used words and syllabified counterparts in Setswana

errors were observed for v-syllable structures.

At least six cv-syllable structures were observed. One, the cv structure was evident in words such as *pele* [pe-le-] ‘following’. Two, the cwv structure was observed in words like *kwala* [kwa-la-] ‘write’. Three, the ccv syllable structure was observed in words such as *tlase* [tla-se-] ‘low’. Four, the ccwv syllable structure was observed in words such as *sengwe* [se-ngwe-]‘something’. Five, we observed the cccv syllable structure in words like *botlhokwa* [bo-tlho-kwa-] ‘important’. Six, we observed the cccwv structure in words such as *tshwanetse* [tshwa-ne-tse-] ‘must’.

We also observed three c-syllable types. One, the m syllable was evident in words such as *mmogo* ‘together’ where it appeared at the word-initial position [m-mo-go-]. Two, the n syllable was observed at the word-medial position in words like *dintlha* [di-n-tlha-] ‘details’. Three, the ŋ syllable appeared at the word-final position in words like *neng* [ne-ng-] ‘when’.

4.2.2 Least used words

The rarest words from the Setswana corpus appeared no more than once in the corpus. The original words together with the syllables are presented in table 5. Similar to the Sepedi list, the Setswana list contains some instances of incorrect spelling such as *adiminsanang* [a-di-mi-n-sa-na-ng-]. Even so, the syllabification system was able to insert justifiable syllable boundaries at the expected spaces. For instance, the additional n in *adimi-n-sanang* is followed by a correct syllable boundary. Furthermore, like the Sepedi list, there are numerous instances of non-Setswana words on the list.

Three v-syllable structures were observed. That is, at the word-initial placement in words like *adileng* [a-di-le-ng-] ‘laid out’, the word-medial position in words such as *abiotiki* [a-bi-o-ti-ki-] ‘abiotic’, and the word-final location in the untranslated English acronym for Autism Centers of Excellence, that is *acae* [a-ca-e-].

Five cv-syllable structures were also observed. That is, the cv syllable in words like *adikarabo* [a-di-ka-ra-bo-] 'of answers', the cwv syllable in words like *abelwaneng* [a-be-lwa-ne-ng-] 'shared', the ccv syllable in words such as *adimanwe* [a-di-ma-nwe-] 'borrowed each other', and the ccwv syllable in words like *adimetsweng* [a-di-me-tswe-ng-] 'borrowed for'.

Finally, three c-syllable types were observed. One, the m syllable was observed in words like *adimlweng* [a-di-m-lwe-ng-]. Although the word is incorrectly spelt, the syllable boundaries are in the expected places. Two, the word-medial position l syllable is evident in words such as *abillweng* [a-bi-l-lwe-ng]. The second lateral in the word is unfortunately a typo. Even so, the syllabification system managed to insert justifiable boundaries following the order of letters in the word. Finally, the ŋ syllable was observed in the word-final position in words such as *adimeng* [a-di-me-ng-] and in the word-medial position in words like *abengditirelo* [a-be-ng-di-ti-re-lo-].

As we expected, the Setswana syllabic 'r' is not covered by the Sesotho rules for syllabification as described in Sibeko (2022) and Sibeko and van Zaanen (2022a). Unfortunately, a proper Setswana word containing the 'r' c-syllable is not present in both lists of Setswana words. Even so, the word *abderrahmane* [a-bde-rra-hma-ne-] contains consecutive 'r' letters. In this occurrence, the expected syllable boundary between the '*rra*', syllable, i.e. [r-ra-] is missing.

5 Discussion

As stated earlier in this article, the Sotho-Tswana languages are mutually intelligible to a great extent. Even though some vocabulary choices may be ambiguous, the ambiguity does not affect syllable breaks. This article set out to evaluate the Sesotho rule-based syllabification system on both Sepedi and Setswana words. We used the Autshumato machine translation corpora for both Sepedi and Setswana. The texts were translated from English texts as a pivot language. As a result, they contain somewhat similar information.

The v-syllable structures showed consistently correct syllable placement in both Sepedi and Setswana. All v-syllable structures argued by Sibeko (2022) were identified for both Sepedi and Setswana. All word-initial, word-medial, and word-final v-syllable structures were correctly identified. This consistency in the accuracy of the syllable breaks indicates that the current Sesotho syllabification system is ideal for identifying v-syllables in both Sepedi and Setswana. Unfortunately, single-letter words cannot be broken down into syllables. Even so, no unexpected outputs were observed for single-letter vowel-only words.

The syllabification system inserted consistently correct syllable breaks in words containing the m and n syllabic consonants on both Sepedi and Setswana texts. Unfortunately, the ŋ could only be identified at the word-end position in Sepedi. As such, we were not able to observe its behaviour when it appears at word-initial and word-medial positions. Even so, the word-medial ŋ syllable was correctly identified in the Setswana list. Furthermore, the Sepedi list did not contain any instances of the l syllable. However, it was observed in the Setswana list. As a result, we can safely assume that the current syllabification system can insert correct syllable boundaries for the l consonant even in Sepedi as the l syllable behaves similarly in all three Sotho-Tswana languages.

The unexpected structure of the *dmi* syllable highlights a need for clear rules governing the behaviour of nasal consonants that follow other consonants. To this point, the rules are only descriptive when the nasal consonant comes before the other consonants. It might be interesting to also investigate this in future studies.

Although the system attempted to identify syllable boundaries in non-Sotho-Tswana words, that is English words, the discord between the rules as implemented in the syllabification system and the structure of the orthography of English words could not be ignored.

All expected syllable boundaries in the correctly spelt words in Setswana were successfully identified by the syllabification system. We however missed an instance of consecutive r syllable in both the Sepedi and the Setswana lists. It would have been interesting to analyse actual Setswana words with such instances. Nonetheless, we noticed the absence of a syllable break between consecutive r letters in the non-Setswana examples. This finding confirms our initial assumption that the current Sesotho syllabification system does not identify the r syllabic consonants.

We also noticed inconsistencies in the spelling of words like *aaforika* and *aaferika* 'Africa' in the Setswana list of one hundred rarest used words. Both words were justifiably broken into syllables according to the given incorrect spelling, see table

5. Although this is unimportant in the identification of syllables, it does affect the counts of syllables as it may exaggerate syllable counts and types identified from a text.

The syllabification system's inability to recognise diacritics such as those used in Sepedi proved unproblematic for our selected words. That is, Sepedi words with diacritics were correctly broken into syllables. Even so, we are not aware of all possible placements of letters with accents in the written Sepedi words. As a caution, we recommend that the update to the syllabification system include letters with diacritics.

Overall, we recommend that the Sesotho rule-based syllabification be updated to cover all three standardised Sotho-Tswana languages. We also recommend that diacritics be included and specifically handled in the recommended Sotho-Tswana syllabification system. Equally important, we recommend that updated rules should also cover specific rules for handling the Sepedi and Setswana r syllable.

Limitations

The results of this article are limited by our sampling method which included the use of the hundred most used words and the hundred least used words in each of the languages as evidenced by the Autshumato corpora. Future studies could consider developing gold-standard syllable information annotated corpora for Sepedi and Setswana. The corpora could then be used for evaluating the usability of the TEX-based Sesotho syllabification system on Sepedi and Setswana texts. In this article, we were limited by the lack of such corpora and were therefore limited only to the evaluation of the rule-based syllabification system. The lists used did not contain correct Sepedi examples of words containing consecutive r consonants. As a result, we are unable to draw concrete conclusions on the rule-based syllabification system's performance on such words.

Ethics Statement

This article utilizes publicly available resources. The authors have taken measures to ensure that the data used is properly cited and attributed to the original sources and that any potential biases or limitations in the data are acknowledged.

References

Connie R Adsett, Yannick Marchand, Vlado Kes, et al. 2009. Syllabification rules versus data-driven methods in a language with low syllabic complexity: The case of italian. *Computer Speech & Language*, 23(4):444–463.

Etienne Barnard, Marelie H Davel, Charl Van Heerden, Febe De Wet, and Jaco Badenhorst. 2014. The NCHLT corpus of the South African languages. In *Proceedings of the 4th International Workshop Spoken Language Technologies for Under-resourced Languages*, pages 194–200.

Sekgaila Chokoe. 2020. Spell it the way you like: The inconsistencies that prevail in the spelling of Northern Sotho loanwords. *South African Journal of African Languages*, 40(1):130–138.

Katherine Demuth. 2007. Sesotho speech acquisition. *The international guide to speech acquisition*, pages 526–538.

Patrick Dickens. 1978. A preliminary report on Kgalagadi vowels. *African Studies*, 37(1):99–106.

Thabo Ditsele. 2014. Why not use Sepitori to enrich the vocabularies of Setswana and Sepedi? *Southern African Linguistics and Applied Language Studies*, 32(2):215–228.

Aditi Sharma Grover, Gerhard B van Huyssteen, and Marthinus W Pretorius. 2010. The South African Human Language Technologies audit. In *Proceedings of the Seventh International Conference on Language Resources and Evaluation (LREC'10)*, pages 2847–2850.

Aditi Sharma Grover, Gerhard Beukes. van Huyssteen, and Marthinus W. Pretorius. 2011. The South African Human Language Technology audit. *Language resources and evaluation*, 45:271–288.

Samson Mbizo Guma. 1982. *An outline structure of Southern Sotho*, 2nd edition. Shooter and Shuter Publishers, Pietermaritzburg, South Africa.

Pali Lehohla. 2011. Census in brief. *Statistics South Africa*. government printing works: Pretoria.

Katjie Sponono Mahlangu. 2015. *The growth and development of isiNdebele orthography and spelling (1921-2010)*. Ph.D. thesis, University of Pretoria.

Leketi Makalela. 2009. Harmonizing South African Sotho language varieties: Lessons from reading proficiency assessment. *International Multilingual Research Journal*, 3(2):120–133.

Zvinaiye Patricia Makaure. 2021. *The contribution of phonological processing skills to early literacy development in Northern Sotho-English bilingual children: A longitudinal investigation*. Ph.D. thesis, The University of South Africa, Pretoria.

Litsépiso Matlosa. 2017. Sesotho orthography called into question: The case of some Sesotho personal names. *Nomina Africana: Journal of African Onomastics*, 31(1):51–58.

Cindy McKellar. 2022a. *Autshumato Monolingual Sepedi Corpus*. ONLINE. South African Centre for Digital Language Resources. Available at: https://repo.sadilar.org/handle/20.500.12185/582 Accessed: 28 Jan 2023.

Cindy McKellar. 2022b. *Autshumato Monolingual Setswana Corpus*. ONLINE. South African Centre for Digital Language Resources. Available at: https://repo.sadilar.org/handle/20.500.12185/584 Accessed: 28 Jan 2023.

Victor Mojela. 2016. Etymology & figurative: The role of etymology in the lemmatization of Sotho terminology. In *The 10th International Conference of the Asian Association for Lexicography (AsiaLex2016) 1-3 June 2016 Manila, The Philippines*, page 93.

Carmen Moors, Illana Wilken, Karen Calteaux, and Tebogo Gumede. 2018a. Human Language Technology audit 2018: Analysing the development trends in resource availability in all South African languages. In *Proceedings of the Annual Conference of the South African Institute of Computer Scientists and Information Technologists*, pages 296–304.

Carmen Moors, Illana Wilken, Tebogo Gumede, and Karen Calteaux. 2018b. Human Language Technology audit 2017/18. Technical report, CSIR Meraka Institute.

Mildred Nkolola-Wakumelol, Liketso Rantsoz, and Keneilwe Matlhaku. 2012. Syllabification of consonants in Sesotho and Setswana. In H S Nginga-Koumba-Binza and S Bosch, editors, *Language Science and Language technology in Africa: Festschrift for Justus C. Roux*, pages 10–13. Sun Express, Stellenbosch, South Africa.

Thapelo J Otlogetswe. 2017. Setswana syllable structure and distribution. *Nordic Journal of African Studies*, 26(4):28–28.

Thapelo J Otlogetswe and Goabilwe N Ramaeba. 2022. Nickname creation through shortening Setswana personal names. *South African Journal of African Languages*, 42(2):200–206.

Danie Prinsloo. 2011. Tribute to Professor Louis Jacobus Louwrens: This issue of the south african journal of african languages is dedicated to Professor Louis Jacobus Louwrens. *South African Journal of African Languages*, 31(1):1–5.

Tebogo Rakgogo and Evangeline Zungu. 2021. The onomastic possibility of renaming the Sepedi and Sesotho sa Leboa (Northern Sotho) language names to restore peace, dignity and solidarity. *Literator (Potchefstroom. Online)*, 42(1):1–14.

Republic of South Africa. 1996. *Constitution of the Republic of South Africa*. Department of Justice, Pretoria.

Boikanyego Sebina. 2014. First language attrition in the native environment. *LANGUAGE*, 6:53–60.

Johannes Sibeko. 2022. Tshebediso ya melao kabong ya dinoko tsa Sesotho. *Southern African Linguistics and Applied Language Studies*, 40(4):494–506.

Johannes Sibeko and Mmasibidi Setaka. 2022. An overview of Sesotho blark content. *Journal of the Digital Humanities Association of Southern Africa*, 4(01).

Johannes Sibeko and Menno van Zaanen. 2022a. Developing a text readability system for Sesotho based on classical readability metrics. In *Responding to Asian diversity*, pages 571–572.

Johannes Sibeko and Menno van Zaanen. 2022b. Sesotho syllabification systems. *Southern African Centre for Digital Language Resources*. Available at: https://repo.sadilar.org/handle/20.500.12185/555 [accessed: 3 jan 2023].

Luan Staphorst. 2022. Ongehoord: Voices unaccented; voices unharmonized. Afrikaans and South Africa's first peoples in discourses of higher education transformation. *Unpublished MA dissertation, Nelson Mandela University*.

Suyanto Suyanto, Ade Romadhony, Febryanti Sthevanie, and Rezza Nafi Ismail. 2021. Augmented words to improve a deep learning-based indonesian syllabification. *Heliyon*, 7(10):e08115.

Hein Willemse. 2018. The hidden histories of Afrikaans. *Whiteness Afrikaans Afrikaners: Addressing Post-Apartheid Legacies, Privileges and Burdens*, page 115.

Carien Wilsenach. 2019. Phonological awareness and reading in Northern Sotho–understanding the contribution of phonemes and syllables in grade 3 reading attainment. *South African Journal of Childhood Education*, 9(1):1–10.

Philimon Nhlanhla Zulu, Gerrit Botha, and Etienne Barnard. 2008. Orthographic measures of language distances between the official South African languages. *Literator: Journal of literary criticism, comparative linguistics and literary studies*, 29(1):185–204.

Towards a Swahili Universal Dependency Treebank: Leveraging the Annotations of the Helsinki Corpus of Swahili

Kenneth Steimel
Indiana University
ksteimel@iu.edu

Sandra Kübler
Indiana University
skuebler@indiana.edu

Abstract

Dependency annotation can be a laborious process for under-resourced languages. However, in some cases, other resources are available. We investigate whether we can leverage such resources in the case of Swahili: We use the annotations of the Helsinki Corpus of Swahili for creating a Universal Dependency treebank for Swahili. The Helsinki Corpus of Swahili provides word-level annotations for part of speech tags, morphological features, and functional syntactic tags. We train neural taggers for these types of annotations, then use those models to annotate our target corpus, the Swahili portion of the Global Voices Corpus. Based on the word-level annotations, we then manually create constraint grammar rules to annotate the target corpus for Universal Dependencies. In this paper, we describe the process, discuss the annotation decisions we had to make, and we evaluate the approach.

1 Introduction

Swahili is the most-widely spoken Bantu language with an estimated 16 million native speakers (Simons and Fennig, 2018) and 50-100 million L2 speakers. Swahili serves as a national language of Tanzania, Kenya, Uganda, and the DRC, is a working language of the African Union, and serves as lingua franca for the East African Community.

While not a typical under-resourced language in general, there are no syntactic treebanks available for Swahili. Since dependency annotation is a costly endeavor and requires experts in the syntactic framework as well as in the language, we investigate whether we can leverage existing resources to automate the creation of a treebank as much as possible. We investigate an approach where we use the Helsinki Corpus of Swahili (Hurskainen, 2004a) and its annotations as a starting point. We then create automatic taggers for the word-level annotation based on this corpus. After applying these taggers to our target corpus, the Swahili section of the Global Voices Corpus (Tiedemann, 2012), we use a rule-based approach to convert the word-level annotation to Universal Dependency (UD) annotations (de Marneffe et al., 2021). The word-level annotations available in the Helsinki Corpus of Swahili consist of part of speech (POS) tags, based on a POS tagset that has more fine grained information than the Universal Dependency part of speech tagset. Additionally, the corpus contains morphological features and functional syntactic tags, which are based on a constraint grammar framework.

In the process of converting the morphological and syntactic information into the Universal Dependency framework, we encountered challenges based on the fact that little work has been done on UD annotations for Bantu languages. We will discuss some of these cases along with the annotation decisions we have made. The treebank, all rules and code are available at `https://git.steimel.info/ksteimel/SWH_UDT`. The treebank will be included in the next release of UD.

The remainder of this paper is structured as follows: section 2 reports on related work, section 3 gives an overview of the system used for converting the annotations, and section 4 describes the corpora we use. In section 5, we describe the word-level annotations, and in section 6, we describe the rules for the dependency annotation. Section 7 looks into the quality of our annotations, and section 8 concludes.

2 Related Work: NLP Approaches for Swahili

Political and economic significance promote research on Swahili making it one of the more well-studied Bantu languages in natural language processing. Rule-based systems, data driven approaches, and unsupervised methods have been adopted for Swahili. Hurskainen (1992) presents the first research into morphological analysis of

Proceedings of the Fourth workshop on Resources for African Indigenous Languages (RAIL 2023), pages 86–96
May 6, 2023 ©2023 Association for Computational Linguistics

Swahili. The SWATWOL morphological analyzer uses a finite-state two level morphology (Koskenniemi, 1983) to tag words. A constraint grammar system is used to disambiguate when multiple analyses are provided by the finite state-system (Hurskainen, 1996). These components are combined together into the Swahili language manager (SALAMA) (Hurskainen, 2004b). The SALAMA system is extended to include a shallow constraint grammar parser and a deeper grammar-based dependency parser. Though the dependency parser in SALAMA would appear invaluable to the present work, the parser is not freely available and the dependency structure is not provided as part of the Helsinki Corpus of Swahili (Hurskainen, 2004a). Littell et al. (2014) develop a similar finite state morphological analyzer for Swahili. However, their approach involves using an online crowd-sourced dictionary (`kamusi.org`) to ensure wide lexical coverage.

Using corpora developed by rule-based methods, De Pauw et al. (2006) adopt a data driven approach instead. They train part of speech taggers on the Helsinki Corpus of Swahili (Hurskainen, 2004a), which was built using the SALAMA language manager system described above. They use a variety of different off the shelf taggers including a Hidden Markov Model (TnT), SVMs (SVMtool), memory-based taggers (MBT) and a maximum entropy model tagger (MXPOST). The best performance is achieved with the maximum entropy model, though all models reach an accuracy of more than 90%. The maximum entropy model does particularly well with out-of-vocabulary words.

Swahili has also been the focus of research on unsupervised morpheme discovery. Hu et al. (2005) use a string-edit-distance (SED) heuristic to learn the morphology of Swahili. This heuristic goes through all pairs of words in a corpus and creates an alignment between the pairs using edit distance with specific penalties for substitution, addition and deletion. Then, finite-state automata describing pairs of related strings are collapsed together with aligned sequences of characters mapping onto the same state. This process iterates; the finite state automata produced combine with other automata. In the end, the places where the FSA diverges are morpheme boundaries. The authors report high performance when compared to other unsupervised morpheme discovery heuristics such as successor frequency (Harris, 1955).

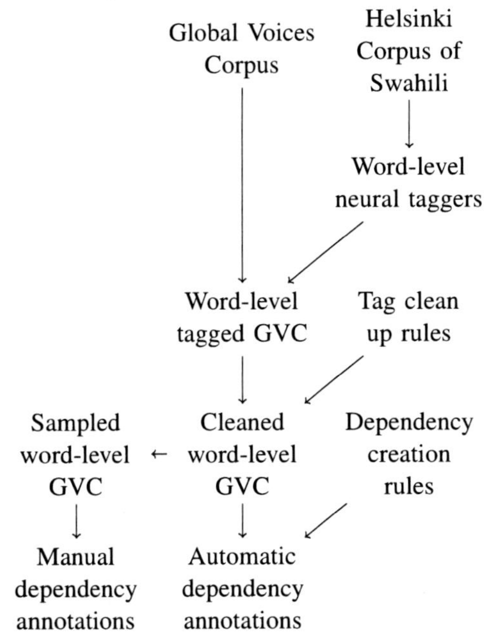

Figure 1: Diagram of the steps involved in creating the Universal Dependency Treebank for Swahili.

Recently, researchers have developed corpora for question answering and emotion classification in Swahili (Martin et al., 2022). In addition, a transformer model for Swahili has been developed (Martin et al., 2022).

3 System Overview

Since no dependency treebank is available, we create the dependency trees automatically, using the annotations in the Helsinki Corpus of Swahili. This corpus contains syntactic information in the form of word-level constraint grammar labels, which need to be converted into Universal Dependency annotations. For this conversion, we use a number of neural tagging models, post-processing rules, and dependency arc creation rules.

The smaller higher-quality, manually annotated, portion of the treebank undergoes a similar series of steps but before dependency creation rules are applied, a portion of the treebank is sampled. This sample is then manually annotated. Figure 1 displays the different steps and resources involved in the process.

word	gloss	POS	syntax	lemma	msd
Afisa	officer	N	@SUBJ	afisa	9/6-SG
Elimu	Education	N	@<P	elimu	9/10-SG
alisimama	stand	V	@FMAINVintr	simama	SUB-PREF=1-SG3 TAM=PAST
kwa	for	PREP	@ADVL	kwa	_
amri	command	N	@<P	amri	9/10-SG
ya	of	GEN-CON	@GCON	ya	9-SG
Mwenyekiti	Chairman	N	@<NH	mwenyekiti	1/2-SG

Table 1: Tags for a single sentence in the HCS.

<table>
<tr><th>id</th><th>word</th><th>lemma</th><th>UD POS</th><th>HCS POS</th><th>Morph. features</th></tr>
<tr><td>1</td><td>Afisa</td><td>afisa</td><td>NOUN</td><td>N</td><td>NounCl=9|Num=Sing</td></tr>
<tr><td>2</td><td>Elimu</td><td>elimu</td><td>NOUN</td><td>N</td><td>NounCl=9|Num=Sing</td></tr>
<tr><td>3</td><td>alisimama</td><td>simama</td><td>VERB</td><td>V</td><td>Mood=Ind|
NounCl[subj]=1|Num[subj]=Sing|
Pers[subj]=1|Pol=Pos|Subcat=Intr|
Tense=Past|Voice=Act</td></tr>
<tr><td>4</td><td>kwa</td><td>kwa</td><td>ADP</td><td>PREP</td><td>_</td></tr>
<tr><td>5</td><td>amri</td><td>amri</td><td>NOUN</td><td>N</td><td>NounCl=9|Num=Sing</td></tr>
<tr><td>6</td><td>ya</td><td>ya</td><td>ADP</td><td>GEN-CON</td><td>NounCl=9|Num=Sing</td></tr>
<tr><td>7</td><td>Mwenyekiti</td><td>mwenyekiti</td><td>NOUN</td><td>N</td><td>NounCl=1|Num=Sing</td></tr>
</table>

Table 2: CONLL-U representation of the sentence in Table 1, focusing on the relevant columns only.

4 Corpora

The corpus situation for Swahili is somewhat difficult. We use both the Helsinki Corpus of Swahili (HCS) (Hurskainen, 2004a) and the Swahili section of the Global Voices corpus (GVC) (Tiedemann, 2012) in this work. Because of licensing limitations, we are unable to annotate the Helsinki Corpus of Swahili with dependencies and redistribute it. For this reason, we leverage the word-level annotations of this corpus to create a POS tagger using the Helsinki Corpus of Swahili POS tagset, a POS tagger for UD POS tags, a morphological analyzer, and a word-level constraint-grammar syntactic tagger. We then use these taggers to annotate the Swahili portion of the Global Voices corpus on the word level. In a final step, we create Universal Dependency annotations based on all of these annotations via a rule-based approach.

The texts contained in the Helsinki Corpus of Swahili are primarily from legislative assemblies, a collection of stories, and news articles. In terms of annotations, the Helsinki Corpus of Swahili is a silver standard corpus created by the SALAMA finite state transducer and disambiguator (Hurskainen, 1999). In the corpus, each word is annotated with its lemma, POS tag, a series of morphological tags, and a functional syntactic tag (constraint grammar) describing the word's role in the sentence are included for each word. Table 1 shows the word-level annotation for the sentence *Afisa Elimu alisimama kwa amri ya Mwenyekiti* (Eng.: The education officer stood for the Chairman's command) from the HCS.

Table 2 shows the conversion of this sentence to CONLL-U format[1]. The HCS uses multiple ways to express the noun class or noun class agreement of a word. For example, nouns (which inherently have a noun class) indicate the noun class of the singular form, the noun class of the plural form and whether the given noun is singular or plural (i.e. 9/10-SG). Noun class agreement prefixes on a verb follow a different convention where noun class, number, and person are indicated (e.g., 1-SG3). Adpositions such as *ya*, meanwhile, indicate noun class agreement as simply a noun class followed by the number (i.e., 9-SG). Additionally, for some POS tags, certain morphological features are assumed as the default by the HCS, and only

[1]For more details on CONLL-U format, see `https://universaldependencies.org/format.html`

Orthographic representation	Wa-Mauritania	M-Jordan	Ki-China
Morpheme analysis	2-Mauritania	1-Jordan	7-China
English Gloss	Mauritanians	Jordanian	China

Table 3: Tokenization examples of Swahili demonyms.

features which diverge from this default are included. For example, active voice and positive polarity are frequently not explicitly annotated in the HCS annotations, but passive voice and negative polarity are.

The Global Voices Corpus, in contrast, is a large massively multilingual corpus with parallel texts in 46 languages. The GVC consists of news articles from around the world. Because the corpus features articles by citizen journalists, social media text is included as well. Unlike the HCS, the GVC consists of plain text without any word-level annotations. For our treebank, we use the section of the GVC with parallel texts in Swahili and English. This section of the corpus consists of 29 698 Swahili sentences, 546 000 words.

5 Creating Word-Level Annotations

Our ultimate goal is the creation of a Universal Dependency Treebank for Swahili. As a first step, we need to annotate the Global Voices Corpus (GVC) for word-level information, based on which we can then apply the rules that will construct the dependency annotations.

We trained word-level neural tagging models using a sample of 789 691 words, corresponding to 35 925 sentences, from the Helsinki Corpus of Swahili (HCS). A common neural architecture was used for the following word-level tagging models: UD POS tags, language specific POS tags from the HCS, morphological features, and functional syntactic tags. This architecture consists of a two layer bidirectional GRU-LSTM using learned character and word embeddings. Because of the large number of morphological tags, we developed a second architecture that models individual morphological features as single tags. This model is very similar in design to the other neural tagging architecture. However, instead of using argmax to predict a single tag, this model predicts all tags that exceed a threshold (0.5) after a sigmoid activation.

We then automatically tagged the Global Voices Corpus (GVC) with these neural models. From the automatically tagged GVC data, 150 short sentences (length 8–30 words) and 30 longer sentences (length 20–50 words) were randomly sampled for manual annotation. Then, the rule system was applied to the remainder of the GVC to create the UD annotations.

Integrating Swahili into the Universal Dependency framework required us to make annotation decisions regarding tokenization, conversion of part of speech tags, handling of particular constructions in Swahili. We detail these decisions below.

Tokenization When tokenizing, we took special consideration to ensure that demonyms with hyphens were not separated, but compounds were split apart. Demonyms such as those shown in Table 3 are frequently present in the Global Voices corpus. The regular expressions used for tokenization ensured that hyphens after noun class prefixes were not separated from the rest of the word.

Following UD guidelines, compounds of coordinating conjunctions and pronouns are separated into their component tokens. For example, *naye* is separated into *na yeye* (Eng.: and he/she) and *nasi* is separate into *na sisi* (Eng: and you all).

Converting POS Tags to UD The POS tags for the Helsinki Corpus of Swahili are relatively close to Universal Dependency POS tags. In general, the conversion is a many-to-one mapping: the Helsinki corpus tags annotate a number of distinctions that are not featured in Universal Dependencies. Additionally, all POS tags reserved for punctuation in the Helsinki Corpus of Swahili tagset (i.e., COLON, HYPHEN, etc.) are mapped to PUNCT. Table 4 shows the correspondence between the two POS tags annotations.

In some cases, additional information was required to determine the appropriate Universal Dependency tag. For example, in HCS, EXCLAM is typically used for interjections such as *jamani* (Eng.: hey there). However, it is also used for exclamation marks. For those cases, we assign PUNCT.

Both relative pronouns and verbs with relative markers received the Helsinki POS tags REL-LI

Helsinki Corpus	Universal Dependency
A-UNINFL	ADJ
ABBR	SYM
ADJ	ADJ
ADV	ADV
AG-PART	ADP
CC	CCONJ
CONJ	SCONJ
CONJ/CC	CCONJ
DEM	DET
EXCLAM	INTJ
GEN-CON	ADP
GEN-CON-KWA	ADP
INTERROG	PRON
N	NOUN
NUM	NUM
NUM-ROM	NUM
POSS-PROM	SCONJ
PREP	ADP
PREP/ADV	ADV
PRON	PRON
PROPNAME	PROPN
REL-LI	PRON
REL-LI-VYO	PRON
REL-SI	PRON
REL-SI-VYO	PRON
TITLE	PROPN
V	VERB
V-BE	AUX
V-DEF	VERB

Table 4: Correspondence between Helsinki Corpus of Swahili and Universal Dependencies POS tags.

or REL-LI-VYO. In such cases, we use the functional syntactic tag assigned to the word for disambiguation: if the word has a verbal functional tag, then we assign the UD tag V. In all other cases, we assign PRON.

Morphological Features Unlike the conversion of POS tags, which is a relatively straightforward process, morphological tag extraction is considerably more complex.

Morphological features in Universal Dependency consist of attribute-value pairs. These are represented in the CONLL-U format with attributes separated from their associated values by '=' and each pair is separated by '|'. The Universal Dependency annotation guidelines (Nivre et al., 2017) provide morphological features to accommodate noun classes in Bantu languages. These features are indicated using different values for the NounClass attribute. However, these features are not sufficient since verbs can have multiple noun class markers indicating the noun class of the subject, object, and relative head.

For example, the word *aliyoitumia* has markers indicating noun class, person, and number for the subject, object, and relative head, see the analysis in example (1).

(1) *a-li-yo-i-tum-ia*
3SG-PST-4.REL-9.OBJ-use-APPL

those that he/she used for it

To address this issue, we use layered morphological features. For `Person`, `Number`, and `NounClass`, additional subtypes such as `rel`, `subj`, and `obj` are added. Until recently, this was not a documented possibility in Universal Dependencies, however other treebanks have established these layered features as a precedent. One example is the Basque Universal Dependency treebank (Aranzabe et al., 2015). Though subtypes are not described in the documentation of the conversion process (Aranzabe et al., 2015), this treebank includes verbs with multiple number features using subtypes to indicate the type. Unlike the Basque Universal Dependency treebank, we do not use subtypes with the *case* of the agreeing element indicated for Swahili. Rather, the subtypes simply specify the function of the agreeing element. For example, where the Basque corpus uses `Number[nom]`, the Swahili corpus uses `Number[subj]`. The Basque option is not usable for Swahili as Swahili does not have overt case, and adopting a covert case analysis for all languages like Swahili does not follow the principles of Universal Dependency.

6 Creating Dependency Annotations

6.1 Dependency Guidelines

We adhere to the guidelines laid out by Universal Dependency (Nivre et al., 2017). This section outlines some specifics for how we applied these guidelines to Swahili. The Universal Dependency guidelines state that "[t]he copula be is not treated as the head of a clause, but rather the nonverbal predicate" (de Marneffe et al., 2020). The guidelines also advise that "[t]he cop relation should only be used for pure copulas that add at most TAME categories to the meaning of the predicate".

In the Swahili treebank, we make a distinction between the "verbal" copula *kuwa* and other copulas like *ni*, the negated form *si*, emphatic forms like *ndiyo* and locative copulas like *uko*[2]. We analyze *kuwa* as a verb while the other copulas are given the POS tag COP and are not considered the head of their clause.

6.2 Rule application

To create rules for correcting common issues with the neural taggers and generate dependency arcs, CG3 was used (Bick and Didriksen, 2015). CG3 is an extended variant of constraint grammar with implementations for compiling and applying constraint grammar rules, allowing us to develop and apply complex rules.

Addressing errors in word-level tags Initially, rules were written to remedy errors with the word-level tags produced by the neural POS models. To correct errors produced by the automatic tagger, `SUBSTITUTE` and `ADD` commands were used to change one tag to another, add a missing tag, or remove an errant tag. These word-level tag correction rules were applied before all rules creating dependency arcs.

In many cases, tag rewrite rules were leveraged to rewrite a word-level tag if three or more of the other word-level tags indicated that an error had occurred. The first example in Table 5 displays a rule that replaces `NOUN` with `VERB` in cases where other taggers indicate that the word in question is actually a verb. More specifically, the language specific POS tagger must assign this word a `V` tag, and it must have the morphological feature specifying polarity and one of a number of functional syntactic tags indicating that this word is serving as a verb in the sentence for the rule to apply.

Dependency arc creation To create dependency arcs from sentences plus the word-level annotations, we created ordered regular expression rules, such that highly specific rules were followed by more generic versions using more lax restrictions; and occasionally we used fallback rules. Some phenomena were addressed using a single generic rule without more specific or lax versions. For example, the bold phrase in the sentence in example (2) shows an example of multiple noun phrases linked together in an associative noun phrase chain.

(2) *Biti ni katibu mkuu w-a MDC*
Biti COP secretary major ASSOC.1 MDC
, ki-na-cho-ongoz-wa ***na***
, 7.SUBJ-PRES-7.REL-lead with/by
Wa-ziri Mkuu w-a zamani
minister major ASSOC.1 past
w-a nchi hiyo *, Morgan*
ASSOC.1 country DEM , Morgan
Tsvangirai .
Tsvangirai .

Biti is the secretary general for Movement for Democratic Change, led by former Prime Minister Morgan Tsvangirai.

Without taking noun class agreement into consideration, the noun phrase in bold is ambiguous, i.e., both dependency analyses in Figure 2 would be possible.

As the interlinear analysis in example (2) indicates, *zamani* is a class 9 noun, the associative adposition *wa* is class 1, and *Waziri* is class 1. The associative agrees in noun class with the noun that its parent noun modifies. Thus the syntactic analysis in the dependency analysis on the right of Figure 2 is the correct one. The specific version of the rule, shown as the second rule in Table 5, leverages this agreement.

More generic rules are applied if no match for a specific rule is found. A generic rule may apply because of errors in the morphological tags produced by the tagging model or because of missing agreement between the two tokens[3]. In this particular case, associative adpositions in different noun classes are often polysemous. For example, *wa* can indicate that the noun modified by its parent noun is class 1, as in the example above, or classes 2, 3, or 11. The neural taggers can leverage the surrounding context; however errors still occur with some frequency. A generic rule is thus used to combat errors in the morphological annotations. This rule, shown as the third rule in Table 5, has no agreement constraints.

Fallback rules are applied in cases where criteria using morphological and functional tags both

[2]Locative copulas like *uko* could perhaps be annotated as an adverbial. However, this only affects the label. The non-verbal predicate following *uko* would still be the head of the clause.

[3]For example, some adpositions like *wa* agree with the noun class of the preceding noun and would match a specific rule form. However, other adpositions like *katika* do not indicate the noun class of the preceding noun in any way.

```
SUBSTITUTE NOUN VERB TARGET V (0 (/FMAINV/r) LINK 0 (/Polarity=/r) );
```

```
# Go from a nominal to another nominal with a genative connector in between,
# the first nominal and the genative connector have to agree in noun class
ADDRELATION nmod EXTENDED_NOMINAL TO
  (0 $$NOUN_CLASS
    LINK 1* GCON BARRIER mainv
    LINK 0 $$NOUN_CLASS
    LINK 1 EXTENDED_NOMINAL) ;
```

```
ADDRELATION REVERSE nmod EXTENDED_NOMINAL (T:no_parent) TO
  (-1 ADP
    LINK -1* EXTENDED_NOMINAL BARRIER mainv);
```

Table 5: Example rule for error correction in word-level tags.

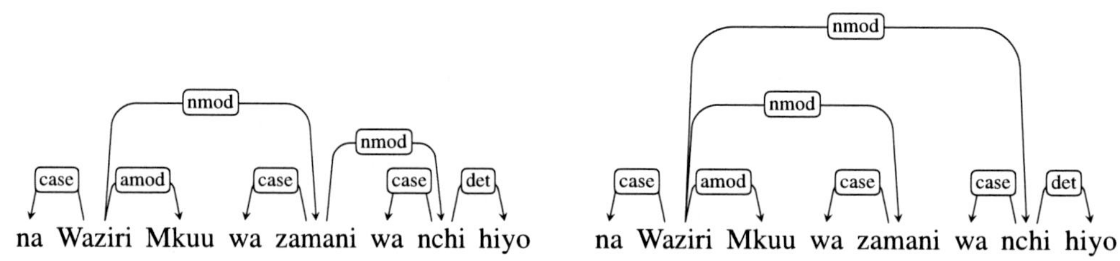

Figure 2: Two possible dependency analyses for the noun phrase chain from example (2).

fail. Instead, simple linear ordering patterns conditioned on POS are used in fallback rules.

Table 6 shows how often specific, generic, and fallback rule types are used to address each type of phenomenon. While the highly specific rules are able to disambiguate between different possible arcs more effectively, these specific rules are triggered less frequently.

7 Quality of Annotations

7.1 Word-Level Tagging Results

Before we trained the neural tagging models, we set aside 2 000 sentences from the Helsinki Corpus of Swahili, 1 000 sentences for validation and 1 000 sentences for testing the model's performance. Table 7 shows the results of this evaluation. All models exceed 94% accuracy, and all but the multilabel morphological tagger reach an accuracy of 97% and higher; corresponding F-scores for POS tagging, and functional role are in the same range. As discussed in section 5, the multilabel tagger outputs a tag if it exceeds a threshold of 0.5. While this allows the tagger to be more flexible and consider combinations of morphological features that were not present in the training data, it also does not enforce co-occurrence restrictions between morphemes. The multilabel model can predict both NounClass=9 and NounClass=7 for the same noun, though this should not be permitted. These restrictions are automatically followed when using the monolithic morphological tagger.

Note that the test data are derived from the source corpus, the Helsinki Corpus of Swahili, and therefore the exact performance of the models on the target corpus (GVC) cannot be determined. During the manual corpus creation process, we corrected UD POS tags and added depedency arcs but did not correct other word level tags. In the future, other word level tags will also be corrected.

7.2 Strengths and Limitations in Generated Trees

Out of 29 698 sentences, the dependency creation rules rules generate spanning trees for 4 994 sentences. 3 499 of these trees are projective dependency trees. When examining particular linguistic phenomena, the rules do well at some and

Phenomenon	Rule type	Number of rule applications	Percentage of rule applications
amod	Specific	487	37.12%
	Generic	825	62.88%
case	Specific	2438	25.06%
	Generic	7292	74.94%
det	Specific	1030	91.15%
	Generic	100	8.85%
det	Specific	292	82.95%
	Generic	60	17.05%
case	Generic	140	10.26%
	Fallback	1224	89.74%
nummod	Specific	247	18.14%
	Generic	1115	81.86%
nmod	Specific	8152	72.28%
	Generic	3126	27.72%
nsubj	Specific	155	0.36%
	Generic	13237	30.57%
	Fallback	29903	69.07%
obj	Specific	535	1.36%
	Generic	19355	49.34%
	Fallback	19336	49.29%

Table 6: Rule type frequency for dependency creation rules on Global Voices Corpus.

Task	Number of tags	Accuracy	Macro-average F-score	Weighted-average F-score
Functional role tagging	39	97.53	92.01	97.51
Helsinki POS tagging	55	98.99	93.13	98.96
UD POS tagging	15	98.98	97.81	98.98
Multilabel morphological tagging	99	94.74	42.35	95.04
Monolithic morphological tagging	7 397	97.63	72.87	97.52

Table 7: Model accuracy in relation to tagset size for bidirectional GRU-based models.

produce incorrect or incomplete trees when confronted with others.

Associative chains In Swahili, complex noun phrases are often constructed using chains of associative adpositions. Our system of rules does well with these constructions. Figure 3 shows the tree generated for the associative chain at the beginning of the sentence in example (3). While the associative chain is handled correctly, the locative noun phrase *nchini Cambodia* should be modifying *Watumiaji* (users), at the beginning of the text. However, there are no morphological features that can help the rules disambiguate the attachment of this locative noun phrase.

(3) *Wa-tumiaji w-a mitandao y-a*
1-users 1-ASSOC network 9-ASSOC
jamii nchini Cambodia pia
society country Cambodia also
wa-me-hamas-ish-wa ku-weka
3PL-PERF-motivate-CAUS-PASS 15-set
picha z-a alama y-a
pictures 10-ASSOC sign 9-ASSOC
kampeni
campaign

Social media users in Cambodia are also encouraged to replace their profile photos with icons of the campaign.

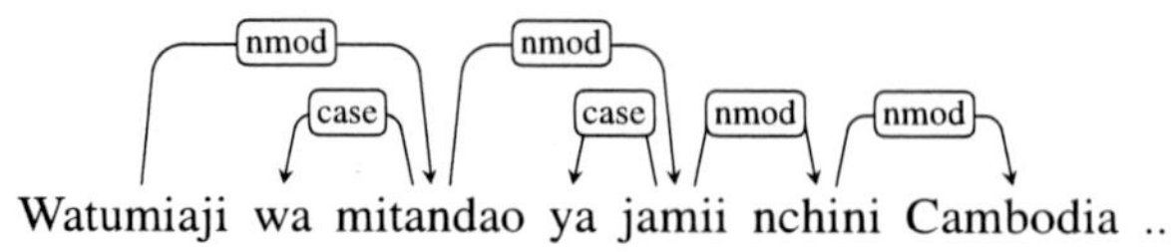

Figure 3: Initial associate chain in example 3

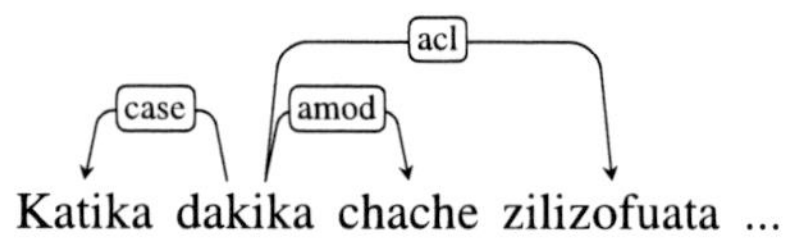

Figure 4: A tree for a short headless relative clause

Relative clauses Both headless and headed relative clauses are often handled correctly by the system of rules. Only headless relative clauses are shown here due to space constraints. Example (4) displays a phrase with a headless relative clause. The noun *dakika* (Eng.: minutes) is modified by the relative clause *zilizofuata* (Eng.: following). The intervening adjective *chache* does not interfere with the rules and is also connected to *dakika*, as appropriate.

(4) *Ikiwa* *i-ta-tok-ea* ,
if 9-FUT-come.from-PASS ,
basi *siku* *z-a* *ahadi*
then day 10-ASSOC vow
z-a *ndoa* *ku-pewa*
10-ASSOC marriage 15-give
u-muhimu *u-na-o-stahili*
14-importance 14-PRES-14.REL-deserve
“ *Mpaka* *ki-fo*
“ until 7-death
ki-ta-ka-po-tu-tengan-isha
7-FUT-CONT-16-1PL-be.separated-CAUSE
” *zi-me-pita* ?
” 10-PERF-pass ?

If this will happen, gone are the days when the marriage vows are to be taken seriously “Til death do us part”?

Root identification Identifying the root of the clause using rules is difficult. This is particularly true in cases where topicalization of some kind has occurred.

In example (4), the fronted adverbial clause *Ikiwa itatokea* (Eng.: If this will happen) interferes with the current rules for root identification. Instead of assigning *kupewa* root status, the verb in the adverbial clause *itatokea* is erroneously labeled as the root. While *itatokea* is a verbal form and thus a possible root, it is the head of the subordinate clause.

8 Conclusion

Our work is concerned with creating a Universal Dependency treebank for Swahili leveraging the annotations in the Helsinki Corpus of Swahili. We show that we can train neural taggers to annotate UD POS tags, language specific POS tags, morphological tags, as well as functional syntactic tags, and that we can use those annotations on a new corpus to create regular expression rules to derive a dependency annotation. The results are not perfect: for about 30% of the sentences, our methods do not create fully connected trees. But our annotations can be improved in the future. It is, of course, possible to add more rules to our framework to cover more cases. However, any new rule will be very specific and will thus only improve a very small number of cases. We consequently argue that additional improvement should come from training a robust parser and manually correcting the parse trees. We are planning to investigate robust parsing methods that will provide reliable parses when trained on the available annotations.

9 Limitations

It is certain that there are errors in the automatic and manual annotations. Our conversion procedure is limited by the information available in the Helsinki Corpus of Swahili. And while the first author, who manually annotated the portion of the Swahili treebank, has extensive training in Bantu syntax, he is not a native speaker of Swahili. We hope that this initial step inspires future expansion and/or correction of the corpus.

10 Ethics Statement

Working on an under-resourced language is always accompanied by the danger of disenfranchising the language community. However, dependency annotations require a syntactic background, and there are often not enough speakers of the language with such a training. We hope that the Swahili community will adopt and improve our treebank. We have consciously chosen a corpus the can be freely distributed, rather than working with the Helsinki Corpus of Swahili, which comes with restrictive licensing requirements.

References

Maria Jesus Aranzabe, Aitziber Atutxa, Kepa Bengoetxea, Arantza Diaz de Ilarraza, Iakes Goenaga, Koldo Gojenola, and Larraitz Uria. 2015. Automatic conversion of the Basque Dependency Treebank to Universal Dependencies. In *Proceedings of the Fourteenth International Workshop on Treebanks and Linguistic Theories (TLT14)*, pages 233–241.

Eckhard Bick and Tino Didriksen. 2015. CG-3 - Beyond classical constraint grammar. In *Proceedings of the 20th Nordic Conference of Computational Linguistics (NODALIDA 2015)*, pages 305–308.

Marie-Catherine de Marneffe, Filip Ginter, Yoav Goldberg, Jan Hajič, Christopher Manning, Ryan McDonald, Joakim Nivre, Slav Petrov, Sampo Pyysalo, Sebastian Schuster, Natalia Silveira, Reut Tsarfaty, Francis Tyers, and Dan Zeman. 2020. Universal Dependencies.

Marie-Catherine de Marneffe, Christopher D. Manning, Joakim Nivre, and Daniel Zeman. 2021. Universal Dependencies. *Computational Linguistics*, 47(2):255–308.

Guy De Pauw, Gilles-Maurice De Schryver, and Peter W Wagacha. 2006. Data-driven part-of-speech tagging of Kiswahili. In *International Conference on Text, Speech and Dialogue*, pages 197–204. Springer.

Zellig S. Harris. 1955. From phoneme to morpheme. *Language*, 31(2):190–222.

Yu Hu, Irina Matveeva, John Goldsmith, and Colin Sprague. 2005. Refining the SED heuristic for morpheme discovery: Another look at Swahili. In *Proceedings of the Workshop on Psychocomputational Models of Human Language Acquisition*, pages 28–35, Ann Arbor, Michigan. Association for Computational Linguistics.

Arvi Hurskainen. 1992. A two-level computer formalism for the analysis of Bantu morphology. an application to Swahili. *Nordic Journal of African Studies*, 1(1).

Arvi Hurskainen. 1996. Disambiguation of morphological analysis in Bantu languages. In *Proceedings of the 16th Conference on Computational Linguistics*, pages 568–573.

Arvi Hurskainen. 1999. Salama: Swahili language manager. *Nordic Journal of African Studies*, 8:139–157.

Arvi Hurskainen. 2004a. Helsinki corpus of Swahili. *Compilers: Institute for Asian and African Studies (University of Helsinki) and CSC.*

Arvi Hurskainen. 2004b. Swahili language manager: A storehouse for developing multiple computational applications. *Nordic Journal of African Studies*, 13(3):363–397.

Kimmo Koskenniemi. 1983. Two-level model for morphological analysis. In *IJCAI*, volume 83, pages 683–685.

Patrick Littell, Kaitlyn Price, and Lori Levin. 2014. Morphological parsing of Swahili using crowdsourced lexical resources. In *Proceedings of the Ninth International Conference on Language Resources and Evaluation (LREC'14)*, pages 3333–3339, Reykjavik, Iceland. European Language Resources Association (ELRA).

Gati Martin, Medard Edmund Mswahili, Young-Seob Jeong, and Jiyoung Woo. 2022. SwahBERT: Language model of Swahili. In *Proceedings of the 2022 Conference of the North American Chapter of the Association for Computational Linguistics: Human Language Technologies*, pages 303–313, Seattle, United States. Association for Computational Linguistics.

Joakim Nivre, Željko Agić, Lars Ahrenberg, Maria Jesus Aranzabe, Masayuki Asahara, Aitziber Atutxa, Miguel Ballesteros, John Bauer, Kepa Bengoetxea, Riyaz Ahmad Bhat, Eckhard Bick, Cristina Bosco, Gosse Bouma, Sam Bowman, Marie Candito, Gülşen Cebiroğlu Eryiğit, Giuseppe G. A. Celano, Fabricio Chalub, Jinho Choi, Çağrı Çöltekin, Miriam Connor, Elizabeth Davidson, Marie-Catherine de Marneffe, Valeria de Paiva, Arantza Diaz de Ilarraza, Kaja Dobrovoljc, Timothy Dozat, Kira Droganova, Puneet Dwivedi, Marhaba Eli, Tomaž Erjavec, Richárd Farkas, Jennifer Foster, Cláudia Freitas, Katarína Gajdošová, Daniel Galbraith, Marcos Garcia, Filip Ginter, Iakes Goenaga, Koldo Gojenola, Memduh Gökırmak, Yoav Goldberg, Xavier Gómez Guinovart, Berta Gonzáles Saavedra, Matias Grioni, Normunds Grūzītis, Bruno Guillaume, Nizar Habash, Jan Hajič, Linh Hà Mỹ, Dag Haug, Barbora Hladká, Petter Hohle, Radu Ion, Elena Irimia, Anders Johannsen, Fredrik Jørgensen, Hüner Kaşıkara, Hiroshi Kanayama, Jenna Kanerva, Natalia Kotsyba, Simon Krek, Veronika Laippala, Phng Lê Hồng, Alessandro Lenci, Nikola Ljubešić, Olga Lyashevskaya, Teresa Lynn, Aibek Makazhanov, Christopher Manning, Cătălina Mărănduc, David Mareček, Héctor Martínez Alonso, André Martins, Jan Mašek, Yuji Matsumoto, Ryan McDonald, Anna Missilä, Verginica Mititelu, Yusuke Miyao, Simonetta Montemagni, Amir More, Shunsuke Mori, Bohdan Moskalevskyi, Kadri Muischnek, Nina Mustafina,

Kaili Müürisep, Lng Nguyễn Thị, Huyền Nguyễn Thị Minh, Vitaly Nikolaev, Hanna Nurmi, Stina Ojala, Petya Osenova, Lilja Øvrelid, Elena Pascual, Marco Passarotti, Cenel-Augusto Perez, Guy Perrier, Slav Petrov, Jussi Piitulainen, Barbara Plank, Martin Popel, Lauma Pretkalniņa, Prokopis Prokopidis, Tiina Puolakainen, Sampo Pyysalo, Alexandre Rademaker, Loganathan Ramasamy, Livy Real, Laura Rituma, Rudolf Rosa, Shadi Saleh, Manuela Sanguinetti, Baiba Saulīte, Sebastian Schuster, Djamé Seddah, Wolfgang Seeker, Mojgan Seraji, Lena Shakurova, Mo Shen, Dmitry Sichinava, Natalia Silveira, Maria Simi, Radu Simionescu, Katalin Simkó, Mária Šimková, Kiril Simov, Aaron Smith, Alane Suhr, Umut Sulubacak, Zsolt Szántó, Dima Taji, Takaaki Tanaka, Reut Tsarfaty, Francis Tyers, Sumire Uematsu, Larraitz Uria, Gertjan van Noord, Viktor Varga, Veronika Vincze, Jonathan North Washington, Zdeněk Žabokrtský, Amir Zeldes, Daniel Zeman, and Hanzhi Zhu. 2017. Universal dependencies 2.0. LINDAT/CLARIAH-CZ digital library at the Institute of Formal and Applied Linguistics (ÚFAL), Faculty of Mathematics and Physics, Charles University.

Gary F Simons and Charles D Fennig. 2018. Ethnologue: Languages of the world, twenty. *Dallas: SIL International. Retrieved from www. ethnologue. com. Accessed*, page 2018.

Jörg Tiedemann. 2012. Parallel data, tools and interfaces in OPUS. In *Proceedings of the Eight International Conference on Language Resources and Evaluation (LREC'12)*, Istanbul, Turkey. European Language Resources Association (ELRA).

Comparing methods of orthographic conversion for Bàsàá, a language of Cameroon

Alexandra O'Neil, Daniel Swanson
Robert Pugh, Francis Tyers
Indiana University
Bloomington, IN USA

Emmanuel Ngué Um
University of Yaoundé
Yaoundé, Cameroon

Abstract

Orthographic standardization is a milestone in a language's documentation and the development of its resources. However, texts written in former orthographies remain relevant to the language's history and development and therefore must be converted to the standardized orthography. Ensuring a language has access to the orthographically standardized version of all of its recorded texts is important in the development of resources as it provides additional textual resources for training, supports contribution of authors using former writing systems, and provides information about the development of the language. This paper evaluates the performance of natural language processing methods, specifically Finite State Transducers and Long Short-term Memory networks, for the orthographical conversion of Bàsàá texts from the Protestant missionary orthography to the now-standard AGLC orthography, with the conclusion that LSTMs are somewhat more effective in the absence of explicit lexical information.

1 Introduction

Orthographic standardization is a process that many languages of the world have undergone throughout history and many are still undergoing. Although there are numerous benefits to the standardization of a language's writing system, it can also present challenges for language communities. These challenges include contention between speakers that are used to using different representations, discomfort from speakers that relate to their language solely as an oral language, addressal and mitigation of the impact of colonialism on the language and community, debate about how to best represent sounds in the language, and hesitance in adoption of the writing system by all speakers (Limerick, 2018).

As referenced in the set of potential challenges above, communities often have differing means of representing their language prior to the coordinated effort to implement a uniform system (Mosel, 2004). While one of the goals of orthographic standardization is to create a consistent medium that speakers can use to understand one another and communicate their own thoughts, texts and data written in formerly used orthographies remain relevant in both the history and development of the language. To preserve this information it is necessary to convert former orthographies to the new standard. Furthermore, it is preferable to begin this process shortly following the standardization of the system, as this increases opportunity to work with speakers that are knowledgeable in the previously used systems.

Additionally, conversion of former orthographies into the current standard is beneficial since some speakers may not be willing to switch to the new standard. For a period of time following the adoption of the new orthography, speakers may continue to use a variety of orthographies in their own writing, following whichever orthography they previously learned (Jahani, 1989). Some speakers may be compelled to continue to use a non-standard system due to an emotional attachment to an orthographic system. For example, reasons for maintaining an orthographic preference range from positive experience, such as associating a system with how one's grandparents taught them, to a reaction to a traumatic experience, such as psychologically and physically abusive school environments where one writing system was emphasized (Arndt, 2019). Regardless of a speaker's reason for continuing use of a different orthography, it is constructive to the community to ensure that users of the new orthography are still able to understand writings in other orthographies and develop a method to easily convert these texts (Person, 2009).

In this paper, we investigate and compare the usefulness of finite-state transducers (FSTs)

Proceedings of the Fourth workshop on Resources for African Indigenous Languages (RAIL 2023), pages 97–105
May 6, 2023

and long short-term memory neural networks (LSTMs) for the to the task of converting a prior orthography for the Bàsàá language to the current standard, with the conclusion that LSTMs slightly outperform FSTs in the absence of lexical information.

2 Bàsàá

Bàsàá is a Bantu language spoken by approximately 300,000 speakers in Cameroon (Eberhard et al., 2022). While it has many characteristic features of a Bantu language, it is commonly perceived to have more syllable structure variation and flexibility in noun classes when compared with other Bantu languages, as discussed in Section 2.1. The history of Bàsàá also accounts for a variety of writing systems from different missionaries and different standardization efforts, as outlined in Section 2.2.

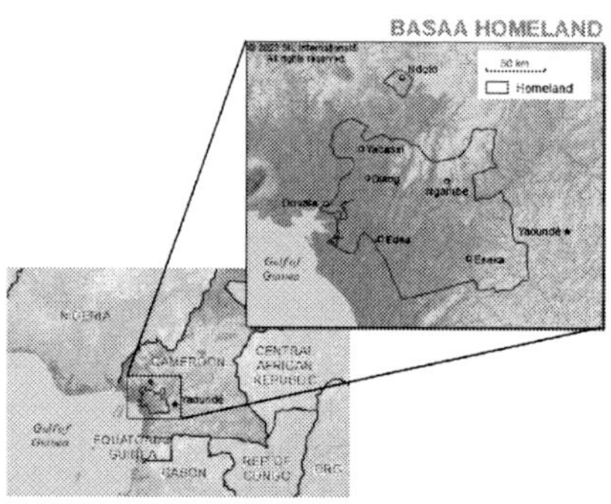

Figure 1: Map depicting the primary regions where Bàsàá is spoken: southern, central and littoral Cameroon. (Njock, 2019)

2.1 Linguistic Profile

A phonetic inventory of Bàsàá is laid out in Makasso and Lee (2015), which includes 7 phonemic vowels (see Figure 2) with short-long contrasts and 30 consonants (see Figure 3). Additionally, Bàsàá utilizes a high-low tone system. While it is a Bantu language, it atypically allows for closed syllable structure in addition to open syllable structure. Although it does have a noun class system, the surface distinctions between the classes are sometimes neutralized. Nouns are not required to start with a consonantal onset and verbs are not required to end in a vowel. These factors result in a higher diversity of permissible syllable structures in Bàsàá when compared with other Bantu languages (Hyman, 2003).

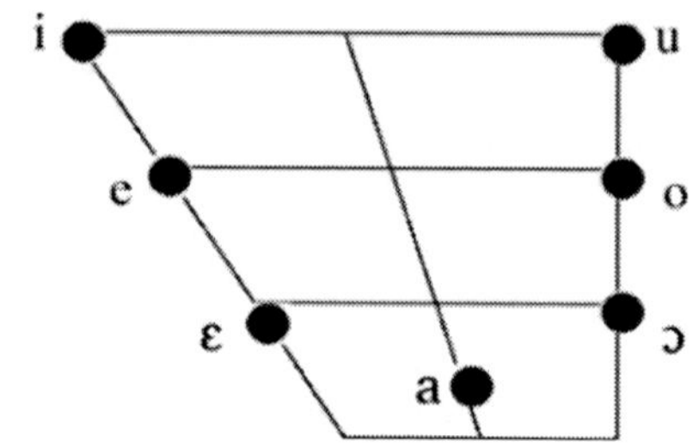

Figure 2: Vowel inventory in Bàsàá (Makasso and Lee, 2015). [ɛ] and [ɔ] are contrasted with [o] and [e] by diacritics in the missionary orthographies

2.2 Orthographic History

The orthographic history of Bàsàá contains multiple writing systems as English, German, and French colonialists who transcribed the language chose different methods of representation. The alphabets created for Bàsàá, and for many of the languages of Cameroon, were primarily influenced by the first languages of the transcriptionists, commonly French, English, or German, and often failed to properly mark important contrasts in the language (Bird, 2001). The two most prominent orthographies established prior to the current one are attributed to Protestant missionaries and Catholic missionaries and are referred to in this paper as the Protestant and Catholic orthographies, neither of which marked tone.

While the first attempt to implement a standard writing system, using an orthography developed for Western African language in Bamako (United Nations Educational and Organization, 1966), wasn't successful, a national committee was established to develop a writing system that would facilitate a pan-Cameroonian literacy in all the languages of the country. Central to this endeavor was the establishment of a system that could capture all of the contrasting sounds across Cameroonian languages. The inclusion of all contrasts would allow any literate speaker of a Cameroonian language to read and pronounce the words of a text in any of the languages of Cameroon, irrespective of comprehension (Hartell, 1993).

The national effort culminated in the establishment of the General Alphabet of the Cameroonian Languages (AGLC) by the National Committee for the Unification and Harmonisation of the Alphabets of Cameroon Languages in 1979 (Maurice Tadadjeu, 1979). The characters of this alpha-

	Bilabial	Alveolar	Post alveolar	Palatal	Velar	Labialized velar	Uvular	Glottal
Plosive	p	t			k	kʷ gʷ		
Affricate			ʧ ʤ					
Implosive	ɓ							
Prenasalized	ᵐb	ⁿd	ⁿʤ		ᵑg			
Nasal	m	n		ɲ	ŋ	ŋʷ		
Tap		ɾ̥ ɾ						
Fricative	ɸ β	s			x ɣ		χ	h ɦ
Approximant	w			j				
Lateral approximant		l						

Figure 3: Consonant inventory in Bàsàá (Makasso and Lee, 2015).

bet are predominately Latin, and thus similar to the English, German, and French alphabets, however the alphabet integrates symbols from the International Phonetic Alphabet to fully represent the phonetic inventory of Cameroonian languages. The symbols in the full AGLC are listed in Table 1.

Consonants	b,ɓ,c,d,ɗ,f,g,',h, j,k,l,m,n ŋ,p,q,r,s,t,v,w,ẅ,x,y,yˀ,z
Vowels	a,ɑ,ɛ,e,ə,æ,ɤ,i,ɨ,o,ɔ,ø,œ,u,ʉ

Table 1: Alphabet of the Cameroonian Languages. The AGLC alphabet was designed to work as a unifying and intelligible alphabet for speakers of all Cameroonian language.

Bàsàá utilizes a subset of this system in accordance with the language's phonetic contrasts. Latin letters are used alongside ɓ, ŋ, ɛ, and ɔ with acute, grave, and circumflex accents to denoting tone. While this orthography is supported by the Academy of Languages of Cameroon, the former missionary orthographies are still used by some speakers and are generally used in earlier texts written in Bàsàá, necessitating a method of conversion of missionary orthographies to the AGLC standard.

Comparing the three writing systems, the first major discrepancy is found in tone marking and vowels. The Protestant and Catholic writing systems do not mark tone, but instead use acute, grave, and circumflex accents to mark different vowels. The Protestant system represents [e] by using an acute accent mark, é, while a [ɛ] is represented by a plain e. Likewise, the Protestant system uses the circumflexed ô, to mark [o], but a plain o in the orthography represents [ɔ]. On the other hand, the Catholic orthography marks [ɛ] and [ɔ] by è and ò, while the plain e and o represent [e] and [o]. However, in the AGLC orthography, acute, grave, and circumflex accents are used to represent tone and the ɛ and ɔ are already contrasted in the orthography by the addition of the symbols ɛ and ɔ. Tone is also marked on syllabic nasal consonants in the AGLC system.

The consonants in the orthography also require consideration in the conversion process. The [ɓ] and [ŋ] sounds are represented by b and ñ in the missionary orthographies, while the AGLC orthography distinguishes [b] from [ɓ] with the characters b and ɓ. Instead of ñ, the [ŋ] is represented by ŋ in the AGLC orthography. In addition to these consonants, the missonary orthographies transcribe the sound tʃ as tj, the AGLC system uses c. One sentence is presented in the three orthographies below to exemplify some of the differences in the orthographies.

AGLC:	Mɛ̀ yè lɛ mɛ ɓɔl nyɔɔ̄ nì màkɔ̀ɔ̀.
Protestant:	Me yé le me bol nyoo ni makôô.
Catholic:	Mè ye lè mè bòl nyòò ni makoo.

3 Prior work

Negotiation between orthographies is a common issue in many languages, and as such a number of previous studies have explored techniques to aid in orthographic conversion and/or normalization. This work builds on existing research describing the Bàsàá language and the use of natural language processing for low-resource languages. This section outlines existing work on Bàsàá in Section 3.1, Finite State Transducers (FST) in Section 3.2, and Long Short-term Memory (LSTM) networks in Section 3.3. While research concerning FSTs and LSTM networks in low-resource settings is extensive, this section focuses on examples that closely mirror the goals of this paper.

3.1 Research on Bàsàá

Existing work on Bàsàá has profiled the linguistic inventory of the language (Makasso and Lee, 2015; Hyman, 2003), generated dictionaries (Lemb and de Gastines, 1973), designed learning materials (Moreton et al., 1968), and, more recently, facilitated the development of resources that integrate computational and NLP methods with Bàsàá to enhance the resources available for documentation, such as the bilingual speech corpus developed to assist in automatic phonetic transcription (Hamlaoui et al., 2018).

Nikitin et al. (2022) approaches the task of orthography conversion in Bàsàá by using Bidirectional Encoder Representations from Transformers (BERT), which often performs well due to the large amount of resources and training that went into the model. However, for this task, BERT was only able to beat the baseline after extensive pre-processing of the text. The importance of extensive pre-processing the text and only marginally better performance than the baseline suggests that BERT is not well-suited to this task.

3.2 Finite State Transducers

Finite State Transducers (FST) work as a translator between a set of input strings and a set of output strings. In the case of language, the input string can utilize linguistic rules and produce an output that adheres to those rules. As the input of the FST relies on linguistic rules, the model often performs well in low-resource environments, as the models do not rely on large amounts of training data or computational resources. While FST models require some amount of linguistic or computational efforts to build, various tools have been created which automate various parts of the process to help alleviate these boundaries (Khanna et al., 2021), although the performance of FST models benefits greatly from the generation of detailed, language-specific rules.

In general, FSTs do not necessarily specify a unique mapping between input and output strings, which can cause problems for tasks like orthography conversion that generally need a single output. This can be addressed by adding additional rules to constrain the transducer. However, if determining appropriate rules is difficult and a corpus is available, it can also be addressed by adding weights, which are scores that can be applied either to a whole-word input-output pair or to a subword mapping. Then, for a given input, each output has a weight equal to the sum of all the applicable weights derived from the corpus, with only the form with the lowest total being output.

FSTs have been implemented in many low-resource settings, as well as for the application of orthographic conversion, transliteration, and text normalization. Washington et al. (2021) developed a transducer to assist in orthographic conversion and morphological analysis of Zapotec and found that even an incomplete transducer could yield positive results. Similar efforts use an FST to develop a morphological generator and analyzer while simultaneously addressing the issue of missing diacritics (Alkhairy et al., 2020), demonstrating the easy expansion of an FST to create more resources for a language. Manohar et al. (2022) extend the use of FSTs to text-to-speech (TTS) applications in low-resource settings, generating a model that converts between Malayalam phonemes and graphemes.

While the use of FSTs in low-resource settings is well-attested, the inclusion of tones has proven difficult. Ngué Um et al. (2022) built an FST for Ewondo, a Cameroonian language. In this study, the ambiguous nature of combined versus combining tone markings produces difficulty for the analyzer. While both the combined and combining accents can be analyzed by the FST, it results in errors in the morphological generation. An expansion of the FST for Bàsàá would also need to address this issue.

3.3 Long Short-Term Memory Networks

The LSTM is a recurrent neural network architecture that allows information about long-term dependencies to be incorporated, providing additional context for the generation of the output. LSTM networks have been applied to many deep learning tasks, such as machine translation, optical character recognition (OCR), and speech recognition.

LSTMs have been combined with OCR tasks to assist languages in digitization and orthographic normalization of historic texts. Azawi et al. (2013) found that LSTMs perform well for the conversion of German historic texts as they are able to handle unseen examples. Similarly, Simistira et al. (2015) found using LSTMs for OCR produces a lower character error rate than leading methods of

OCR for Greek polytonic script.

Additionally, LSTMs have recently gained popularity for their utility in TTS tasks, such as grapheme-to-phoneme conversion. Adriana (2019), Liu et al. (2018), and Behbahani et al. (2016) successfully implemented LSTM models for grapheme-to-phoneme conversion in Romanian, Mongolian, and Persian.

4 Methodology

This paper compares the accuracy of a Finite State Transducer (FST), a weighted FST, and a Long Short-term Memory (LSTM) model for the task of orthographic conversion of Bàsàá. Section 4.1 describes the data the models trained on, Section 4.2 describes the simple baseline metric used for comparison, Section 4.3 explains the use of an unweighted FST, Section 4.4 details the implementation of the weighted FST, and Section 4.5 outlines the LSTM model.

4.1 Data

The methods in this study use a text corpus comprised of 12,000 sentences in the Protestant orthography together with transliterations into the AGLC orthography. Of these sentences, 10,000 are used for training, 1,000 for validation, and 1,000 for testing. Pre-processing of the text consisted of lower-casing the characters.

4.2 Baseline

The baseline searches the target sentences for the most frequent translation of a source word and replaces the source word with that token. In the event that the source word does not appear in the data, the source word is output in its original form without conversion. The baseline here is a naïve approach to the problem, but is representative of the current lack of existing work on orthographic conversion in the language.

4.3 Unweighted FST

The unweighted FST consists of a set of character mappings compiled using the lexicon compiler Lexd (Swanson and Howell, 2021) which includes every pair of source and target characters found in the training data. Mapping each character individually and without context creates a large number of output forms, which we resolve by selecting a single output form at random. Additionally, we added four rules which restrict the output in cases where the phonological context is unambiguous. Specifically, that nasals will never have a tone diacritic in the AGLC orthography if they precede a vowel (this is 3 rules, one each for m, n, and ŋ), and that where the missionary orthography has tj the AGLC orthography will always have c (as opposed to converting the t and the j separately as tj).

4.4 Weighted FST

Where the unweighted FST treats every mapping as equally probable, the weighted FST sets a weight for each path which has been seen in the training data, with more frequent source-target pairs receiving lower (better) weights. Then, rather than selecting randomly, the output with the lowest weight is used.

4.5 Neural seq2seq model

Following previous work that has shown that character-based neural seq2seq architectures perform well for orthographic normalization and conversion (Rosca and Breuel, 2016; Orife, 2018), we trained an encoder-decoder model with global attention (Luong et al., 2015) to convert missionary orthographies into the AGLC orthography. Both the encoder and decoder are unidirectional Long short-term memory networks (Hochreiter and Schmidhuber, 1997) consisting of 2 layers of 1,000 hidden units each. We used the OpenNMT-py library (Klein et al., 2020) to train the model and generate predictions on the held-out datasets.

5 Results

We compare the four systems using word- and character-error rates (WER and CER). WER and CER are calculated automatically by comparing the outputs of each of the systems to the output of the target file. Following the presentation of WER and CER for each of the systems, we provide examples of the output from each model. Information on the differences in orthographical representation for the source and target texts can be found in Section 2.2.

5.1 Word- and Character-error Rates

Results of all systems apart from the unweighted FST were relatively similar, with baseline model performing better than both the FST systems and on par with the seq2seq model. The seq2seq model achieved the best character-error rate, while

System	CER	WER
Baseline	15.61	41.11
Unweighted FST	40.31	90.72
Weighted FST	18.06	55.10
LSTM	13.27	42.03

Table 2: Comparison between the 4 models.

the baseline shows a marginally better word-error rate. This can be explained by the fact that the baseline operates at the word level. Thus, a mistake results in selecting the wrong word form, which likely has multiple characters that are different than the correct word form. The seq2seq model, on the other hand, predicts at a character level, and may make only a single character error in a word, such as a missed tonal diacritic.

5.2 Error Analysis

To better understand the performance of these models, we present examples of outputs of the models for three different sentences and discuss which errors are common for each of the models. The examples are taken from the development set output for each of the models.

Source:	*malét a nhundus binan.*
Target:	màlêt à ǹhundus binan.
Baseline:	màlêt à nhundus bìnan.
Unweighted FST:	màlět à ŋhúńdus bǐŋan.
Weighted FST:	màlět à ŋhúńdus bǐŋan.
LSTM:	màlêt à ǹhundus binan.

Table 3

In the sentences in Table 3, we see that the FSTs have a tendency to overgenerate the letter ŋ when the source orthography has an n. Additionally, it shows that the LSTM network is successful in generating the tone of a syllabic nasal. While the baseline often can predict tone on a syllabic nasal, this token is not in the training data, so the baseline just outputs the original token.

The sentences in Table 4 show that the most systems are able to understand that the accents in the source orthography are not indicative of an accent on the target orthography. However, the unweighted FST tends towards adding accents even in the absence of accents in the target form. Overall, we see the LSTM perform well on the assignment of tone and characters in this example, with the baseline being almost perfect apart from the tone on the second token.

Source:	*nledek mut u nnéégа bé.*
Target:	ǹlɛ̀dɛk mût u nnēegà ɓe.
Baseline:	ǹlɛ̀dɛk mùt u nnēegà ɓe.
Unweighted FST:	ǹlɛ̄dɛk mût ù ŋnêègâ ɓè.
Weighted FST:	ǹlɛ̀dɛk mùt ù nnēegà ɓe.
LSTM:	ǹlɛ̀dɛk mût u nnēegà ɓe.

Table 4

Source:	*kal nye le me ñke.*
Target:	kăl nyɛ lɛ mɛ̀ ŋ̀kɛ̂.
Baseline:	kăl nyɛ lɛ mɛ̀ ŋkɛ̀.
Unweighted FST:	kāl ńyɛ lɛ̆ mɛ̄ ŋ̀kɛ.
Weighted FST:	kâl nyɛ lɛ mɛ̀ ŋkɛ̀.
LSTM:	kal nyɛ̄ lɛ mɛ̀ ŋ̀kɛ̂.

Table 5

In the sentences in Table 5, although the LSTM comes close, it is not able to identify the rising tone in the first token and marks the tone of the second token as mid. The weighted and unweighted FST correctly predict the characters, but otherwise are very inconsistent with tone diacritics, although it is evident that the weighted FST outperforms the unweighted FST.

6 Conclusion

The results of this paper contribute to the discussion concerning the relative benefits of NLP methods versus more simplistic baselines in low-resource settings. The baseline outperforms the unweighted and weighted FSTs and LSTM network in regards to WER. As Bàsàá is a tone language, changes in the tone of one character can create minimal pairs and thus WER is a more realistic metric for evaluating the utility of a model. However, the baseline simply outputs the original word for any out-of-vocabulary (OOV) tokens, meaning that the performance of the baseline is strongly impacted by OOV tokens. While this has a minimal impact on this dataset, a dataset with more OOV tokens would perform worse.

While the baseline performs well on the Protestant orthography, it would likely perform even better on the Catholic orthography as it uses grave accent marks instead of acute accent marks. Although the Catholic and AGLC orthography use the grave accents to mark different things, the presence of grave marks in the target is much more likely than acute accent marks, which only appear when deconstructing rising and falling tones on long vowels. The method of handling OOV tokens would therefore perform better for a source text written in the Catholic orthography, as the probability of coincidentally having an output that matches the input form is much higher when the source orthography uses grave accents.

In this paper, the unweighted and weighted FST were written using very minimal linguistic rules, which is evidenced in their relatively poor performance. The weighted FST greatly reduced the impact of the lack of detailed rules, but would clearly still benefit from their addition.

This paper presents a preliminary investigation of the application of FSTs and LSTM networks to the topic of orthographic conversion. While the simplistic baseline performs surprisingly well for this dataset, we believe that the comparable performance of the weighted FST and LSTM network is promising and necessitates further development of these models, specifically the inclusion of more linguistic rules for the weighted FST and augmentation of the training data for the LSTM network.

Limitations

This paper attempts to make a broader statements about the applicability of current NLP methods for text conversion by discussing the results of these models on Bàsàá. The case of Bàsàá is challenging as the representation of tones is difficult for many models. However, this study still benefits from the roman-based, alphabetic orthography of the language and the resources that are available to languages with a Latin-based, alphabetic orthography. Additionally, Bàsàá utilizes a transparent orthography that also facilitates automatic methods of conversion. Other results and challenges are likely to arise when applying these models to a language that utilizes a non-Latin-based, non-alphabetic, and/or opaque orthography.

As this project is intended to present a starting point for extended research on orthographic conversion, we have begun by providing an overall comparison and brief error analysis. However, we plan to implement a more systematic error analysis to guide future work. The current error analysis highlights some patterns that are observed in the data, but a more thorough review of the outputs will help in the development of the current system for Bàsàá.

Ethics Statement

The motivation of this work is to compare current NLP methods in a low-resource setting and discuss how the different systems might apply in different contexts based on the results, contributing overall to the discussion on how NLP methods can be used to benefit language communities and support the creation of more linguistic resources. While the hope is to support the language community, the integration of computational methods also poses the risk of language commodification and a dispossession of intellectual property of a community. This study is submitted with the belief that the current benefits associated with the application of this research outweigh this risk.

Acknowledgements

This research was supported in part by Lilly Endowment, Inc., through its support for the Indiana University Pervasive Technology Institute.

References

STAN Adriana. 2019. Input encoding for sequence-to-sequence learning of romanian grapheme-to-phoneme conversion. In *2019 International Conference on Speech Technology and Human-Computer Dialogue (SpeD)*, pages 1–6. IEEE.

Maha Alkhairy, Afshan Jafri, and David A Smith. 2020. Finite state machine pattern-root arabic morphological generator, analyzer and diacritizer. In *Proceedings of the Twelfth Language Resources and Evaluation Conference*, pages 3834–3841.

Jochen S Arndt. 2019. Engineered zuluness: Language, education, and ethnic identity in south africa, 1835–1990. *The Journal of the Middle East and Africa*, 10(3):211–235.

Mayce Al Azawi, Muhammad Zeshan Afzal, and Thomas M Breuel. 2013. Normalizing historical orthography for ocr historical documents using lstm. In *Proceedings of the 2nd International Workshop on Historical Document Imaging and Processing*, pages 80–85.

Yasser Mohseni Behbahani, Bagher Babaali, and Mussa Turdalyuly. 2016. Persian sentences to phoneme sequences conversion based on recurrent neural networks. *Open Computer Science*, 6(1):219–225.

Steven Bird. 2001. Orthography and identity in cameroon. *Written Language & Literacy*, 4(2):131–162.

David M. Eberhard, Gary F. Simons, and Charles D. Fennig. 2022. *Ethnologue: Languages of the World*, twenty-fifth edition. SIL International.

Fatima Hamlaoui, Emmanuel-Moselly Makasso, Markus Müller, Jonas Engelmann, Gilles Adda, Alex Waibel, and Sebastian Stüker. 2018. BULBasaa: A bilingual basaa-French speech corpus for the evaluation of language documentation tools. In *Proceedings of the Eleventh International Conference on Language Resources and Evaluation (LREC 2018)*, Miyazaki, Japan. European Language Resources Association (ELRA).

Rhonda L. Hartell. 1993. Alphabets of africa. *SIL International.*

Sepp Hochreiter and Jürgen Schmidhuber. 1997. Long short-term memory. *Neural computation*, 9(8):1735–1780.

Larry M Hyman. 2003. Basaá (a43). *The Bantu languages*, pages 257–282.

Carina Jahani. 1989. *Standardization and orthography in the Balochi language*. Ph.D. thesis, Acta Universitatis Upsaliensis.

Tanmai Khanna, Jonathan N Washington, Francis M Tyers, Sevilay Bayatlı, Daniel G Swanson, Tommi A Pirinen, Irene Tang, and Hèctor Alòs i Font. 2021. Recent advances in apertium, a free/open-source rule-based machine translation platform for low-resource languages. *Machine Translation*, 35(4):475–502.

Guillaume Klein, François Hernandez, Vincent Nguyen, and Jean Senellart. 2020. The opennmt neural machine translation toolkit: 2020 edition. In *Proceedings of the 14th Conference of the Association for Machine Translation in the Americas (Volume 1: Research Track)*, pages 102–109.

Pierre Lemb and François de Gastines. 1973. *Dictionnaire basaá-français*, avec un préface par meinrad hebga edition. Collège Libermann, Douala.

Nicholas Limerick. 2018. Kichwa or quichua? competing alphabets, political histories, and complicated reading in indigenous languages. *Comparative Education Review*, 62(1):103–124.

Zhinan Liu, Feilong Bao, and Guanglai Gao. 2018. Mongolian grapheme to phoneme conversion by using hybrid approach. In *Natural Language Processing and Chinese Computing: 7th CCF International Conference, NLPCC 2018, Hohhot, China, August 26–30, 2018, Proceedings, Part I 7*, pages 40–50. Springer.

Minh-Thang Luong, Hieu Pham, and Christopher D Manning. 2015. Effective approaches to attention-based neural machine translation. *arXiv preprint arXiv:1508.04025*.

Emmanuel-Moselly Makasso and Seunghun J. Lee. 2015. Basaá. *Journal of the International Phonetic Association*, 45(1):7179.

Kavya Manohar, AR Jayan, and Rajeev Rajan. 2022. Mlphon: A multifunctional grapheme-phoneme conversion tool using finite state transducers. *IEEE Access*, 10:97555–97575.

Etienne Sadembouo Maurice Tadadjeu. 1979. *Alphabet général des langues camerounaises / General Alphabet of Cameroon Languages*. Université de Yaoundé, SIL Internationale, University of Yaoundé, SIL International.

Rebecca L Moreton et al. 1968. Cameroon basaa. *Inspection copy available from Foreign Languages Program, Center for Applied Linguistics*.

Ulrike Mosel. 2004. Dictionary making in endangered speech communities. *Language documentation and description*, 2:39–54.

Emmanuel Ngué Um, Émilie Eliette, Caroline Ngo Tjomb Assembe, and Francis Morton Tyers. 2022. Developing a rule-based machine-translation system, ewondo–french–ewondo. *International Journal of Humanities and Arts Computing*, 16(2):166–181.

Ilya Nikitin, Brian O'Connor, and Anastasia Safonova. 2022. Tone prediction and orthographic conversion for basaa. *arXiv preprint arXiv:2210.06986*.

Pierre Emmanuel. Njock. 2019. *àsàa - French - English - German Dictionary.* Dallas: Webonary.org.

Iroro Orife. 2018. Attentive sequence-to-sequence learning for diacritic restoration of yorùbá language text. In *Interspeech*.

Kirk R Person. 2009. Heritage scripts, technical transcriptions, and practical orthographies: a middle path towards educational excellence and cultural preservation for thailands ethnic minority languages. In *Proceedings from the international conference on national language policy: Language diversity for national unity*.

Mihaela Rosca and Thomas Breuel. 2016. Sequence-to-sequence neural network models for transliteration. *arXiv preprint arXiv:1610.09565*.

Fotini Simistira, Adnan Ul-Hassan, Vassilis Papavassiliou, Basilis Gatos, Vassilis Katsouros, and Marcus Liwicki. 2015. Recognition of historical greek polytonic scripts using lstm networks. In *2015 13th International Conference on Document Analysis and Recognition (ICDAR)*, pages 766–770. IEEE.

Daniel Swanson and Nick Howell. 2021. Lexd: A finite-state lexicon compiler for non-suffixational morphologies. In Mika Hämäläinen, Niko Partanen, and Khalid Alnajjar, editors, *Multilingual Facilitation*. University of Helsinki Library.

Scientific United Nations Educational and Cultural Organization. 1966. *Meeting of a group of experts for the unification of alphabets of national languages. Bamako, Mali, 28 February 5 March 1966. Final report*. United Nations Educational, Scientific and Cultural Organization, UNESCO.

Jonathan Washington, Felipe Lopez, and Brook Lillehaugen. 2021. Towards a morphological transducer and orthography converter for western tlacolula valley zapotec. In *Proceedings of the First Workshop on Natural Language Processing for Indigenous Languages of the Americas*, pages 185–193.

Vowels and the Igala Language Resources

Mahmud Mohammed Momoh
Prince Abubakar Audu University
P.M.B 1008, Anyigba, Nigeria
mahmoodmohammed19@yahoo.com

Abstract

The aim of this article is to provide some insight into the link between diacritic orthography and the implicit sounds in these orthographies that are applied in writing the Igala Language corpus. 30 vowels were identified (5 short vowels, and 25 mid to long vowels of different variety) plus 8 diphthongs. Examples in the form of sentences and interpretation were provided. The article combines up to seven diacritic forms in order to better tackle the oft encountered problem of pronouncing words in texts written in foreign language by non-native speakers and learners with supporting indicators provided to guide end users on how to pronounce the words using the diacritic forms and vocal representation of these forms that are herein provided in the double slash oral transcription of the words.

Keywords: vowels, Igala, Language, Resources

1. Introduction

The Igala language is mainly spoken in the East Senatorial District of Kogi State, Nigeria (Oguagha, 1980) within a geographical coordinate lying between 6 3^0 and 8^0 north of latitude and 6 3^0 and 7 4^{0}east of longitude (Saleh and Yunusa, 2013). The people occupy an area that is roughly around 4,982 miles of the Niger-Benue rivers by-pass numbering over 2 million speakers of the language (Saleh and Yunusa, 2013). Wikipedia.com[1] pointed out that; "the Igala is Yoruboid branch of the Volta–Niger language family, spoken by the Igala, Agatu, Idoma, and Bassa people". In the same vein Obayemi, (1980) recognized Igala as being, "among the more conspicuous entities in the Niger-Benue confluence area.

In this study, the key priority is to point out some important vowels and lexicons applicable to day-to-day communication in Igala land. It should be emphasized that the words indicated in this work are by no means 'self-exhaustive', for this is but just a drop out of the ocean of words in existence within the Igala lexicographical system. The Latin letters with their associated phonetic symbols and sound were used as reference points.

2 Vowels and Words in Igala Language

The *Oxford Advanced Learner's Dictionary of English* defined lexicon as; "all the words and phrases used in a particular language or subject; all the words and phrases used and known by a particular person or group of people" (Hornby, 2015). With respect to the Igala as with other languages, lexical formation begins with conjoining strings of phones or alphabets to form morphemes from which words are created. Currently, no known homemade or standard alphabetical or orthographical system exists for writing the Igala language except for the esoteric signs and markings; usually on the floor, used by traditional witchdoctors, which is not known to the vast majority of the people and that also did not serve formal purposes within society. In the midst of this foibles induced by this lack of inbred phonemes, writers beginning from the modern era, are known to either select the Latin phonetic symbols or the Arabic phonemes to replicate or transcribe words of Igala origin, what is at times referred to in West Africa as a'jami or ajami (Mc Laughlin, 2017).

Notwithstanding the fact that Igala is a tone-based language (Rodriguez, 2014; Dawson et al. 2015; Adeniyi, 2016), while attempting to study the structure of the Igala language, most of the attention of scholars has been on parts of speech, without much effort been dedicated towards tones and sounds with the result that without a prior knowledge of the language words written are hard to pronounce, in some cases not even with the English translation of these provided, and as for those categories of writers who tried to express tones using diacritic orthographies, without a prior knowledge of diacritic by the readers, it is still hard for the readers to decipher what was written,

[1] https://en.wikipedia.org/wiki/igala

Proceedings of the Fourth workshop on Resources for African Indigenous Languages (RAIL 2023), pages 106–114
May 6, 2023

besides, through occasional failures of writers to provide double slash transcription boxes or oral parenthesis of sounds represented by orthographic symbols in their works, the fact that these symbols produce certain sounds from place to place and from one writer to the other makes it very hard for readers to grasp with the sound frame being inferred by these writers.

Abraham (2017; 2019) as well as, Emah and Ojonugwa (2020) while using diacritic orthography to write words, partly to show how differences in pitch change word meanings as was once observed by Yip (2002), failed to provide double slash transcription of the sounds represented by the orthographic symbols incorporated. Kigalaonline.wordpress.com[2] made an attempt that came close to remedying the above stated shortcomings but ended up identifying just three form each for the five main vowels and two supplementary vowels (ó and é to sound /ó:/ and /é:/ [Sic] - or as in the more commonly recognized phonological form /eu/ and /ei/), which gave only seventeen vowels at the expense of the 30 vowels + 8 diphthongs recognized in this very paper. This shortcoming is not limited to the Igala language alone. Other likewise languages that are still plodding around the threshold of traditional education by the start of the 20th Century, mostly in respect of the low-resourced language groups in Africa are also faced with this very problem, a development Ken Lodge, observed thus:

> Traditional education largely ignores spoken languages… little attention is paid to the details of speech in an objective way. We therefore need a method of describing speech in objective, verifiable terms as opposed to the lay approaches which typically describes sound as "hard", "soft", "sharp", and so on which can only be understood by the person using such description (Lodge, 2009).

In the context of this particular paper thus, Latin alphabets were adopted for fashioning Igala sounds, words, and phrasal forms using diacritic symbols bearing phonemic modes similar to Blench (2011). All the English phonemes were adopted except the letters, Q, V, S, X, and Z which were discarded consonants for lack of relevance as it is with Yoruba (Kasali et al. 2021) while the letter 'c' is applied only in combination with the letter 'h' to produce the digraph /tʃ/ that is used for writing words such as *ūchōnā* (somebody's name meaning 'creator' or just 'the creator' in a more general sense of the word), as can be had with English words as chicken and kitchen. More also, the letter 'c' is not used in writing /k/ sounding words that are often written with the letter 'c' such as can /kæn/, neither can it be devoted to writing a sound /s/ bearing word such as ceiling for this would have been *silīni* /si:lini/ or actually *chílīni* /tʃi:lini/ because of the still the more total absence of the 's' consonant within the Igala lexical system. Similarly, rather than write the word quantity with the letter 'q', in our own Igala orthography, the spelling of quantity would appear as 'kwontity'.

Writing vowels during word formation often involves the embracement of any one out of some three alternative styles. The first is the exclusive use of plain alphabets in which case only vowels that are unadorned with glyphs would be put to use. This first form does not embody the use of diacritic in any way and if vowel are to be crafted, that would depend upon the efficacious amalgam of plain alphabets to produce words that are not delineated in the existing letter ordering as in the spelling of the word Igalaa in wiktionary.org[3] in which case the underlined double 'a' in that word Igalaa does not merely suggest a long vowel (i.e.; /a:/) but a repetition of the vowels as /a/ + /a/ to give a sound much like a gliding 'are are'. The second form of these on-hand modes which this author here assume to be actually impractical depend exclusively on the use of diacritic, if not in writing the plain orthographic characters but in the scrawling of the oral parenthesis of words as in the *Webster's II New College Dictionary*. The third style involves the commixing of the other two diametrical forms, i.e.; the adoption of both the plain vowels and the diacritic–based vowels. Any of these three forms is cogent enough provided they goose-step along the conventional morphophonemic norms. It is the third form of these approaches- that of mixing plain Latin alphabet with Latin diacritic symbols, that would be utilized in this particular work.

In the oral parenthesis provided in the *Webster's II New College Dictionary* and thesaraus.yourdictionary.com,[4] short vowels were represented with the application of the breve- a form of diacritic that is presented like the lower half of a cycle above the vowels, i.e.; ă, ĕ, ĭ, ŏ, ŭ,

[2] htpps://kigalaonline.wordpress.com/2017/

[3] https://en.wiktionary.org/wiki/Igalaa

[4] https://thesaraus.yourdictionary.com/

but in writing this work, rather than to vent these letters using the breve, they were written just as plain as possible, i.e.; 'a, e, i, o, u'. Be that said, the other point of departure concern the sounds the other diacritic orthographies used by these esteem dictionaries produced with respect to our own keys here. In the *Webster's II New College Dictionary* (1999), the macron was adopted to produce the unique form of the long vowels ō ~ /eu/ as in the word old /ōld/ in much of a respect used by Dawson et al. (2015) and ā ~ as in the word said /sād/, but in this work, moved by the peculiarity of the Igala language which partially sets it apart from English and the prima facie claim by Wells (2001) that the macron is ratified for initiating a middle locus between the short vowels and the long vowels.

Macrons were therefore used in this work, not for the production of the ā = /ei/ and ō = /eu/ sounds for these are in this work illustrated by the use of the letters 'o' and 'e' with dots on top of them (i.e.; *ȯ* = /eu/ and *ė* = /ei/). Although, there are a few improvements lately, most of the previous writings, following mainly from the recommendation of the 1984 Igala Orthographic Committee which recognized the under dotted ọ and ẹ for the low tones o ~ /o˩/ | e ~ /e˩/ (i.e.; as in the spelling of *ọjọ* /o˩jo˩/ in Okwoli (1996) and Ahiaba (2015), and ẹrẹ /e˩re˩/ in Ayegba et al. (2017) for sounding the falling /o/ and /e/ sounds, while the quartet reserved the plain forms of 'o' and 'e' alphabets for the rising and falling forms of /eu/ and /ei/ sounds as used for Yoruba in aroadedictionary.com, most of these scholars recognized only 7 vowels plus a so called 24 consonant sounds (Ojoaogwu, 2017) or 32 symbols in whole according to Miachi and Armstrong (1986), which meant they left out a number of vowels and therefore downplaying the use of the macron in the work of succeeding writers with the only exceptions being Omachonu (2011) and to an extent, Dawson et al. (2015) who either used it in much of a respect as done in this paper or as was done in the *Webster's II New College Dictionary*.

Thus, the use of the macron in this article follows a model that is similar to its use by Karshima (2012) in respect to the Tiv language or in respect to the Igala word *ìkpā̠* (bag) in Rodriguez (2014); not to be confused with *íkpa* (knock knees), in which *ā* = /æ/ as in the American English pronunciation of the words 'plan' and 'stand' in oxfordlearnersdictionary.com as an intermediate tone between the sound /a/ and /a:/ of the IPA sound system, *ē* = /ɛ/ as in the English word 'a̲ny', i.e.; an intermediate tone between the sound /e/ and /e:/ of the IPA sound system) as was used in respect to the word *ònēkèlē* in Rodriguez (2015) which the author of this very paper would here again rewrite as *ōnēkēlē* (male), *ī* = /i:/ > /x/ > /i/, i.e.; an intermediate tone between the sound /i/ and /i:/ of the IPA sound system, *ō* = /ɔ/ as in the cardinal mid-back rounded 'o' used in sounding the English word 'bu̲t' or the Igala word *ōkō* /ɔkɔ/ in respect to airplane or ship which is in contrast to *òkò* /o˩ko˩/ (millipede) or *okā* /okæ/ (style, i.e.; acrobatic) or *ókō* /o:kɔ/ (money), with 'ō' being an intermediate tone between the sound /o/ and /o:/ of the IPA sound system, *ū* = /u:/ > /x/ > /u/ as in Lithuanian, Livonian, and Maori,[5] i.e.; an intermediate tone between the sound /u/ and /u:/ of the IPA sound system. The x in the oral parentheses represents the indefinite phonemic sound for the diacritic orthographies ī & ū ~ x. Decision to jettison the breve in this paper has a twofold underling. First was to ensure the design of a coherent orthographic system with pure vowels used in their original orthographic forms as it is in most English language texts, notwithstanding whatever graphical modification or characterization that the addition of impending glyphs to the first letter thenceforth might confer. The second reason propped from the need to eschew the immanent supererogatory burden of having to write them with an added character when they could remain plain or without partial alteration and still maintain their functions as short vowels.

The desuetude towards the breve as done here was not a deliberate attempt to undo the merits of the *Webster's II New College Dictionary*, their discretion are still very valid, specifically with respect to the study of the English language. This writer is well abreast with the unequivocal fact that left with a vagaries of indicative keys to choose from, it is always incumbent upon each writer to cherry-pick both the phonotactical and the morphotactical forms that are amenable to the language being worked on (Pretorius and Bosch, 2009), it should however be noted that the use of ā = /ei/ and ō = /eu/, despite not being wrong in any sense, doesn't nonetheless conforms with the original phonological flow pattern enshrined in their root alphabet 'a' which produces the sounds /a/ and /a:/, and 'e' which produces the sounds /e/ and /e:/. Bearing in mind the fact that the middle tone is sometimes perceived to be a conflation of two vowels (i.e.; /e/ + /i/ = /ei/ and /e/ + /u/ = /eu/

[5] https://en.wiktionary.org/wiki/ū

as it is in English), then it would not be totally wrong to say that the editors of the *Webster's II New College Dictionary* were right in their own right to have used the macron in the context they employed it, besides, language analyst do agree that, 'there is no such thing as a standard form when it comes to matters of language' (Laperre 2020) and as Szczegielniak laconically hinted, "spelling or orthography does not consistently represent the sounds of language".[6] Thus, in Igala language, middle tone implies is a position between a long vowel and a short vowel such as the middle sound between the high /a:/ and the low /a/, i.e.; an 'a' that has a higher tone than /a/ but yet is still less pitched than /a:/ represented as x > /a/ < /a:/.

This writer would have loved to have the alphabet ė which is hereby sounded /ei/ written as ȧ, but because most words in the language are already written with the letter 'e' to sound /ei/, as in words such as *ugbede* /ugbeidei/ or *ele* /eilei/, the author therefore chose to maintain the letter ė which comes closer to the now more popular tradition. The decision to use the alphabet ȧ instead of ė would have matched perfectly with the use of the over dotted 'o' (ȯ) to produce the sound /eu/. The use of the macron itself becomes vital considering the fact that, most words in the Igala language are sounded within this mid tone context.

As in writing the Yoruba language or French (Olufemi, 2022; Nolte et al. 2018), the acute and the grave forms of diacritic were also used although with a contrastive difference in phonation between the Igala words written here using this form that is different from French as regards to the word *café*, in which case, the é as in the French and in the form used by Rodriguez (2014) in relation to the word '*édʒú*' ~ /eidʒu:/ (face), is pronounced /ei/, more like the English word rake /reik/, whereas, the orthography *é* as it relates with the Igala and sometimes with the Yoruba; as with the word *òrẹ́* (friend) in (Oshodi, 2016) ~ /oɹre:/, is nonetheless pronounced /e:/ as in English. Thus, we must agree with Cahill, (2019) that, in using diacritic tools, "the challenge is that the tone marks are usually not consistent among scholars", with the result that, a letter é that is pronounced as /e:/ in one instance or by one scholar is pronounced at another instance or by another scholar as /ei/ as in spelling of *wálẹ́* ~ /wa:lei/ (come home) in Dalamu (2019) which is at variance with Oshodi (2016)'s /e:/ above.

Here too, the grave accent (i.e.; *ȁ, ȅ, ȉ, ȍ, ȕ*) was used to indicate the low tones as was done in Yip (2002). The use of certain diacritic marks in this work might be counted as inappropriate as is now apparent with respect to how the macron is used here which is already in conflict with how it was used in the *Webster's II Dictionary* or how any of these marks are represented in other languages such as French, Dutch, Portuguese, Italian, and Mohawk[7] (Finegan, 2012).

A critic might ask to know why 'this author did not use the breve diacritic in writing the short vowels', which has already been reflected upon above. To cover any anomaly that emanates from how certain things are represented in this work, enabling tools with instructions regarding how to pronounce the diacritic forms is provided, with the hope that the writer of this piece and the readers might be on a common wavelength in comprehending what has been put down. Hence, words having these marks which as this writer suppose might not follow the existing methods in some languages, can be pronounced; if not so perfectly, it would be 'nearly perfect'.

The Igala vowels are still yet not limited to the above mentioned accent forms. In this study, it is revealed that some vowels are a combination of double sound of the same vowel either ways raised between short or long vowel and then pitched lowly or highly with the corresponding vowel (like a bend), as was done with respect to that closing tone in the word Igal<u>aa</u>.[8] For this category of vowels, the author came up with the idea of having orthographies with macrons on top of them that are further capped with a grave or the acute diacritic but only two of the short vowels ḕ, ḗ and ṑ, ṓ could meet this requirement, and so the author thought of remedying this problem with the use of the circumflex having either the acute or the grave diacritic mark on top of them, i.e.; ấ, ầ, but only the letter 'a' has this feature out of the other three still missing letters conveying the short vowels (a, i. and u). The next that could be done was to check for diacritic graphemes that have the features that can best solve the 'u' and the 'i' problem (regarding this category of sound), but this author once again stumbled upon the idea of using the 'u' dieresis capped with either the grave or the acute mark, i.e.; ǘ and ǜ, but the 'i' symbols was still missing, and so, the author thought of using the Greek small letter iota with psili and varia (ἲ) and ἴ small letter iota with psili and oxia

[6] https://scholar.harvard.edu/files/adam

[7] https://en.wikipedia.org/wiki/Grave

[8] https://en.wiktionary.org/wiki/Igalaa

which the author found as the only current fitting option for use here.

2.1 Contextual Usage of Vowels

In writing the orthographic forms of Igala vowels, one would thus have 30 of these, with each of the short vowels producing 5 variants each while from the glyph ȯ and ė can be gotten an additional 8 diphthongs. In the *Webster's II New College Dictionary*, orthographic characters and phonetic sounds adhering or being inherent in the long vowels of the English language were written in the forms; /â/ or /ä/ = /a: /, /ê/ = /e: /, /ē/ = /i: /, /ô/ = /o: /, /û/ = /u: /, /ā/ = /ei/, and ō = /eu/. In this work the above 5 high tones were replicated as *á* = /a: /, *é* = /e: /, *í* = /i: /, *ó* = /o: /, *ú* = /u: /. Added to these long vowels are the 5 short vowels *a* = /a/, *e* = /e/, *i* = /i/, *o* = /o/, *u* = /u/. There are also 5 macron diacritic to produce the intermediate of these vowels, *ā*, *ē*, *ī*, *ō*, *ū*, whose vocal forms have been explained above.

There are 5 long vowels that are stressed with falling tones, i.e.; as in *à* = /a˩/, *è* = /e˩/, *ì* = /i˩/, *ò* = /o˩/, *ù* = /u˩/. With the exception of the orthographic symbol 'o' which is capped with the double grave and double acute accent (i.e.; ȍ /o˩˩/ and ő /o::/) used to express the extra-low and the extra-high accent of the /o/ sound, the other four orthographies bearing the primary vowels (a, e, i, and u) whose logographic form (as lone orthographies) expresses the pronouns '*a*' (me), '*e*' (you), '*i*' (s/he or it), and '*u*' (first person me) which do convey emphasis and mood, have dieresis-like rise-rise inflective sounds with one, the combine 'a' (*ấ* = /a:a:/) having a circumflex on top of it with an acute glyph capping the circumflex. Others are, the combined 'e' (*ḗ* = /e:e:/) which has a macron glyphs on top of it with an acute accents capping the macron, one other has a dieresis glyph with a grave accent on top of the glyph (*ǘ* = /u:u:/), and the fourth is the Greek iota with psili and varia with the combined 'i' (*ἴ* = /i:i:/). Each of these 4 vowel begin with short forms of vowels that are succeeded by corresponding long vowels of the same sound bracket within given syllables, more like ending the sound flow in the middle but yet again stressing it forward (an intermittent break that is followed by a change in flow).

Following a reverse, there are also 4 fall-fall inflective sounds, 'a' (*ầ* = /a˩a˩/) took on a circumflex on top of it with a grave glyph on top of the circumflex, 'e' (*ḕ* = /e˩e˩/) has a macron glyph on top of it with a grave accents on top of the macron, 'u' (*ǜ* = /u˩u˩/) has a dieresis glyph with a grave accent on top of the glyph, and the fourth is the Greek iota with psili and oxia 'i' (*ἲ* = /i˩i˩/), to make 4 of these, all having the sound of the pure vowels combined with the corresponding low tones within given syllables, more like ending the flow of the sound in the middle but yet again stressing it lower. Thus, this writer shall try to justify the assumption of the other 30 vowels as adduced.

For letter 'a';

á lōn (we didn't go), *a lȯ* (we went), *ā lȯn* (let us not go), *à l* + (*ȯ capped with an acute diacritic accent* (?) (should we go?), *ấ lōn*? (won't we go?), *ầ lō?* (are we going?).

For letter 'e';

é wán (you didn't come), *e wā* (you came), *ē wān* (don't come), *è wā*? (will you come?), *ḗ wān*? (won't you come?), and *ḕ d'ōmō*? (will you be there?).

For letter 'i';

í wán (s/he didn't come), *i wā* (s/he came), *ī wān* (s/he should not come), *ì wā*? (should, she/he come?), *ἴ wān*? (shouldn't s/he come?), and *ἲ d'ōmō*? (is s/he there?).

For letter 'o';

óna (as for a man), *onā* (dream), *ōna* (road), *ȯkȯ* (millipede), *őgbá* (front), and *ȍgbā* (as demarcation of land).

For letter 'u';

ú kān (I didn't say), *u ka* (I said), *ū ka tān'* (let me not say yet), *ù ká*? (should I say?), *ǘ kān*? (won't I say?), *ǜ kān*? (should I not say?).

2.2 Diphthongs

In writing the Igala token, the 'mid-tones' 'ȯ' and 'ė' with respect to the sounds /eu/ and /ei/ do not always remain the same for some of these sounds could be in context short, intermediate or long in tone, meaning that up to eight varieties of these two sounds can be gotten but in the main time, the author could only come about four glyphs for writing them, that being *ė* = /ei/, *ā* = /eiei/, *ȯ* = /eu/, and *ō̇* = /eueu/. These eight sounds are generated from the first vowels /e/ + /i/ = /ei/ and /e/ + /u/ = /eu/, out of which we have 8 diphthongs, although some of these are not currently portrayed by any orthographic symbol. There would thus be the need for additional symbols, i.e.; dotted '*ė*' or '*ȧ*' and *ȯ* orthographies with a grave or acute accents placed (either ways) on top of the dots on each to sound /eiei˩/ and /eueu˩/ or /eiei:/ and /eueu:/.

The author would take just one example on this in respect of the word ele as is currently spelt which could mean gift or python. Here, the author has spelt them ėlė only as a matter of necessity for if they are to be spelt in their actual sense, the more fitting orthography for these could not all be gotten on the IPA list of symbols on Microsoft word, but this nonetheless (the act of writing them with dotted 'e', i.e.; ėlė) brings one closer to not confusing the spelling of the word as merely ele to mean four, 'well fried', or the other two instances (gift and python). For if the author was to spell the word python correctly, that would probably be, (*ė with an acute on top of the dot*) or (*ė:*) + *lė*, while gift would be, (*ė with an acute on top of the dot*) or (*ė:*) + *l* + (*ė with an acute on top of the dot*) or (*ė:*), while palm kernel oil would just be *ėnė*, 'lies' would be (*ė with a grave on top of the dot*) or (*ė:*˩) + *mī*, as leaf would be (*ė with an acute on top of the dot*) or (*ā*) + *nghmi*. The same applies to the letter ȯ where the fruit of the Palmyra palm ought to be *(ȯ with an acute on top of the dot) + d + (ȯ with an acute on top of the dot)*, *ȯbė* (ant hill), which ought to be *(ȯ with a grave on top of the dot)* or (*ė:*) + *bė*, while 'peep' would have been *ȯ + p + ė* or just '*ȯpė* as in the statement "*kp'ȯpė kā g'ēnē ki yā wā*" (make a peep let's see who's coming).

2.3 Elision and other forms of Vowel Combination

Since the Igala language 'somewhat' follows the 'French Lemon Rule' or the VCV (vowel – consonant – vowel) Rule for it is rare to have situation where vowels follow themselves concurrently during words formation. Even in one instance where this rule is broken as shall be demonstrated below, this is more the result of an elision of a corresponding consonant sound than a naturally fixed format for that word. The only known exception to this rule is in respect to the word *ābū* which means 'how' or 'what', or where', in which case, speakers tend to deliberately elicit the /b/ consonant or both the /b/ and and the succeeding /u/ vowels during communication for only the vowel /a/, or /a/ with /u/ in respect to the word *mà* (them) is educed so that when succeeded with the suffices *ū* (I or me), *ē* (you), *ā* (we), *ī* (she/he/it), and *mà* (them), the word becomes sounded as *ā'ū* (how or what did I, as in the sentence "*ā'ū kā*?" (how or what did I say), *ā'ē* (how or what did you, as in the sentence "*ā'ē mā*?" (how do you know), *ā'ā* (how or what did we, as in the statement, "*ā'ā chė*?" (how or what did we do), *ā'ī* (how or where did she/he/it, as in the sentence, "*ā'ī lė*?" (how or where did she/he/it go), and *ā'ū* mà or *ā'mà* (how or what do they, as in the sentence "*ā'ū mà kō*" or "*ā'mā kō*?" (What or how did they write?). Although, these other forms are used as substitute for *ābū*, they don't however constitute a better alternative to *ābū* which is the actual form of how the word should be used for these are only corrupt versions of that word *ābū*.

More also, when writing sentences in the Igala language, certain letters are omitted from some words to avoid creepiness, muddiness or jumpiness and in the place of these omitted alphabets the apostrophe is used as a way of showing these elisions. The hyphen can be used to write certain words but for a writer who has a better understanding of the parts of speech, the use of the hyphen becomes almost unnecessary, but rather than committing the error of agglutinating the words or creating ambiguity problems in word usage as was observed by Malema et al. (2020), with a better understanding of inherent speech parts, it would have been preferable to have these words hyphenated. Since vowels are not re-echoed, the use of the umlaut or dieresis as is common with some Northern European languages or English is not common since there was no need for any two vowels to be cluttered to be vocalized. More so, since there are currently no homegrown phonemic orthographies at the moment or because the development of a standardized version of the Igala language is still an evolving process, there is the need to check against the practice in the English language sound system where vowels could produce multiple sounds or where certain sounds are repeated even when the repetition is almost nearly unnecessary, as one will have with the repetition of the letter 'l' in the word 'ball', or the repetition of the 'g' in 'egg'.

In English, letters as used in certain words do not usually follow a uniform pattern, i.e., letter 'a' (which could sound as /ei/ as in 'cake' or /æ/ as in 'can' /kæn/, or /o:/ as in ball and as in /a:/ in 'cart'), letter 'e' (which could sound as /e/ as in 'end' or /i/ as in 'elastic' or 'penis'), letter 'i' (which could pronounced as /i/ as in ink or /ai/ as in kite), letter 'o' (which could sound like /o/ as in on or /o:/ as in off, and as /u/ or /u:/ as in oops or ooze when repeated or as /ʌ/, /o/, or /u:/ when letter 'u' comes immediately in front of letter 'o' in a spelling as we have in the words coupling or thought or coup), letter 'u' (which could be pronounced as /u/ as in book or /u:/ as in boom or /ʌ/ as in umbrella, or as /3:/ as in urban when r is placed after letter u). Like the Hungarian language or other languages that do not depend exclusively on the use of the plain alphabet but employs some measure of diacritic to widen the range of available alphabets so as to accommodate more letters that are produced distinctly, while writing the Igala language, we must not necessarily change the sound of a monophony by that mere rule that some words having similar spelling be pronounced differently, neither are additional phoneme added to a vowel or a consonant as a way of changing the sound that the carrying letter is supposed to produce into another phonetic sound as we have with the English words plough or bought, and fort and resort. This problem of pronunciation could pose some headache to a new learner of the English language.

3 Conclusion

This paper provides an overview of vowels used in the Igala language. Vowels are central to word formation and without them speech making becomes impossible. These vowels combine with the consonant sound to form words but this is not to say that without the consonant sounds, certain words cannot be verbalized or written as in the case of the Igala language where certain words can be written without the combination of consonant sounds with the consonant sounds as it applies to the four vowels, a, e. i, u which by standing alone means something. This is largely the result of the fact that, the Igala language has a wide ranging tone system.

4 Limitation of the Study

As an under-resourced indigenous language whose contextual study as a culture transmitting agent is relatively new (Ojoajogwu, 2017), approaches towards formalization of the Igala language in a more modern sense has been done scantily but also indiscriminately in ways that are devoid of any serious scientific consideration, more so that those who made attempt at writing the language are either not language specialist who understand scientific rudiments regarding the rules of language as it relates with grammar and tone pattern and structure, or were individuals who were too hasty in a way that deep thinking regarding the depth and breadth of both grammar and tones contained in the language were not attended to at great depth. It was therefore not surprising that among some of the available materials that contain words, sentences and meanings, one often see variations in diacritic forms used to demonstrate tones and pronunciation from scholar to scholar and in some cases certain diacritic orthographies that can represent some tones are left out. Added to this is also a variation with respect to accent and tribal differences in tones from one area to the other which has further influence the work output of the various writers. This factor therefore contribute to the first limitation of this very study, because understanding the inherent flaws regarding the inappropriate diacritic orthographies adopted by other writers, the very writer developed separate tools representing several tones, which while being scientifically logical, nonetheless, confine exclusively not to any previous methods used by the earlier writers.

Although, prior to this current work, no effort was made to study the oral form of the Igala language from the basic in a more comprehensive form, such as is done in this paper, a fact which accounted for the neglect of some vowel forms represented by special symbols as stated above. But vowels were not the only orthographies left out for even consonant orthographies that present a single symbol as a unit of consonant cluster such as the 'c' with an over dot, i.e.; ċ, or the caron or hacek as it is at times called; č, both of whom represent the sound /ch/ in other world languages, as with respect to the English word 'church', and the symbol ŋ which is supposed to represent a single unit of the cluster /ng/ as in the *word* '*ānyīngā*' (finger nail) which ought to have been '*āɲīŋā*' or the 'ny' cluster (ɲ) is hardly used. While the non-use of these orthographies by previous writer posed some limitation with respect to how this very writer would have written syllables that should carry these orthographies, it was also a limitation of this study because this very writer failed to do otherwise from what has been held down for so long owing to English influence on the writing of the Igala language. While the tilde ñ which bear the /nn/ cluster and which is occasionally used by some of the earlier writers, albeit with some misconception here and there, in this work, words boiling around this very sign were not used and for that reason, the sign was bypassed, but in future attempt, it shall be treated with special consideration.

Added to the above two limitations is the fact that some orthographies representing vowels do not currently exist to exhibit these sounds on the IPA list of symbols on Microsoft word as pointed out in the body of the work, or perhaps these symbols exists but because of the limited knowledge of this author regarding how some of the symbols are pronounced, they could not be accounted for by the author. This fact also poses a limitation of its own. Added to this missing vowels or undiscovered vowels by this author is the absence of a single symbol for the consonant clusters 'kw', 'kp', nw, and 'gh'. This writer is aware that the over dotted p (ṗ), is currently used with respect to writing the Yoruba language, a development that some writers of Igala language have become accustomed to with respect to writing the 'kp' cluster as one would have with the Yoruba name '*Tōṗē*' which is pronounced as /topke/ or /tōkpē/, but this symbolization of the /kp/ sound with 'ṗ' calls for question since it is not the first phone on the cluster. Could it then be that this symbolization is the result of the fact that, there is no over dotted 'k' on the IPA list of symbols or because the 'p' in the combination forms a more voiced phoneme than the 'k' or it is because the people by choice, chose to write like that? As for the 'kw' cluster, should the under lined ḵ (the qaph) merely remain as ق as it is in the Arabic orthography or another use as a single unit for presenting the 'kw' cluster be found in it within the Latin orthographic symbols for those languages whose writing systems are still evolving?

5 Ethical Statement

While there is very little effort towards developing the Igala language into a formalized medium of written communication or the fact that effort towards its preservation should take preference over its deterioration or is key for undertaking a paper work such as the one undertaken here, extra care must be taken towards avoiding unnecessary abuse of content. That fact took a central stage in the consideration of this author while compiling this piece. This writer therefore takes responsibility for whatever infraction that might arise from the consumption or application of this work.

Bibliography

Abdulkadir S. Mohammed. 2001. "British Administration of Igalaland, 1896-1918". *FAIS Journal of Humanities*, 1(4): 130-144.

Adeniyi K. Obafemi. 2016. "Downstep in Igala and Yala (Ikom)". *Journal of West African Languages*, 43(1): 1-21.

Ahiaba Martin. 2015. "Retrieving Ẹbọ as Spirit: The Foundation of Authentic Christian Pneumatology among the Igala, Nigeria. *Cross-Cultural Communication*, 11(3): 7-19.

Albert S. Hornby. 2015. *Oxford Advanced Learner's Dictionary of English*, (Ninth Edition). Oxford University Press, Oxford, UK, Page 896.

Ayegba S. Felix, Abu Onoja, and Musa Ugbede-ojo. 2017. "Igala-English Parallel Corpora for Natural Language Processing Applications. *International Journal of Computer Applications*, 171(9): 3-6. https://www.academia.edu/55595333/

Blench Roger. 2011. *An Atlas of Nigerian Languages*. Kay Williamson Educational Foundation, Cambridge, UK, Page 37.

Cahill Michael. 2019. Tone, orthographies, and phonological depth in African languages. In Samson Lotven, Silvina Bongiovanni, Phillip Weirich, Robert Botne & Samuel Gyasi Obeng (eds.), *African linguistics across the disciplines: Selected papers from the 48th Annual Conference on African Linguistics*. Language Science Press, Berlin, Germany, Pages 103-123.

Dalamu O. Taofeek. 2019. "Decoding Encoded Yorùbá Nomenclature: An Exercise of Linguistic Competence and Performance". *Journal of Language and Education*, 5(1): 16-28.

Dawson Samantha, Michael R. Marlo, Dane Myers, and Christopher Adejo. 2015. "An Overview of Tone in Igala". In *Proceeding of the 46th Annual Conference on African Linguistics*. University of Oregon, Pages 1-16.

Finegan Edward. 2012. Language: Its Structure and Use. Wadsworth Cengage Learning, California, USA, Pages 1-5.

Karshima D.T. 2012. *Comprehensive Tiv Orthography*. Dor- Ter Books Publication, Markurdi, Nigeria, Page 13.

Lappere, Eline. 2020. "There is no such Thing as Standard English". Retrieved on March 19, 2023, from https://www.cambridge.org/elt/

Mc Laughlin Fiona. 2017. "Ajami Writing Practices in Atlantic-Speaking Africa". In *The Atlantic Languages* (Oxford Guide to the World's Languages). Oxford University Press, Oxford, UK. Retrieved on March 25, 2023, from https://people.clas.ufl.edu/fmcl/files/AjamiCIRCRED.pdf

Malema G. Tebalo, Okgetheng B., Motlhanka B., and Rammidi M. G. 2020. "Complex Setswana Parts of Speech Tagging". In Proceedings of the First Workshop on Resources for African Indigenous Languages (RAIL), pages 21-24, Marseilles. European Language Resource Association (ELRA).

Miachi Tom. Armstrong Robert. 1986. Igala Orthography. In *Orthographies of Nigerian Languages IV*. Pages 32-34, Lagos. National Language Center.

Moira Yip. 2002. *Tone*. Cambridge University Press, Edinburg, UK. Pages 1-16.

Nolte Insa, Clyde Ancarno & Rebecca Jones. 2018. ''Inter-religious Relations in Yorubaland: Corpus Method and Anthropological Survey Data''. *Edinburgh University Press Journal,* (13(1): 27-64.

Kasali A.A, Jimoh K.O, Adeagbo M.A, and Bello S.A. (2021). "Web-based Text Editing System for Nigerian Languages". *Nigerian Journal of Technology,* 40(2): 292-301.

Ken Lodge. 2009. *A Critical Introduction to Phonetics.* Continuum International Publishing Group, London; New York, UK; USA, page 3.

Obayemi Ade. 1980. "States and Peoples of the Niger-Benue Confluence Area". In Obaro Ikime (ed.), *Groundwork of Nigerian History.* Heinemann, Ibadan, Nigeria, Pages 144-164.

Oguagha A. Philip. 1981. "The Igala People: A socio-Historical Examination". *ODU Journal of West African Studies,* (21): 168-192.

Ojoajogwu O. Nocholas. 2017. "The Fundamental Arts of the Igala Language". https://www.researchgate.net/publication/

Okwoli P.E. 1996. *Introduction to Igala Traditional Religion.* Pastoral Press, Anyigba, Nigeria.

Olufemi F. Olaseinde. 2022. "Accentuating among Yoruba Learners of French Language in the Higher Institutions". *IOSR Journal of Research and Method in Education (IOSR-JRME),* 12(2): 46-52.

Omachonu G. Sunday. 2011. "Derivational Process in the Igala Numerical System: Some Universal Considerations". *Journal of Universal Language,* 12(2): 81-101.

Oshodi Boluwaji. 2016. "Form and Function of the Yoruba HTS (High Tone Syllable Revisited: Evidence from Ìgbò Second Language Learners of Yoruba". *Cuadernos de Lingüítica de El Colegio de México,* 3(1): 45-72.

Pretorius Laurette and Bosch Sonja. 2009. "Exploiting Cross-linguistic Similarities in Zulu and Xhosa Computational Morphology. In Proceeding of the First Workshop on Language Technologies for African Languages, pages 96-103.

Rodriguez Christopher. 2014. "Overview of the Igala Language". https://www.academia.edu/7951455/

Saleh S. M, and Yunusa O. 2013. "The Misconception and Abuses of Limited Polygamy among Muslims in Igala land". *Anyigba Journal of Arts and Humanities,* 13 (2): 1-15.

Sunday S. Emah, and Sunday Ojonugwa. 2020. "Igala Proverbs as Correctional tools in the Hands of Traditional Elders". *Ogirisi a New Journal of African Studies,* 15(1): 181-196.

Unubi S. Abraham. 2017. "The Used of Conjunction in English and Igala: A Contrastive Analysis". *International Journal of Advanced Multidisciplinary Research,* 4(8): 34-62.

Unubi S. Abraham. 2019. "A Contrastive Study of English and Igala Segmental Phonemes: Implication for ESL Teaches and Learners". *Journal of Biomedical Engineering and medical Imaging,* 6(6): 31-41.

Webster's II New College Dictionary. 1999 Boston; New York Houghton Mifflin Company, Boston; New York: USA, pages 1-100.

Wells C. John. 2001. ''Orthographic Diacritic and Multilingual Computing''. *Language Problems and Language Planning,* 24 (3): 249-272.

Investigating Sentiment-Bearing Words- and Emoji-based Distant Supervision Approaches for Sentiment Analysis

Koena Ronny Mabokela[1,3] **Mpho Raborife**[2] **Turgay Celik**[3]

[1]University of Johannesburg, Applied Information Systems
[2]University of Johannesburg, Institute for Intelligent Systems
[3]University of the Witwatersrand, School of Electrical and Information Engineering
{krmabokela@gmail.com}

Abstract

Sentiment analysis focuses on the automatic detection and classification of opinions expressed in texts. Emojis can be used to determine the sentiment polarities of the texts (i.e. positive, negative, or neutral). Several studies demonstrated how sentiment analysis is accurate when emojis are used (Kaity and Balakrishnan, 2020). While they have used emojis as features to improve the performance of sentiment analysis systems, in this paper we analyse the use of emojis to reduce the manual effort in labelling text for training those systems. Furthermore, we investigate the manual effort reduction in the sentiment labelling process with the help of sentiment-bearing words as well as the combination of sentiment-bearing words and emojis. In addition to English, we evaluated the approaches with the low-resource African languages Sepedi, Setswana, and Sesotho. The combination of emojis and words sentiment lexicon shows better performance compared to emojis-only lexicons and words-based lexicons. Our results show that our emoji sentiment lexicon approach is effective, with an accuracy of 75% more than other sentiment lexicon approaches, which have an average accuracy of 69.1%. Furthermore, our distant supervision method obtained an accuracy of 77.0%. We anticipate that only 23% of the tweets will need to be changed as a result of our annotation strategies.

1 Introduction

South African population is widely diverse and highly multilingual (i.e. origins, cultures, languages, and religions) with distinct language groups including English and Afrikaans (Statista, 2022). The Nguni group is the largest group which includes Seswati, isiNdebele, isiXhosa, and isiZulu. In this instance, our study focuses on the second-largest group—the Sotho-Tswana group comprising Sepedi (*Northern Sotho*) (Mabokela and Manamela, 2013), Sesotho (*Southern Sotho*), and Setswana (Statista, 2022).

Sentiment analysis is a branch of natural language processing (NLP) that studies the emotion (opinions or attitudes) of text. This field has received a lot of attention which led to its numerous successful NLP technologies in various areas (Aguero-Torales et al., 2021; Mabokela et al., 2022a). For example, its popular application has been in social media monitoring, support management, customer feedback (Wankhade et al., 2022) and AI for social good (Mabokela and Schlippe, 2022a).

Emojis being used alongside text messages on social media has become increasingly popular (Jindal and Aron, 2021; Grover, 2021). In recent years there has been more work on sentiment analysis with the use of emojis or emoticons (Grover, 2021; Hakami et al., 2021; Haak, 2021). Emojis have recently become an alternative to emoticons but they differ from emoticons in that emoticons are typographical facial representations (Gavilanes et al., 2018). Emojis are used to express feelings, moods, and emotions in a written message with non-verbal elements (Kralj Novak et al., 2015; Gavilanes et al., 2018).

The use of emojis—as a standardised collection of tiny visual pictograms portrays everything from happy smiles to flags from around the world (Grover, 2021; Gavilanes et al., 2018). The modern-day emojis can be traced back to chatrooms in the 1990s. They were used in conversations to signal a smile, anger or to portray a joke or sarcastic statement (kwan Yoo and Rayz, 2021). According to Emoji Statistics[1], there were 3,633 emojis in total in the Unicode Standard as of September 2021. That means the sentiment lexicon has to be enriched with new emojis that are frequently on social media (Kralj Novak et al., 2015). Therefore, it is necessary to extend the existing emoji lexicons for sentiment labelling.

[1]https://emojipedia.org/stats/

Proceedings of the Fourth workshop on Resources for African Indigenous Languages (RAIL 2023), pages 115–125
May 6, 2023

Many NLP systems require a labelled dataset for machine learning algorithms to produce good results. For this purpose, an annotation method that is not labour-intensive and time-consuming is required. Emojis have received much attention because of their widespread use and popularity in natural language processing (NLP) (Kejriwal et al., 2021). Emoji sentiment lexicons for other languages has been explored as an alternative method which then yielded a significant improvement in sentiment classification (Gavilanes et al., 2018; Haak, 2021; Kralj Novak et al., 2015). However, sentiment annotation and investigation of sentiment via emojis have received little attention for low-resource languages (Hakami et al., 2021).

Several emoji sentiment lexicons were produced by manual construction involving human annotators, automatically and semi-automatic with little human intervention (Grover, 2021). According to our knowledge, there is no published work on analysing the sentiment of emojis in the Bantu languages. In addition, since emojis are perceived as an important part of social media communications, incorporating them is likely to yield a higher-quality sentiment classification (Kejriwal et al., 2021).

Interestingly, emojis have been able to provide more information towards an accurate sentiment of the texts (Ayvaz and Shiha, 2017). Related work has shown that emojis help to detect and determine the sentiment label of the tweets (Go et al., 2009; Wang and Castanon, 2015; Ayvaz and Shiha, 2017; Singh et al., 2019). For this reason, it is interesting that we adopt an automatic approach that employs emoji information to reduce manual effort.

The main objective is to investigate the impact of emojis in the context of sentiment analysis. This comprises two tasks: (i) the usage of emojis to lower the manual effort in creating training data for sentiment analysis systems and (ii) the impact of emojis on the final accuracy of final sentiment analysis systems. For the pre-labelling, we even investigate a novel distance supervision approach to use emoji-based tweets to build a sentiment lexicon from scratch completely language-independent. We evaluate and compare our pre-labelling strategies with frequently used emoji sentiment lexicons provided by (Kralj Novak et al., 2015; Haak, 2021; Hakami et al., 2021). We contribute the following through our study:

- We collected a new sentiment analysis corpus for Sesotho (i.e. 6,314 tweets and 3,168 Sotho-English tweets) and added it to the SAfriSenti corpus.
- We investigate the usage of emoji sentiment lexicons in sentiment labelling strategies to reduce manual annotation effort.
- We leverage the existing emoji sentiment lexicons (Kralj Novak et al., 2015; Hakami et al., 2021; Haak, 2021) to generate a suitable sentiment lexicon for our target languages and provide a solution for the newer emojis which are not yet in the emoji sentiment lexicon.
- To cover tweets without emojis, we leverage sentiment lexicons in a cross-lingual way.
- Since, specific morphemes indicate a mood in our target languages, we also built and analyse morpheme-based language-specific sentiment taggers.

The structure of this paper is as follows: The related work will be discussed in Section 2. In Section 3, we will describe our SAfriSenti sentiment corpus and data collection strategies, as well as quality assurance. In Section 4, we describe the different sentiment annotation strategies. In Section 5, we will present the experiments and evaluation. Section 6, presents the conclusion and future work.

2 Related Studies

Recent efforts have been made to address the challenges of sentiment analysis for under-resourced languages (Mabokela et al., 2022a; Abdullah and Rusli, 2021). For example, a small number of African languages, including a few Nigerian languages (i.e. NaijaSenti Corpus) (Muhammad et al., 2022; Alabi et al., 2022) Swahili (Martin et al., 2021), Tunisian dialects (Medhaffar et al., 2017) and Bambara (Diallo et al., 2021) have been studied for sentiment analysis. Recently, SAfriSenti corpus (Mabokela and Schlippe, 2022b; Mabokela et al., 2022b) was created —it is a multilingual sentiment corpus for South African under-resourced languages. SAfriSenti Corpus is the largest Twitter sentiment corpus to date, with the goal of addressing the challenges of 11 South African languages.

Many current NLP applications are employed for social media data which solely rely on the labelled dataset, preferably manual annotation (Chakravarthi et al., 2022). However, no work has been done for these low-resource languages in the aspect of utilising emoticons or emojis for sentiment labelling. Moreover, high-resourced languages such as English, Spanish, and Arabic explored the emoji- or emoticon-based sentiment analysis with promising progress (Gavilanes et al., 2018; Hakami et al., 2021).

Many studies investigated emojis and word-based sentiment lexicons for sentiment analysis (Cortis and Davis, 2020; Grover, 2021). Additionally, some researchers used sentiment-bearing emojis to collect tweets from Twitter (Go et al., 2009; Pak and Paroubek, 2010). However, emojis for sentiment analysis of low-resource languages have received little research attention (kwan Yoo and Rayz, 2021) and a combination of emojis with sentiment lexicon for sentiment labelling is still an area for investigation. Moreover, only a few studies explored emoji sentiment lexicons for multilingual sentiment analysis (Kralj Novak et al., 2015; Gavilanes et al., 2018). A previous study by (Kralj Novak et al., 2015) created sentiment lexicons by involving 83 annotators to rate each of the 840 emoji as *positive*, *neutral* and *negative*.

Similarly, (Wang and Castanon, 2015) further analysed the impact of emoticons in constructing sentiment lexicons and also training the sentiment classifier. Although it was observed that the performance of the sentiment model increased by 15%, the findings support their claim that a small number of emoticons are powerful and accurate indicators of sentiment polarity. But according to (Guibon et al., 2016), the usage of the emojis can be expanded to numerous additional avenues such as sentiment enhancement and sentiment modification and are not only limited to sentiment expression. Similarly, (Ayvaz and Shiha, 2017) explored the impact of emojis in sentiment analysis but only focused on positive and negative sentiment polarity for the English language. (Kimura and Katsurai, 2017) investigated an automatic construction of an emoji sentiment lexicon. This technique takes the sentiment words from WordNet-Affect and determines how often they occur alongside each emoji.

Consequently, (Gavilanes et al., 2018) created an emoji sentiment lexicon using an unsupervised method based on the emoji descriptions [2]. Based on the analyses of the sentiment of informal texts in English and Spanish, they automatically created sentiment lexica with 840 emojis using the unsupervised system with sentiment propagation across dependencies (USSPAD) approach.

Recently, (Haak, 2021) demonstrated a technique that accurately and quickly identifies the emotions conveyed by emojis without manual annotation. However, a study by (kwan Yoo and Rayz, 2021) examined how emojis are used in tweets and how they can affect the tone and the sentiment of a sentence in the tweets and improved the sentiment analysis accuracy using machine learning techniques. (Hakami et al., 2021) examined the consistency of contextual emoji sentiment analysis in Arabic and European languages. They created the Arabic emoji sentiment lexicon and then compared the sentiment expressed in each of the two language families and cultures.

Some studies attempted to learn emoji embeddings to complement text word embeddings for sentiment classification tasks (Grover, 2021). First, (Eisner et al., 2016) employed a pre-trained emoji embedding strategy using positive and negative, randomly selected Unicode emoji descriptions. (Chen et al., 2018) learnt bi-sense emoji embeddings and train an attention-based LSTM for sentiment classification. By considering only the positive and negative descriptions for each Unicode emoji, the fine-tuning of emoji embeddings can be expedited. However, (Singh et al., 2019) proposed a straightforward method for processing emojis by replacing emojis with their descriptions in tweets and using a pre-trained word embedding strategy that is similar to that of the standard words. Furthermore (Liu et al., 2021) examined and evaluated the impact of supplementing emojis as additional features to improve the sentiment analysis performance. They developed an improved emoji-embedding model based on Bi-LSTM which in turn achieved the best sentiment analysis accuracy on online Chinese texts.

Our study is similar to (Gavilanes et al., 2018), and (Hakami et al., 2021) in that they utilised emoji sentiment lexicons to perform sentiment analysis on tweets with emojis. In this research, we adopt their approach, but we provide some additional steps to construct our emoji sentiment lexicon. Comparing the above-mentioned studies to our study, we utilised the existing emoji sentiment lexicons by (Kralj Novak et al., 2015; Haak, 2021) to construct the initial emoji sentiment lexicon. Simply put, we translate emojis found in the tweets into their textual descriptions and leverage existing

[2]http://emojipedia.org/

emoji sentiment lexicons to create a novel method for effective sentiment annotation of tweets.

3 Languages and Dataset

This section includes statistics regarding our *SAfriSenti*[3] corpus, from the initial collecting of raw data to the final tweets using Twitter API for Academic Research. *SAfriSenti* (Mabokela et al., 2022b; Mabokela and Schlippe, 2022b) corpus was manually annotated by 3 native speakers per target language following strict annotation guidelines. The annotators labelled tweets into 3-classes; positive, negative, and neutral. The corpus contains over 50,000 tweets. About 4% of the tweets were removed for various good reasons while 2% was retained after review. Positive tweets dominate negative tweets in *Sepedi*, *Setswana*, and *Sesotho* monolingual tweets by a higher margin. In addition, we evaluated our annotated sentiment corpus using the inter-annotation agreement metric (i.e., Krippendorff's average value of α=0.7695) which is deemed acceptable.

With a total of about 36% tweets alternating between *Sepedi* and English and 6% between Setswana and English, code-switching between native languages and English is common.

Table 2 shows an extract from the dataset with examples of tweets in *Sepedi*, *Setswana*, *Sesotho*, and English with emojis. We further provide an example for *Sepedi* and *English* code-switched tweets with their associated sentiments. Figure 1 shows examples of tweets with emojis.

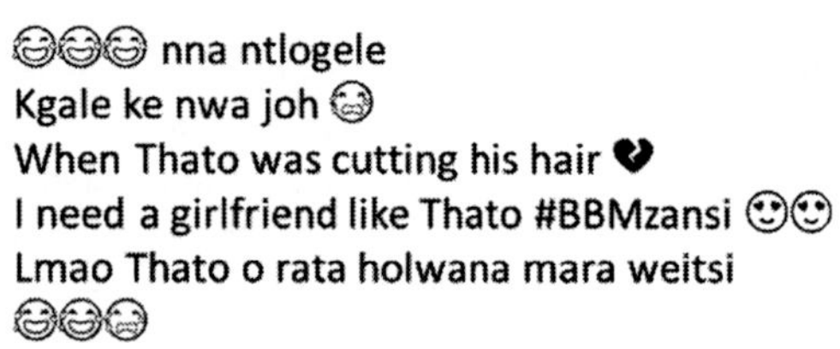

Figure 1: Examples of tweets with emojis

Table 2 presents a summary of the distribution of the tweets in this annotated subset that are monolingual and code-switched. The total monolingual tweets cover 64.4% (32,261) and 35.6% (18,223) of code-switched tweets. As demonstrated in Table 2, our corpus consists of a large number of code-switched tweets for Sepedi-English, Setswana-English and Sesotho-English. Code-switching is common between English and South African Bantu languages. 23.6% of those tweets contain code-switches of *Sepedi* and English. 5.7% of those tweets contain code switches of Setswana and English. 6.3% of those tweets contain code switches of Sesotho and English. *Sepedi*, *Setswana* and *Sesotho* share some common words since the languages are closely related. In our case, a tweet is considered a code-switched tweet if it has more than 3 English words in *Sepedi*, *Setswana* and *Sesotho* tweets.

Lang.	Class	#tweets	Percentage
Sepedi	**POS**	5,153	48%
	NEG	3,270	30%
	NEU	2,355	22%
	Total	10,778	
Setswana	**POS**	3,932	51%
	NEG	2,150	28%
	NEU	1,590	21%
	Total	7,672	
Sesotho	**POS**	3,050	48%
	NEG	2,024	32%
	NEU	1,241	20%
	Total	6,314	
English	**POS**	2,052	27%
	NEG	3,557	48%
	NEU	1,888	25%
	Total	7,497	

Table 1: Statistical summary of monolingual tweets for *Sepedi*, *Setswana*, *Sesotho* and English languages.

Lang.	Class	#tweets	Percentage
Pedi-Eng	**POS**	3,808	32%
	NEG	4,245	36%
	NEU	3,777	32%
	Total	11,830	
Tswa-Eng	**POS**	1,498	52%
	NEG	852	30%
	NEU	512	18%
	Total	2,862	
Sotho-Eng	**POS**	1,278	40%
	NEG	1,060	34%
	NEU	830	26%
	Total	3,168	

Table 2: Statistical summary of code-switched tweets for *Sepedi-English* (Pedi-Eng), *Setswana-English* (Tswa-Eng) and *Sesotho-English* (Sotho-Eng) languages.

4 Methodology

In this section, we will present the different sentiment annotation strategies that we will utilise for this study. For this, we describe how we employ our sentiment lexicons, and morphological sentiment taggers for the target languages and then also

[3]Our dataset will be made available here: https://github.com/Mabokela/SAfriSenti-Corpus

explain how we generate our novel emoji sentiment lexicons from the SAfriSenti corpus.

4.1 Words-Based Sentiment Lexicon

Numerous sentiment lexicons have been produced in various ways, including; manual creation—which is deemed to be a time-consuming and expensive process, and automatic and semi-automatic. Sentiment lexica are typically lists of words with values assigned to them that indicate the word's sentiment. Typically, these are integer values that express the polarity and intensity of the polarity as increasing or decreasing absolute values. For example, values usually range from -5: (very negative) to -1: (weakly negative) and +5: (very positive) to +1: (weakly positive). Sentiment lexicons have been used in many sentiment systems to help determine the semantic orientation of the texts (Nielsen, 2011; Hutto and Gilbert, 2015).

These sentiment lexicons have demonstrated that it is possible to combine the polarity values from a sentence and compute the sentiment on a continuous scale (Kaity and Balakrishnan, 2020). To generate word lexicon entries are chosen as a unit to associate opinion words more accurately. We used a cross-lingual approach by translating the existing English sentiment lexicons such as NRC[4] (Mohammad and Turney, 2013), VADER[5](Hutto and Gilbert, 2015) and AFFIN[6](Nielsen, 2011) to *Sepedi*, *Setswana* and *Sesotho*. Our sentiment lexicons for these targeted languages were constructed and verified by language experts. We still kept the English lexicon as our tweets contain English words. Additionally, some of the sentiment-bearing words were tagged by the annotators during the sentiment annotation process. Table 3 shows the distribution of our sentiment lexicons with words marked with sentiment polarity scores. The total number of words in the sentiment lexicon is 17,715.

Lexicons	#Words
Ours	1,250
AFFIN	7,520
VADER	2,477
NRC	6,468
Total	17,715

Table 3: Distribution of translated words in the sentiment lexicon for Sepedi, Setswana, and Sesotho.

[4]https://saifmohammad.com/WebPages/lexicons.html

[5]https://github.com/cjhutto/vaderSentiment.git

[6]https://github.com/fnielsen/afinn.git

Additionally, we used morphological sentiment taggers to tag the positive and negative tweets using morphemes with negative or positive moods. This is added to our sentiment lexicon. For example, the word *rata*, which means /love or like/ often ends with /-a/ but the ending /-e/ can signify a negation when used with the negative morphemes like /ga se/ and /rate/ which means /ga se rate/. However, the verbal ending with a vowel /-e/ can be the last component of the past tense forms as well as one of the markers of a negative mood (Prinsloo, 2020). In cases where tweets contain /ha se/ (e.g. *bona ha se wena fela motho waka /you are not my only person/*) from Sesotho (i.e. *Southern Sotho*) rather than /ga se/, our sentiment taggers presented limitations. We improved this by incorporating extra grammatical rules to compensate for this Sotho-Tswana language group scenario.

4.2 Emoji-Based Sentiment lexicons

Figure 2 shows the method for obtaining the emojis from tweets. To create the emoji sentiment lexicons, we leverage the information of the existing emoji sentiment lexicon created by (Kralj Novak et al., 2015), (Hakami et al., 2021), and (Haak, 2021). At this point, our emoji approach runs algorithms on both the tweets, emojis, and the description to automatically determine whether an emoji expresses a positive, negative, or neutral sentiment. To extract emoji-containing tweets from the SAfriSenti corpus, we only selected a subset of tweets with emojis by searching for any tweets with emojis. To create our unlabeled emoji sentiment lexicon, we follow the steps summarised below:

- We automatically extract emoji characters from the SAfriSenti corpus using regular expressions and then convert the emojis into a Unicode representation. A Unicode is a string encoding schema that translates characters into bytes.
- We create a list of unique emojis to avoid repetition in the emoji sentiment lexicons. That means emoji that repeats itself only appears once in the lexicon.
- Next, we retrieve the emoji descriptions from the python emoji translation and Emojipedia platform—an emoji dictionary in English with emoji images from different platforms. This is done by searching for the corresponding Unicode to match its description.

- To predict whether an emoji expresses a positive, negative, or neutral sentiment, we follow the approach by (Gavilanes et al., 2018) and also perform a lookup in the existing emoji sentiment lexicon and utilise the word sentiment lexicons to look up the words' polarities from their description without human intervention.

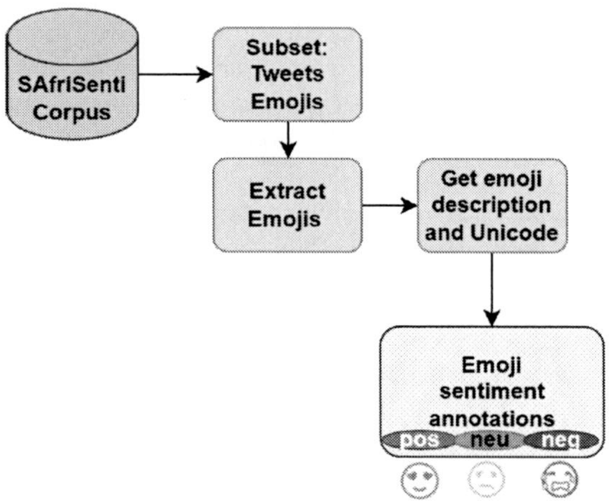

Figure 2: A process to obtain emojis and their description

In addition, we employ emoji sentiment lexicons which were obtained as follows:

- First methods are described in (Kralj Novak et al., 2015; Hakami et al., 2021). This emoji sentiment lexicon was obtained from 4% of 1.6 million tweets that were annotated (i.e. negative, neutral, positive) by 83 different native annotators for 13 European languages. It contains 751 most frequently used emojis on Twitter. The emoji sentiment lexicons were proposed as emoji sentiment rank language-independent resources for automatic sentiment analysis.

- The second method is in (Haak, 2021). This method is based on the intentions of the use of emojis for expressing the sentiment together with the methods used in (Kralj Novak et al., 2015). The emojis are statistically derived by occurrences in sentiment-bearing texts. In this case, the sentiment of the emojis is derived from the texts containing them and the sentiments are determined by using the English VADER lexicon.

4.3 Distant Supervision

In addition to our investigation, we looked at a simple and cheap process of developing an emoji and sentiment lexicon that is language-independent. As illustrated in Figure 3, 4, 5 and 6, we propose the following algorithm for sentiment labelling that leverages the information from emoji sentiment ranking[7] with sentiment-bearing emojis and words (Kranjc et al., 2015):

- $Step\ 1_{emoji_tweets}$: Use emoji unicode to identify and extract a subset of tweets with emojis (see Figure 3).

- $Step\ 2_{emojis}$: classify tweets with sentiment-bearing emojis into the classes *negative*, *neutral* and *positive* (Figure 3).

- $Step\ 3_{lists}$: create lists with sentiment-bearing words and assign a score from the translated word lexicon (Figure 4):
    1. collect all words from *negative*, *neutral* and *positive* tweets.
    2. Then remove words that occur in one or both other lists (Figure 5).

- $Step\ 4_{words}$: classify remaining tweets without sentiment-bearing emojis (e.g. tweets with no sentiment-bearing emojis) into the classes *negative*, *neutral* and *positive* based on highest word coverage with the lists of sentiment-bearing words.

- $Step\ 5_{words+emojis}$: classify all the tweets with and without sentiment-bearing emojis into the classes *negative*, *neutral* and *positive* based on highest word coverage with the lists of sentiment-bearing words and utilising the emoji sentiment lexicon scores (i.e. sentiment score [-1...+1]) from emoji sentiment lexicon (Kralj Novak et al., 2015; Hakami et al., 2021).

5 Experiments and Evaluations

In this section, we will describe our experimental setup, evaluation metrics, and the results. We also show that by acquiring the emoji sentiment lexicon from their descriptions, we then evaluate the proposed sentiment labeling framework in this section.

[7] https://kt.ijs.si/data/Emoji_sentiment_ranking/

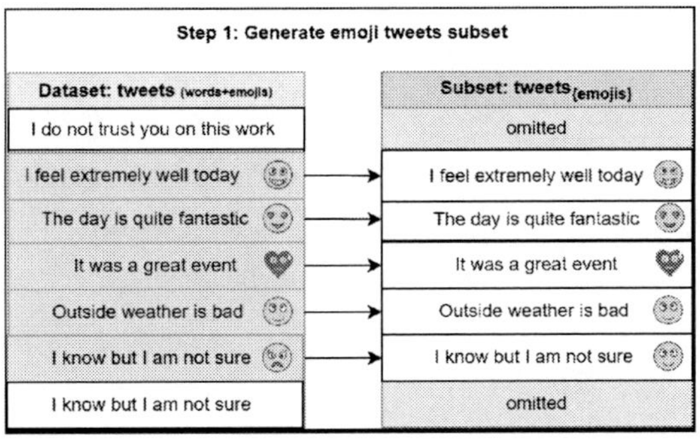

Figure 3: Use unicode to generate emoji tweets subset($step1_{emojisttweets}$).

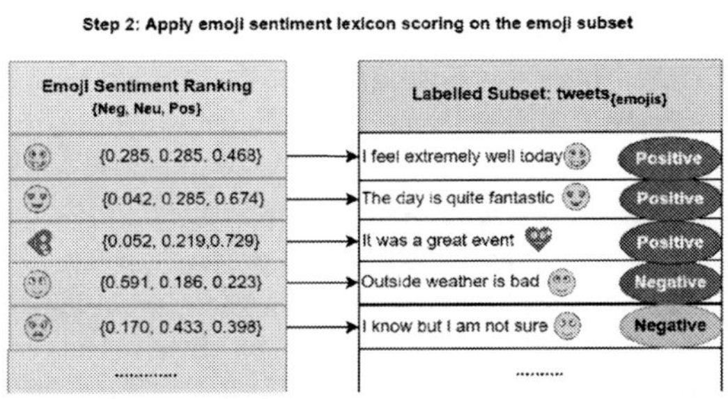

Figure 4: Classify tweets with sentiment-bearing emojis into the 3 classes ($step2_{emojis}$).

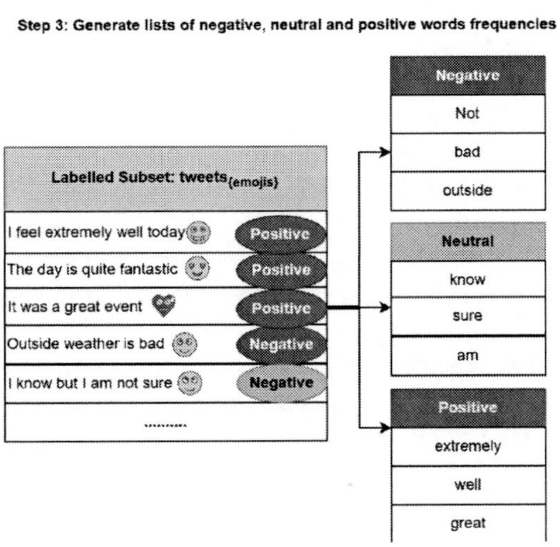

Figure 5: create lists with sentiment-bearing words ($step3_{words}$).

Our objective is to reduce manual annotation effort in creating training datasets for training NLP systems. Additionally, we investigated how to automatically create a sentiment lexicon using emoji scores from the existing emoji sentiment lexicon.

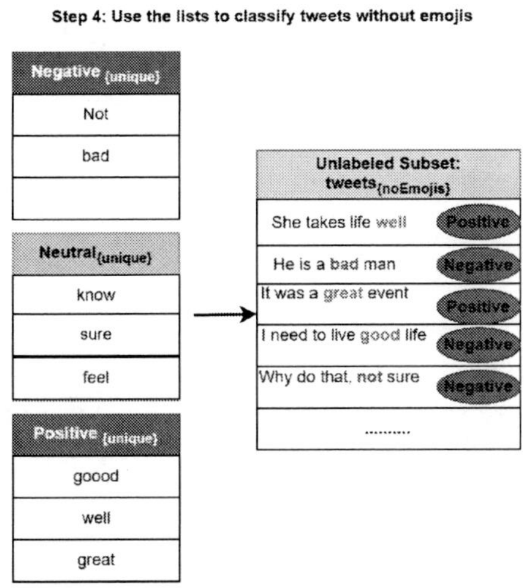

Figure 6: Sentiment-bearing words as indicators for remaining tweets' sentiment classes ($step3_{lists}$).

5.1 Experimental Setup and Metrics

We extracted the tweets with sentiment-bearing emojis for experimentation as in Figure 3. For quality assurance, all tweets have undergone a rigorous pre-processing step to remove noise, punctuations, and superfluous characters without any vital information (Mabokela and Schlippe, 2022b). In total, tweets with emojis are 34,269 which then constitute 72% of tweets in the SAfriSenti corpus. Only a small set of about 2.9% and 5.43% was found in the Setswana-English and Sesotho-English code-switched tweets while the rest of the monolingual tweets contain about 10%-24% of the tweets with emojis. Table 4 demonstrates the distributions of

Lang.	#Emojis	Freq.	Percent
Sepedi	214	7,723	22,1%
Setswana	103	5,260	15,4%
Sesotho	240	4,114	12,0%
English	287	6,103	17,8%
Pedi-Eng	370	8,200	23,9%
Tswa-Eng	78	1,008	2,94%
Sotho-Eng	64	1,861	5,43%
Total	686	34,269	

Table 4: Distribution of unique emojis and tweets with emojis per language.

tweets with emojis. A total of 686 unique emojis are identified from SAfriSenti Corpus across all the target languages. We also extracted emojis from code-switched tweets as well. We assessed our emoji tweets with the sentiment annotation methods defined in Section 4. Additionally, we use sentiment lexicon together with morpheme-based

Approaches	Features	Accuracy	Recall	Precision	F_1 score
Emoji Senti. lexicon (Kralj Novak et al., 2015)	emojis	68.7%	66.3%	65.0%	66.2%
Emoji Senti. lexicon (Hakami et al., 2021)	emojis	70.2%	72.6%	70.8%	71.7%
$SentiLexicon_{words+morph}$	words+morphemes	69.1%	67.1%	64.5%	68.4%
$SentiEmojiLex_{emojis}$	emojis	75.0%	72.6%	73.2%	74.5%
$CombSentiLex_{emojis+words}$	emojis+words	76.3%	72.6%	69.8%	73.9%
$DistSuper_{emojis+words}$	emojis+words	77.4%	76.9%	75.4%	76.3%

Table 5: Accuracy, recall, precision, and macro-F_1 score of the sentiment annotation methods.

sentiment taggers to accurately label the positive and negative moods.

We adhere to the metrics used in previous work (Gavilanes et al., 2018). We evaluated our sentiment labelling approach with accuracy, precision, recall, and macro-F_1. We evaluate our sentiment labelling strategies against manual annotations. We evaluated our approaches using accuracy, precision, recall, and macro-F_1 score using all labels as a multi-class task i.e. positive, neutral, and negative.

To obtain the tweet sentiment score associated with the sentiment label (i.e. negative, neutral, or positive), we used the discrete emoji distribution formula used in (Kralj Novak et al., 2015; Hakami et al., 2021). n emoji may appear in multiple tweets, each of which has been labeled with a sentiment. This creates a discrete distribution:

$\sum N(c) = N, c \in \{-1, 0, +1\}$

which records the distribution of sentiment for the relevant set of tweets. The *N* denotes the number of all the occurrences of the emojis in the tweets, and *N(c)* are the occurrences in tweets with the sentiment label *c*. We considered the multiple occurrences of an emoji in a single tweet. From the above, we formed a discrete probability distribution: (P_-, P_0, P_+), $\sum P(c) = 1$.

The components of the distribution (i.e., P_-, P_0, P_+) denote the sentiment class (negative, neutral, or positive) of the emoji being identified. Then, we estimated the probabilities from relative frequencies:

$$P(c) = \frac{N(c)}{N}$$

Then, the sentiment score *S* of the emoji was calculated as the mean of the distribution:

$$S = (-1 \cdot P(-)) + (0 \cdot P(0)) + (+1 \cdot P(+))$$

In addition, the labels of the emojis are also determined from the existing emoji lexicons, and their agreement is then tested.

5.2 Results

Table 5 shows the percentages of the accuracies, recall, precision, and F_1 score measures for the 4 methods. Our results indicate that the emoji lexicon provided by (Hakami et al., 2021) performs slightly better as compared to the emoji lexicon developed by (Kralj Novak et al., 2015). Furthermore, this is because the emoji sentiment lexicon by (Kralj Novak et al., 2015) has few emojis than the one presented by (Hakami et al., 2021). The accuracy of 68.7% and F_1 score of 66.2% is considered comparable as per the previous work (Gavilanes et al., 2018). We used the sentiment lexicon ($SentiLexicon_{words+morph}$)) to classify the sentiments contained in the tweets based on words. Our $SentiLexicon_{words+morph}$ approach achieved an accuracy of 69.1% with a macro-F_1 score of 68.4%. Thus, the $SentiLexicon_{words+morph}$ performs slightly better with an increased margin of (+0.4%) compared to the emoji lexicon provided by (Kralj Novak et al., 2015).

As per the previous work (Hakami et al., 2021), emojis are classified according to categories namely; facial expressions, body language, human activity, hearts, nature, food, object and symbols, and flags. 50% of our emojis fall within the category of facial expressions having strong indicators for emotions. As shown in Table 5, Distant supervision ($DistSuper_{emojis+words}$) methods perform significantly better than the two existing emoji lexicons and word-based sentiment lexicon. Comparing our emoji sentiment lexicon ($SentiEmojiLex_{emojis}$) with the two existing emoji lexicons (Kralj Novak et al., 2015; Hakami et al., 2021), $SentiEmojiLex_{emojis}$ performs way better with an accuracy of 75%. This means that our $SentiEmojiLex_{emojis}$ approach is more effective in determining the sentiments of the tweets. Furthermore, we tested with $DistSuper_{emojis+words}$ approach—the combination of emoji-bearing sentiment and sentiment-bearing words. This $DistSuper_{emojis+words}$ approach achieved an accuracy of 77.4% as well as an F-score of 76.3%. Our results further show that our $SentiEmojiLex_{emojis}$ together with $DistSuper_{emojis+words}$ approach can be used to do language-independent sentiment labelling of tweets with and without emojis. Comparing $DistSuper_{emojis+words}$ with $DistSuper_{emojis+words}$, we obtained an increased margin of more than (+1.4%).

In addition, a combination of word-based sentiment lexicon and morphological sentiment tagger ($SentiLexicon_{words+morph}$) yielded an increase in accuracy. Our $DistSuper_{emojis+words}$ approach outperforms all the sentiment lexicon approaches used in the experiments. Our results show that obtaining the sentiment labels using emoji definitions performed better. However, using the $SentiEmojiLex_{emojis}$ approach achieved a good F_1 score of 73.9%. It is worth noting that combining emojis and words (i.e $CombSentiLex_{emojis+words}$) also improves accuracy by 1.3% compared to $SentiEmojiLex_{emojis}$. Furthermore, we were able to achieve superior results using $CombSentiLex_{emojis+words}$ compared to utilising the $SentiLexicon_{words+morph}$ approach. Additionally, there is no significant difference in the results obtained for F_1 score, Precision, and Recall in this corpus. This confirms the quality of the SAfriSenti corpus.

6 Conclusion

In this paper, we describe the different sentiment labelling strategies that involve the utilisation of emojis and words to automatically pre-label tweets for low-resource languages. Additionally, we utilised the $SentiLexicon_{words+morph}$ plus the sentiment taggers to perform sentiment labelling. We create our $SentiEmojiLex_{emojis}$ from the existing manually annotated tweets in the SAfriSenti corpus—a multilingual Twitter sentiment corpus for South African languages (i.e. *Sepedi*, *Setswana*, *Sesotho* and English) which will later be extended to other South African languages. We created our $SentiEmojiLex_{emojis}$ by extracting only the tweets that contain emojis and converting the emojis to their corresponding textual descriptions. Furthermore, we leverage the approach by (Gavilanes et al., 2018) to develop our emoji sentiment lexicon. We achieved better accuracy and F_1 score with our $DistSuper_{emojis+words}$. Comparing our $SentiLexicon_{words+morph}$ with the sentiment-bearing words lexicon, our results show that the $SentiEmojiLex_{emojis}$ strategy is more effective and reliable. In addition, by comparing our labelling strategies to existing emoji sentiment lexicons, we obtained comparable results with an accuracy of 75% for $SentiEmojiLex_{emojis}$ and 77% of accuracy for the $DistSuper_{emojis+words}$ approach. Furthermore, we used the $CombSentiLex_{emojis+words}$ and $DistSuper_{emojis+words}$ approaches to label the remaining tweets in the *SAfriSenti* corpus (i.e. 32% (16,215 tweets)). Therefore, developing an automatic sentiment annotation strategy for tweets with emojis is more likely to reduce human annotation effort. Additionally, these methodologies can be readily adapted to other under-resourced African languages, provided the data gathered contains emojis. Our future endeavors include leveraging emoji embedding to formulate context-sensitive sentiment labeling techniques for specialized systems. Moreover, we aim to enhance sentiment classification by incorporating various active learning approaches that incorporate emojis.

7 Acknowledgments

This research work is supported by the National Research Foundation (NRF). First, we acknowledge the NRF for the Black Academics Advancement Programme (BAAP) award (No: BAAP200225506825). We also want to express our deepest gratitude to the annotators who devoted their time and effort, the language experts, and the session facilitators. Finally, we thank the valuable feedback provided by the reviewers.

References

Nur Atiqah Sia Abdullah and Nur Ida Aniza Rusli. 2021. Multilingual sentiment analysis: A systematic literature review. *pertanika journal of science and technology*, 29.

Marvin M. Aguero-Torales, Jose I. Abreu Salas, and Antonio G. Lopez-Herrera. 2021. Deep learning and multilingual sentiment analysis on social media data: An overview. *Applied Soft Computing*, 107:107373.

Jesujoba O. Alabi, David Ifeoluwa Adelani, Marius Mosbach, and Dietrich Klakow. 2022. Multilingual Language Model Adaptive Fine-Tuning: A Study on African Languages. *arXiv e-prints*, page arXiv:2204.06487.

Serkan Ayvaz and Mohammed Shiha. 2017. The effects of emoji in sentiment analysis. *International Journal of Computer and Electrical Engineering*, 9:360–369.

Bharathi Raja Chakravarthi, Ruba Priyadharshini, Vigneshwaran Muralidaran, Navya Jose, Shardul Suryawanshi, Elizabeth Sherly, and John P. McCrae. 2022. Dravidiancodemix: sentiment analysis and offensive language identification dataset for dravidian languages in code-mixed text. *Language Resources and Evaluation*, 56:765 – 806.

Yuxiao Chen, Jianbo Yuan, Quanzeng You, and Jiebo Luo. 2018. Twitter sentiment analysis via bi-sense emoji embedding and attention-based lstm. *Proceedings of the 26th ACM international conference on Multimedia*.

Keith Cortis and Brian Davis. 2020. Over a decade of social opinion mining. *Artificial Intelligence Review*, abs/2012.03091:4873–4965.

Mountaga Diallo, Chayma Fourati, and Hatem Haddad. 2021. Bambara language dataset for sentiment analysis. In *Practical ML for Developing Countries Workshop. ICLR 2021, Virtual Event*.

Ben Eisner, Tim Rocktäschel, Isabelle Augenstein, Matko Bosnjak, and Sebastian Riedel. 2016. emoji2vec: Learning emoji representations from their description. In *SocialNLP@EMNLP*.

Milagros Fernández Gavilanes, Jonathan Juncal-Martínez, Silvia García-Méndez, Enrique Costa-Montenegro, and Francisco Javier González-Castaño. 2018. Creating emoji lexica from unsupervised sentiment analysis of their descriptions. *Expert Syst. Appl.*, 103:74–91.

Alec Go, Richa Bhayani, and Lei Huang. 2009. Twitter sentiment classification using distant supervision. *Processing*, 150.

Vandita Grover. 2021. Exploiting emojis in sentiment analysis: A survey. *Journal of The Institution of Engineers : Series B*, pages 1–14.

Gaël Guibon, Magalie Ochs, and Patrice Bellot. 2016. From Emojis to Sentiment Analysis. In *WACAI 2016*, Brest, France. Lab-STICC and ENIB and LITIS.

Fabian Haak. 2021. Emojis in lexicon-based sentiment analysis: Creating emoji sentiment lexicons from unlabeled corpora. In *Proceedings of the LWDA 2021 Workshops: FGWM, KDML, FGWI-BIA, and FGIR*, pages 279–286. CEUR-WS.

Shatha Ali A. Hakami, Robert Hendley, and Phillip Smith. 2021. Arabic emoji sentiment lexicon (Arab-ESL): A comparison between Arabic and European emoji sentiment lexicons. In *Proceedings of the Sixth Arabic Natural Language Processing Workshop*, pages 60–71, Kyiv, Ukraine (Virtual). Association for Computational Linguistics.

C.J. Hutto and Eric Gilbert. 2015. Vader: A parsimonious rule-based model for sentiment analysis of social media text. In *Proceedings of the 8th International Conference on Weblogs and Social Media, ICWSM 2014*, pages 218–225.

Kanika Jindal and Rajni Aron. 2021. A systematic study of sentiment analysis for social media data. *Materials Today: Proceedings*.

Mohammed Kaity and Vimala Balakrishnan. 2020. Sentiment lexicons and non-English languages: A survey. *Knowledge and Information Systems*, 62:4445–4480.

Mayank Kejriwal, Qile Wang, Hongyu Li, and Lu Wang. 2021. An empirical study of emoji usage on twitter in linguistic and national contexts. *Online Social Networks and Media*, 24:100149.

Mayu Kimura and Marie Katsurai. 2017. Automatic construction of an emoji sentiment lexicon. *Proceedings of the 2017 IEEE/ACM International Conference on Advances in Social Networks Analysis and Mining 2017*, page 1033–1036.

Petra Kralj Novak, Jasmina Smailovic, Borut Sluban, and Igor Mozetic. 2015. Sentiment of emojis. *PloS one*, 10.

Janez Kranjc, Jasmina Smailovic, Vid Podpecan, Miha Grcar, Martin Znidari, and Nada Lavrac. 2015. Active learning for sentiment analysis on data streams: Methodology and workflow implementation in the clowdflows platform. *Inf. Process. Manag.*, 51:187–203.

Byung kwan Yoo and Julia Taylor Rayz. 2021. Understanding emojis for sentiment analysis. In *FLAIRS Conference*.

Chuchu Liu, Fan Fang, Xu Lin, Tie Cai, Xu Tan, Jianguo Liu, and Xin Lu. 2021. Improving sentiment analysis accuracy with emoji embedding. *Journal of Safety Science and Resilience*, 2:246–252.

Koena Ronny Mabokela, Turgay Celik, and Mpho Raborife. 2022a. Multilingual Sentiment Analysis for Under-Resourced Languages: A Systematic Review of the Landscape. *IEEE Access*, 11:15996 – 16020.

Koena Ronny Mabokela and Madimetja Jonas Manamela. 2013. An integrated language identification for code- switched speech using decoded-phonemes and support vector machine. In *2013 7th Conference on Speech Technology and Human - Computer Dialogue (SpeD)*, pages 1–6.

Koena Ronny Mabokela, Mpho Raborife, and Turgay Celik. 2022b. Safrisenti: Towards a creation of multilingual sentiment corpus for south african under-resourced languages. *ACM Trans. Asian Low-Resour. Lang. Inf. Process.*

Koena Ronny Mabokela and Tim Schlippe. 2022a. AI for Social Good: Sentiment Analysis to Detect Social Challenges in South Africa. In *The South African Conference for Artificial Intelligence Research (SACAIR 2022)*.

Koena Ronny Mabokela and Tim Schlippe. 2022b. A Sentiment Corpus for South African Under-Resourced Languages in a Multilingual Context. In

The 1st Annual Meeting of the ELRA/ISCA Special Interest Group on Under-Resourced Languages (SIGUL 2022), page 70–77.

Gati Lother Martin, Medard Edmund Mswahili, and Young-Seob Jeong. 2021. Sentiment Classification in Swahili Language Using Multilingual BERT. *African NLP Workshop, EACL 2021*, abs/2104.09006.

Salima Medhaffar, Fethi Bougares, Y. Estève, and Lamia Hadrich Belguith. 2017. Sentiment analysis of tunisian dialects: Linguistic ressources and experiments. In *WANLP@EACL*.

Saif M. Mohammad and Peter D. Turney. 2013. Crowdsourcing a word-emotion association lexicon. *Computational Intelligence*, 29(3):436–465.

Shamsuddeen Hassan Muhammad, David Ifeoluwa Adelani, Sebastian Ruder, Ibrahim Said Ahmad, Idris Abdulmumin, Bello Shehu Bello, Monojit Choudhury, Chris Chinenye Emezue, Saheed Salahudeen Abdullahi, Anuoluwapo Aremu, Alipio Jeorge, and Pavel Brazdil. 2022. NaijaSenti: A Nigerian Sentiment Corpus for Multilingual Sentiment Analysis.

Finn Årup Nielsen. 2011. A new ANEW: evaluation of a word list for sentiment analysis in microblogs. *CoRR*, abs/1103.2903.

Alexander Pak and Patrick Paroubek. 2010. Twitter as a corpus for sentiment analysis and opinion mining. In *LREc*, pages 1320–1326.

D.J. Prinsloo. 2020. Lexicographic treatment of negation in sepedi paper dictionaries. *Lexikos*, 30:1–25.

Abhishek Singh, Eduardo Blanco, and Wei Jin. 2019. Incorporating emoji descriptions improves tweet classification. In *Proceedings of NAACL-HLT*, page 2096–2101.

Statista. 2022. African countries with the largest population as of 2020.

Hao Wang and Jorge A. Castanon. 2015. Sentiment expression via emoticons on social media. In *2015 IEEE International Conference on Big Data (Big Data)*, pages 2404–2408.

Mayur Wankhade, Annavarapu Rao, and Chaitanya Kulkarni. 2022. A Survey on Sentiment Analysis Methods, Applications, and Challenges. *Artificial Intelligence Review*, pages 1–50.

A Appendix: Language Information

Northern Sotho, also known as Sesotho sa Leboa, is a Sotho-Tswana language primarily spoken in the northeastern regions of South Africa. It is also commonly referred to as Sepedi or Pedi. The South African National Census of 2011 reports that it is the first language of over 4.6 million people, accounting for 9.1% of the population, thus ranking it as the 5th most spoken language in South Africa. The Sepedi language is most frequently used in the Mpumalanga, Gauteng, and Limpopo provinces.

Tswana, known by its indigenous name **Setswana**, is a Bantu language spoken in Southern Africa by approximately 8.2 million individuals. It belongs to the Bantu language family within the Sotho-Tswana branch of Zone S, and shares close ties with the Northern Sotho, Southern Sotho, Kgalagadi, and Lozi languages. Setswana is an official language in Botswana and South Africa and serves as a lingua franca in Botswana and certain parts of South Africa, particularly in the North West Province. Tswana-speaking ethnic groups can be found across more than two provinces in South Africa, mainly in the North West, where approximately four million people speak the language.

Sesotho, also referred to as Southern Sotho, is a Southern Bantu language belonging to the Sotho-Tswana ("S.30") group. It is primarily spoken in Lesotho, where it serves as both the national and official language, as well as in South Africa (particularly in the Vaal and Free State), where it is one of the 11 official languages. It is also recognized as one of the 16 official languages of Zimbabwe. As with all Bantu languages, Sesotho is an agglutinative language that utilizes numerous affixes, and derivational and inflectional rules to construct complete words.

Natural Language Processing in Ethiopian Languages: Current State, Challenges, and Opportunities

Atnafu Lambebo Tonja [1,*], Tadesse Destaw Belay[2,*], Israel Abebe Azime[3,*], Abinew Ali Ayele[4,5,*], Moges Ahmed Mehamed[6,*], Olga Kolesnikova[1], Seid Muhie Yimam[5,*],

[*]EthioNLP, [1]Instituto Politécnico Nacional, Mexico, [2]Wollo University, Ethiopia, [3] Saarland University, Germany, [4]Bahir Dar University, Ethiopia,[5]Universität Hamburg, Germany, [6]Wuhan University of Technology, China.

Abstract

This survey delves into the current state of natural language processing (NLP) for four Ethiopian languages: Amharic, Afaan Oromo, Tigrinya, and Wolaytta. Through this paper, we identify key challenges and opportunities for NLP research in Ethiopia. Furthermore, we provide a centralized repository on GitHub that contains publicly available resources for various NLP tasks in these languages. This repository can be updated periodically with contributions from other researchers. Our objective is to identify research gaps and disseminate the information to NLP researchers interested in Ethiopian languages and encourage future research in this domain.

1 Introduction

Due to the rise of its applications in many fields, Natural Language Processing (NLP), a sub-field of Artificial Intelligence (AI), is receiving a lot of attention in terms of research and development (Kalyanathaya et al., 2019). NLP tasks such as Machine Translation (MT), Sentiment or Opinion Analysis, Parts of Speech (POS) Tagging, Question Classification (QC) and Answering (QA), Chunking, Named Entity Recognition (NER), Emotion Detection, and Semantic Role Labeling is currently highly researched areas in different high-resource languages.

Because of the advancement of deep learning and transformer approaches, modern NLP systems rely largely on the availability of vast volumes of annotated and unannotated data to function well. The majority of the languages in the world do not have access to such enormous information tools, despite the fact that a few high-resource languages have received more attention. Ethiopia is a country with more than 85 spoken languages, but only a few are presented in NLP progress. Figure 1 shows a search result for articles found in the ACL anthology for high and low-resource languages. As

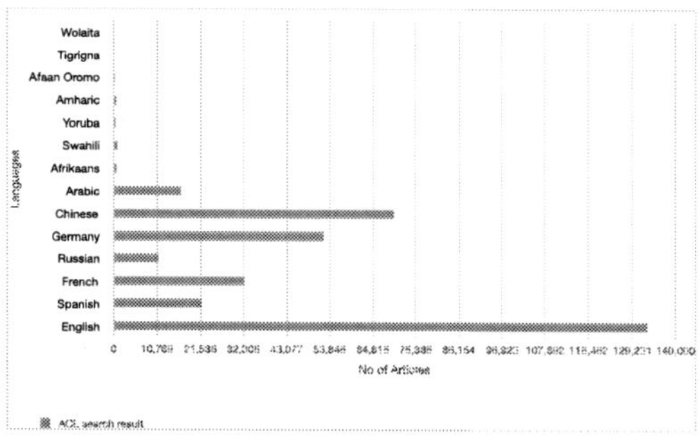

Figure 1: ACL paper search results for high and low-resource languages.

we can see from Figure 1, the search result for low-resource languages shows a very insignificant number of research works, while high-resource languages like English dominate in the ACL anthology paper repository. This might be a reflection of the unavailability of resources in the digital world, like in other high-resource languages, which affected the NLP progress in low-resource languages in general and Ethiopian languages in particular.

In this paper, we overview research works done in the area of selected NLP tasks for four Ethiopian languages. We cover mainly the following 4 languages, namely Amharic (Amh), Afaan Oromo (Orm), Tigrinya (Tir), and Wolaytta (Wal). We also reviewed works on a small set of local languages including Awigna (Awn) and Kistane(Gru), specially for the machine translation tasks. The contributions of this paper are as follows: **(1)** Reporting the current state-of-the-art NLP research for Ethiopian languages. **(2)** Discussing NLP progress in Ethiopian languages and the main challenges and opportunities for Ethiopian NLP research. **(3)** Collecting and presenting publicly available resources for different NLP tasks in Ethiopian languages in one GitHub repository that can be extended periodically in collaboration with other researchers. The collected publicly available datasets and models for Ethiopian languages are in our GitHub repository[1].

[1]Link to the survey GitHub repository

Proceedings of the Fourth workshop on Resources for African Indigenous Languages (RAIL 2023), pages 126–139
May 6, 2023

2 Language Details

This paper assesses the progress of NLP research for four Ethiopian languages: Amharic, Afaan Oromo, Tigrinya, and Wolaytta. As Ethiopia is a multilingual, multicultural, and multi-ethnic country, those selected languages have more speakers and native speakers in the country. Additionally, we have searched papers in the major eight Ethiopian languages and taken the top four based on frequency from the ACL anthology. This section gives some descriptions of those four targeted languages.

Amharic: is an Ethio-Semitic and Afro-Asiatic language. It is the official working language of the Federal Democratic Republic of Ethiopia (FDRE). It has about 57 million speakers, which makes it the second most spoken Semitic language in the world, where 32 million of them are native speakers (Eberhard et al., 2022). Other known names for this language are Amarigna and Amarinya.

Afaan Oromo: is a Cushitic language family. The language name may be written in different alternatives: (Afan, Afaan, affan) Oromo, or simply Oromo. There are over 50 million native Oromo speakers (Eberhard et al., 2022).

Tigrinya: (alternatively: Tigregna, Tigrinya or Tigrigna) is a Semitic language family spoken in the Tigray region of Ethiopia and in Eritrea. The language uses Ge'ez script with some additional alphabets that have been created for the Tigrinya language and are closely related to Ge'ez and Amharic. The language has around 9.9 million native speakers (Eberhard et al., 2022).

Wolaytta: (alternatively: Wolayita, Wolaytegna, Wolaytigna, Welaitta, and Welayita) is an Omotic language family spoken in the Wolaytta zone of Ethiopia. Both Afan Oromo and Wolaytta are written in the Latin alphabet.

3 Low-resource Languages

Researchers concerned with NLP have used data availability (either in the form of labeled, unlabeled, or auxiliary data) and NLP tools and resources as criteria for defining low-resource languages (Ranathunga et al., 2021). According to the work by Gereme et al. (2021), low-resource languages lack the tools and resources important for NLP and other techno-linguistic solutions. In addition, low-resource languages lack new language technology designs. Due to all these limitations, it is very difficult to develop new powerful methods for language applications (Tonja et al., 2023). For resource-rich languages such as English, Germany, French, Spanish and etc, the size of the dataset is not a problem because researchers have created a large set of corpora and tools for many NLP tasks. However, many other languages are deemed to be low-resource languages (Fesseha et al., 2021a). With this intuition, Ethiopian languages such as Amharic (Gereme et al., 2021), Afaan Oromo (Abate et al., 2019), Tigrinya (Osman and Mikami, 2012), Wolayitta (Tonja et al., 2023) are "low-resource" languages due to lack of data resources, linguistic materials, and tools. This affected the development of different NLP tasks and tools.

4 Possible Resource Sources and Tools

Data is one of the crucial building blocks for any NLP application. The availability of data is one of the criteria to categorize one language as a high or low-resource language (Ranathunga et al., 2021). As discussed in Section 3 Ethiopian languages belong to low-resource languages due to the unavailability of data. Table 1 shows some possible digital data sources for different NLP tasks.

Like data, NLP tools are also one of the building blocks for NLP applications, and the unavailability of these tools for a certain language also directly affects the development of NLP applications for that language. Table 2 shows available NLP tools for Ethiopian languages. As it can be seen from Tables 1 and 2, there are still very few sources to gather digital data and tools, available for Ethiopian languages.

5 NLP Tasks and Their Progress

In this section, we discuss what work has been done, what datasets of what sizes were used, what methods or approaches the authors proposed, and the availability of their dataset and models for NLP tasks and their progress in selected Ethiopian languages. We focused on Machine Translation (MT), Part-of-speech (POS) tagging, Named Entity Recognition (NER), Question Classification (QC), Question Answering (QA), text classification, and text summarization tasks due to the large number of works done for the targeted low-resource languages. The available models, the datasets for the tasks, and their links are found in Table 7.

5.1 POS Tagging

POS tagging is one of the popular NLP tasks that refer to categorizing words in a text (corpus) in

Sources		Link
Religion books	Bible	https://www.bible.com/
	Quran	
Multilingual data repositories	Opus	https://opus.nlpl.eu
	Lanfrica	https://lanfrica.com
	Masakhane	https://github.com/masakhane-io
	Hugging face	https://huggingface.co/
News medias	Fana	https://www.fanabc.com
	EBC	https://www.ebc.et
	BBC	https://www.bbc.com
	DW	https://www.dw.com
	Walata	https://waltainfo.com/
Social medias	Twitter	https://twitter.com/
	Facebook	https://www.facebook.com/
	Reddit	https://www.reddit.com/
Text Corpus	Amharic Text Corpus	Amharic Corpus at Mendeley

Table 1: Possible data sources

Author (s)	Tool's name	Tool's task	Language (s) support	Resource link
Yimam et al. (2021); Belay et al. (2022b)	amseg	Segmenter, tokenizer, transliteration, romanization and normalization	Amh	amseg
Gasser (2011)	HornMorpho	Morphological analysis	Amh, Orm, Tig	HornMorpho
Seyoum et al. (2018)	lemma	Lemmatizer	Amh	Lemmatizer

Table 2: Available language tools that are developed for low-resource Ethiopian languages.

correspondence with a particular part of speech, depending on the definition of the word and its context (Pailai et al., 2013).

Table 3 summarizes the current state of POS tagging research for selected Ethiopian languages. The table shows the name(s) of the author(s), the size of the dataset, the method used, the accuracy score of the models, and the availability of datasets and models in public repositories.

For Amharic, seven studies are listed, which used different approaches such as Conditional Random Fields (CRF), Maximum Entropy (MaxEnt), Support Vector Machines (SVM), CRFSuit, and Memory-Based Tagger (MBT). The highest accuracy score was achieved using the CRFSuit approach by Gashaw and Shashirekha (2020). For Afaan Oromo, two studies are listed that used the Hidden Markov Model (HMM) and Brill's tagger. The highest accuracy score was achieved using Bill's tagger by Ayana (2015). For Tigrinya, two studies are listed that used CRF and Long Short-Term Memory (LSTM). The highest accuracy score was achieved by the LSTM approach in Tesfagergish and Kapociute-Dzikiene (2020) and for Wolayitta, one study is listed, that used HMM and achieved an accuracy score of 92.96.

From Table 3, we can conclude that POS tagging is less researched for Ethiopian languages, the majority of the works were found for Amharic than for the other languages. From the works discussed in Table 3 only the work by Yimam et al. (2021) made their models and datasets available for public use.

5.2 Named Entity Recognition (NER)

In this section, we present works related to Named Entity Recognition (NER) for Ethiopian languages.

For **Amharic**, Mehamed (2019) conducted the NER experiment on a corpus of 10,405 tokens using the CRF classifier. Alemu (2013) conducted the experiments on a manually developed corpus of 13,538 words with the Stanford tagging scheme. Tadele (2014) used a hybrid of machine learning (decision trees and support vector machines) and rule-based methods. The datasets for these works are not available. The work done by the Masakhane NLP group (Adelani et al., 2021) analyzed a 10 African languages dataset and conducted an extensive empirical evaluation of state-of-the-art methods across both supervised and transfer learning settings, including Amharic. The data and models are available on GitHub. Gambäck and Sikdar (2017); Yimam et al. (2021); Sikdar and Gambäck (2018) built a deep learning-based NER system for Amharic using the available SAY project

Languages	Author(s)	Size	Approach	Score	Dataset	Model
Amharic	Adafre (2005)	1000	CRF	74.00	No	No
	Gambäck et al. (2009)	210,000	MaxEnt	94.52	No	No
	Tachbelie and Menzel (2009)	210,000	SVM	85.50	No	No
	Gebre (2010)	206,929	SVM	90.95	No	No
	HIRPSSA and Lehal (2020)	210,000	CRF	94.08	No	No
	Yimam et al. (2021)	210,000	CRF	92.27	Yes	Yes
	Gashaw and Shashirekha (2020)	109,676	CRFSuit	95.10	No	No
	Tachbelie et al. (2011)	210,000	MBT	93.51	No	No
Afaan Oromo	Wegari and Meshesha (2011)	1621	HMM	91.97	No	No
	Ayana (2015)	17,473	Bill's tagger	95.60	No	No
Tigrinya	Tedla et al. (2016)	72,080	CRF	90.89	Yes	No
	Tesfagergish and Kapociute-Dzikiene (2020)	72,080	LSTM	91.00	No	No
Wolayitta	Shirko (2020)	14,358	HMM	92.96	Yes	No

Table 3: Summary of related works for selected Ethiopian languages in POS tag tasks, **Size** shows the number of tokens used during the experiment, **Score** shows the outperformed model results evaluated using accuracy score, **Dataset** and **Model** shows the availability of dataset and models in publicly accessible repositories.

NER dataset. Jibril and Tantğ (2022) proposed a transformer-based NER recognizer for Amharic using a new annotated 182,691 word dataset. All available NER datasets for Ethiopian languages are shown in Table 7.

For **Afan Oromo**, the work by Legesse (2012) implemented the first NER system using a hybrid approach (rule-based and statistical) which contains 23k words. Abdi (2015) deals with NER in a hybrid (machine learning and rule-based) approach using the data from the work of Legesse (2012). Abafogi (2021) adopted boosting NER by combinations of such approaches as, machine learning, stored rules, and pattern matching using 44k words out of which around 7.8k were named entities. Gardie and Solomon (2022) developed a NER system using 12,479 data instances and BiLSTM, word embedding, and CNN approaches. However, none of the datasets in the above Afan Oromo works are publicly available.

For **Tigrinya**, the research by Yohannes and Amagasa (2022b) proposed a method for NER using a pre-trained language model, TigRoBERTa. The dataset contains 69,309 manually annotated words. Later Yohannes and Amagasa (2022a) employed Tigrinya NER with an addition of 40,627 words.

The only NER work attempted **Wolaytta** Language was conducted by Biruk (2021) using a machine learning approach. Figures 2 and 3 show NER publication types and dataset availability for targeted Ethiopian languages, respectively. We can summarize that NER is a little more developed than the POS tagging for Afan Oromo, Tigriyna, and Wolaytta languages. However, like POS tagging, only small Amharic NER datasets shown in Figure 3 are available.

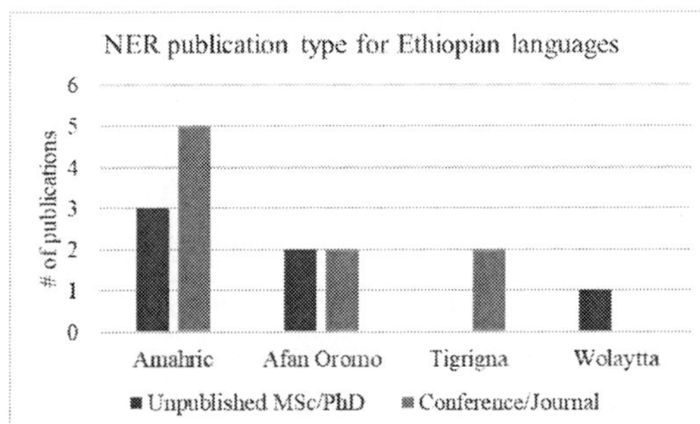

Figure 2: NER publication types for Ethiopian languages: the figure description is the same as in Figure 4. Wolaytta has no published works in conferences/journals.

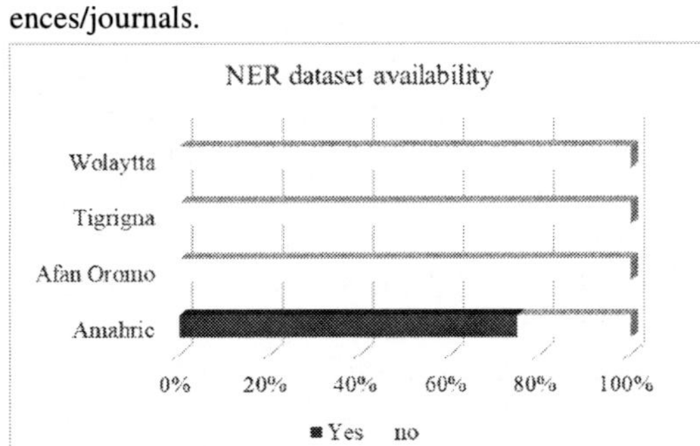

Figure 3: NER dataset availability per language: as it can be seen relatively more NER datasets are available only for the Amharic language.

5.3 Machine Translation (MT)

With the increasing popularity of computational tasks and the Internet's expanding reach to diverse, multilingual communities, the field of MT is rapidly progressing (Kenny, 2018). While impressive translation results have been achieved for language pairs with abundant resources, such as

English-Spanish, English-French, English-Russian, and English-Portuguese, MT systems struggle in environments with limited resources, where insufficient training data for certain languages is the main obstacle. In this section, we discuss the MT progress for Ethiopian languages in three categories: **(i)** ***English Centeric-*** works done for the above target Ethiopian languages with English pair, **(ii)** ***Ethiopian - Ethiopian -*** works done for Ethiopian language pairs without involving other languages, and **(iii)** ***Multilingual MT -*** works done for Ethiopian languages with other languages in a multilingual setting.

Table 4 summarizes several studies on MT in selected Ethiopian languages, focusing on the three categories. The studies vary in size of the parallel dataset, approach, score, availability of dataset, and model for public use. For English-centric language pairs, five studies used Amh-Eng language pairs. Biadgligne and Smaïli (2021) used NMT, and the size of their dataset was 231,898, while Gezmu et al. (2021) used NMT and had a dataset size of 145,364. Ashengo et al. (2021) used RN-NMT, and their dataset size was 8,603. The study by Biadgligne and Smaïli (2022) used NMT, and their dataset size was the same as that of Biadgligne and Smaïli (2021). Belay et al. (2022a) used NMT with a dataset size of 1,140,130. Finally, four studies used language pairs: Orm-Eng, Tir-Eng, and Wol-Eng. These studies applied different approaches such as SMT, NMT, and hybrid, with dataset sizes ranging from 6,400 to 336,000.

Three studies used Amharic (Amh) and other local language pairs, with different approaches and parallel dataset sizes. The study by Mekonnen (2019) used Amh-Awn language pairs, with a parallel dataset size of 5,000 and an SMT approach, while the study by Woldeyohannis and Meshesha (2018) worked on Amh-Tir language pairs with a parallel dataset size of 27,000 and an SMT approach. Finally, the study by Ashengo et al. (2021) used Amh-Gur language pairs with a parallel dataset size of 9,225 and an NMT approach. The performance in these studies ranged from 7.73 to 17.26 in BLEU scores. For multilingual MT, we found two studies by Lakew et al. (2020) and Vegi et al. (2022) that included Ethiopian languages with other African languages.

In Table 4, we can see some of the notable findings of the studies, for example, Solomon et al. (2017) achieved a high BLEU score of 47.00 with their SMT approach, although their parallel dataset size was small (6,400). The study by Berihu et al. (2020) used a hybrid approach and achieved a high BLEU score of 67.57 with a parallel dataset size of 32,000. Kidane et al. (2021) used NMT with a large parallel dataset size (336,000), but their BLEU score was relatively low (15.52). Tonja et al. (2021) and Tonja et al. (2023) used NMT for Wal-Eng language pairs, with parallel dataset sizes of 26,943, but their scores were relatively low (13.8 and 16.1, respectively). Lastly, in multilingual MT studies, the work by Lakew et al. (2020) made the datasets and models available for public use. More analysis of MT studies for the selected languages are discussed in Appendix A.

5.4 Question Answering and Classification

Even though question classification (QC) and question answering (QA) have been largely studied for various languages, they have barely been studied for Amharic, Afaan Oromo, Tigrinya, and Wolaytta. Some of the QC and QA work conducted for these languages are discussed below.

For **Amharic**, the work by Habtamu (2021) implemented a Convolutional Neural Network (CNN) based Amharic QC model using around 8k generic Amharic questions from different websites and labeled into 6 classes, similar to the question classes proposed by Li and Roth (2006). The work done by Taffa and Libsie (2019) developed Amharic non-factoid QA for biography, definition, and description questions. Yimam and Libsie (2009) developed an Amharic QA system for factoid questions. However, the datasets of the aforementioned works are still not available for further investigation. Nega et al. (2016) presented machine learning (SVM) based Amharic QC using a total of 180 questions collected from the Agriculture domain. Lastly, the work done by Belay et al. (2022b) built a QC dataset from a Telegram public channel called Ask Anything Ethiopia and developed deep learning-based Amharic question classifiers. Nega et al. (2016) and Belay et al. (2022b) datasets are released in a GitHub repository (see Table 7).

For **Afaan Oromo**, the work by Chaltu (2016) proposed the Afaan Oromo list, definition, and description QA system. Daba (2021) improved the result of Chaltu (2016) work for Afaan Oromo non-factoid questions. AMARE (2016) conducted the **Tigrinya** factoid QA system using 1200 questions. No QC or QA works have been done previously for **Wolaytta** language. Figures 4 and 5 show QC/QA publication types and dataset availability

Categories	Author(s)	Lang. pairs	Size	Approach	Score	Dataset	Model
English centeric	Biadgligne and Smaïli (2021)	Amh-Eng	231,898	NMT	32.44	No	No
	Gezmu et al. (2021)	Amh-Eng	145,364	NMT	32.20	Yes	No
	Ashengo et al. (2021)	Amh-Eng	8,603	RNNMT	21.46	No	No
	Biadgligne and Smaïli (2022)	Amh-Eng	231,898	NMT	37.79	No	No
	Belay et al. (2022a)	Amh-Eng	1,140,130	NMT	37.79	No	No
	Solomon et al. (2017)	Orm-Eng	6,400	SMT	47.00	No	No
	Meshesha and Solomon (2018)	Orm-Eng	6,400	SMT	27.00	No	No
	Adugna and Eisele (2010)	Orm-Eng	21,085	SMT	17.74	No	No
	Chala et al. (2021)	Orm-Eng	40,000	NMT	26.00	No	No
	Gemechu and Kanagachidambaresan (2021)	Orm-Eng	10,000	NMT	41.62	No	No
	Tedla and Yamamoto (2016)	Tir-Eng	31,279	SMT	20.90	No	No
	Tedla and Yamamoto (2017)	Tir-Eng	31,279	SMT	20.00	No	No
	Berihu et al. (2020)	Tir-Eng	32,000	Hybrid	67.57	No	No
	Azath and Kiros (2020)	Tir-Eng	17,338	SMT	23.27	No	No
	Kidane et al. (2021)	Tir-Eng	336,000	NMT	15.52	Yes	No
	Tonja et al. (2021)	Wal-Eng	26,943	NMT	13.80	No	No
	Tonja et al. (2023)	Wal-Eng	26,943	NMT	16.10	No	No
	Abate et al. (2019)	Amh-Eng	40,726	SMT	13.31	Yes	No
	Abate et al. (2019)	Orm-Eng	14,706	SMT	14.68	Yes	No
	Abate et al. (2019)	Tir-Eng	35,378	SMT	17.89	Yes	No
	Abate et al. (2019)	Wal-Eng	30,232	SMT	10.49	Yes	No
Local -Local	Mekonnen (2019)	Amh-Awn	5,000	SMT	17.26	No	No
	Woldeyohannis and Meshesha (2018)	Amh-Tir	27,000	SMT	9.11	No	No
	Ashengo et al. (2021)	Amh-Gur	9,225	NMT	7.73	No	No
Multilingual	Lakew et al. (2020)	Amh-Eng	373,358	NMT	20.86	Yes	Yes
	Lakew et al. (2020)	Orm-Eng	14,706	NMT	32.24	Yes	Yes
	Lakew et al. (2020)	Tir-Eng	917,632	NMT	32.21	Yes	Yes
	Vegi et al. (2022)	Amh-Eng	46,000	NMT	24.17	Yes	No
	Vegi et al. (2022)	Orm-Eng	7,000	NMT	12.13	Yes	No

Table 4: Summary of related works for selected Ethiopian languages in MT task, **Lang. pairs** is language pairs used for translation, **Size** shows the number of parallel sentences used in each paper, **Score** shows the outperformed model results evaluated using BLEU score, **Dataset** and **Model** shows the availability of dataset and models in publicly accessible repositories, respectively.

for Ethiopian languages, respectively.

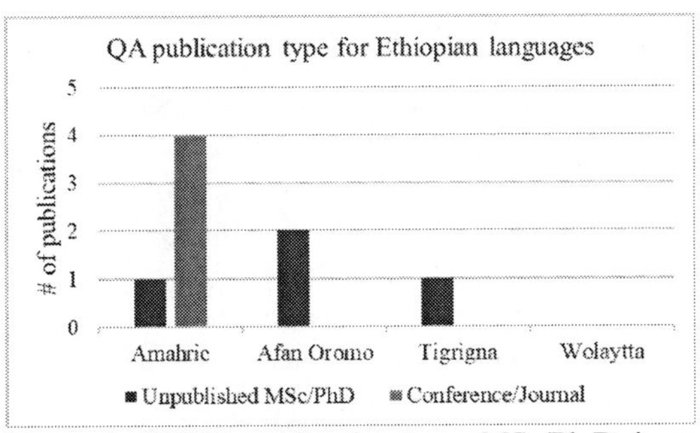

Figure 4: QC/QA publication type: MSc/Ph.D. is an unpublished master or Ph.D. thesis uploaded in local universities repositories and archives. A Conference/Journal label is a work that is published in a conference or journal.

From Table 4 and 5, we can conclude that QC and QA are less researched for Ethiopian languages, compared to the other NLP tasks. Most of the conducted works are unpublished MSc or Ph.D. theses. Relatively, Amharic has received more attention for QA and QC tasks.

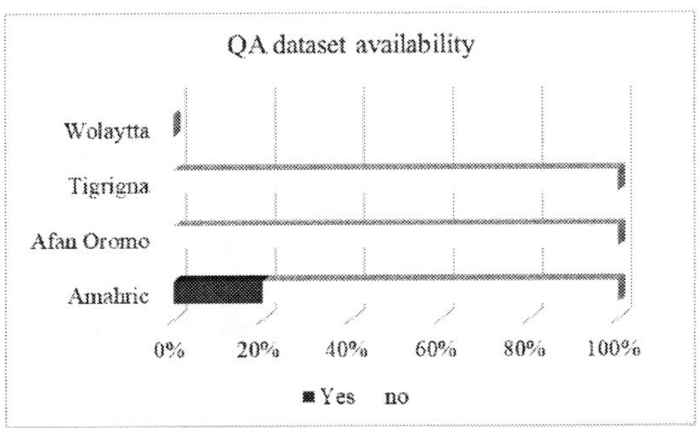

Figure 5: QA dataset availability per language: as it can be seen some QC datasets are available for Amharic but not for the other languages.

5.5 Text Classification

5.5.1 Hate Speech

Despite many works conducted on hate speech detection for resource-rich languages, low-resource languages such as Amharic, Afan Oromo, Tigrinya, and Wolaytta, are less researched. Table 5 presents a summary of the related works in hate speech detection for selected Ethiopian languages. The table includes the name of the language, the author(s) of the paper, the size of the dataset used, the algorithm used, the score obtained, and the availability of the

Languages	Author(s)	Size	Algorithm	Score	Dataset	Model
Amharic	Mossie and Wang (2018)	6,120	Word2Vec	85.34	No	No
	Mossie and Wang (2019)	14,266	CNN-GRU	97.85	No	No
	Abebaw et al. (2022)	2,000	MC-CNN	74.50	Yes	No
	Bawoke (2020)	30,000	BILSTM	90.00	No	No
	Ayele et al. (2022)	5,267	RoBERTa	50.00	Yes	Yes
Afaan Oromo	Ababu and Woldeyohannis (2022)	12,812	BiLSTM	88.00	No	No
	Defersha and Tune (2021)	13,600	L-SVM	63.00	No	No
	Kanessa and Tulu (2021)	2,780	SVM+TF-IDF	96.00	No	No
Tigrinya	Bahre (2022)	7,793	NB+TF-IDF	79.00	No	No

Table 5: Summary of related works for selected Ethiopian languages in hate speech tasks, **Size** shows the number of sentences used during the experiment, **Score** shows the outperformed model results evaluated using F1 score, **Dataset** and **Model** shows the availability of dataset and models in publicly accessible repositories, respectively.

dataset and model in publicly accessible repositories.

For **Amharic**, five studies were conducted with different approaches. Mossie and Wang (2018) used Word2Vec to detect hate speech in a dataset of 6,120 sentences and achieved an F1 score of 85.34. In another study, Mossie and Wang (2019) used CNN-GRU in a dataset of 14,266 sentences and achieved an F1 score of 97.85. Abebaw et al. (2022) used MC-CNN in a dataset of 2,000 sentences, achieving an F1 score of 74.50. Bawoke (2020) used BILSTM on a dataset of 30,000 sentences, achieving an F1 score of 90.00. Lastly, Ayele et al. (2022) used RoBERTa on a dataset of 5,267 sentences, achieving an F1 score of 50.00.

For **Afaan Oromo**, three studies were conducted, and none of them made their dataset or model publicly accessible. Ababu and Woldeyohannis (2022) used BiLSTM on a dataset of 12,812 sentences, achieving an F1 score of 88.00. Defersha and Tune (2021) used L-SVM on a dataset of 13,600 sentences, achieving an F1 score of 63.00. Kanessa and Tulu (2021) used SVM+TF-IDF on a dataset of 2,780 sentences, achieving an F1 score of 96.00. Bahre (2022) used NB+TF-IDF on a dataset of 7,793 sentences in the **Tigrinya** language and achieved an F1 score of 79.00. The dataset and model used in this study were not publicly accessible. In summary, Table 5 shows that hate speech detection in Ethiopian languages is one of the topics of research interest. However, similar to other tasks there is still a lack of publicly accessible datasets and models, which could hinder the development and evaluation of future research. It is worth noting that only two of the nine studies made their dataset and model publicly accessible. We can also see from Table 5 that for the Wolayitta language, there is no literature found for the hate speech task. Additionally, the F1 scores obtained vary greatly among the different studies, indicating that for all tasks the results are not comparable since the datasets are different.

5.5.2 Sentiment Analysis

Table 6 summarizes recent studies on sentiment analysis tasks for selected Ethiopian languages, including Amharic, Afaan Oromo, and Tigrinya. The studies utilize various algorithms such as Role2Vec, Naïve Bayes, LSTM, SVM, hybrid, and XLNet. For **Amharic**, Yimam et al. (2020) achieved the highest F1 score of 58.48% using Role2Vec with a dataset and a model publicly available, while Abeje et al. (2022) achieved the highest accuracy of 90.10% using LSTM. For **Afaan Oromo**, the highest accuracy of 93.00% was achieved by Oljira (2020) using Naïve Bayes, while Rase (2020) achieved 87.70% accuracy using LSTM. In contrast, Wayessa and Abas (2020) achieved 90.00% accuracy using SVM. For **Tigrinya**, Tela (2020) achieved an F1 score of 81.62% using XLNet with a 4000 manually labeled dataset. For **Wolaita**, similar to the hate speech task, there is no literature found for the sentiment analysis task. None of the datasets and models for Afaan Oromo, Tigrinya, and most of the works for Amharic are publicly accessible, hence results are not also comparable. This suggests that more work needs to be done in creating publicly accessible datasets and models for sentiment analysis tasks in Ethiopian languages. In conclusion, the studies in Table 6 indicate the potential for sentiment analysis in Ethiopian languages. The results show that the models' performance varies depending on the algorithm, dataset, and model availability. Still, there is a need for further research to create publicly accessible datasets and models to improve the models' performance

Languages	Author(s)	Size	Algorithm	Score	Dataset	Model
Amharic	Yimam et al. (2020)	9,400	F-Role2Vec	58.48	Yes	Yes
	Philemon and Mulugeta (2014)	600	Naïve Bayes	51.00	No	No
	Abeje et al. (2022)	2,000	LSTM	90.10 (accuracy)	Yes	No
	Alemneh et al. (2020)	30,000	hybrid	98.00(accuracy)	No	No
Afaan Oromo	Oljira (2020)	3000	Naive Bayes	93.00	No	No
	Rase (2020)	1,452	LSTM	87.70	No	No
	Wayessa and Abas (2020)	1,810	SVM	90.00	No	No
	Yadesa et al. (2020)	341	dictionary + contextual valance shifter	86.10	No	No
Tigrinya	Tela (2020)	4,000	XLNet	81.62	No	No

Table 6: Summary of related works for selected Ethiopian languages in sentiment analysis tasks, **Size** shows the annotated dataset used during the experiment, **Score** shows the outperformed model results evaluated using F1 score, **Dataset** and **Model** shows the availability of dataset and models in publicly accessible repositories, respectively.

and make them available for use in different applications.

5.5.3 News Classification and Text Summarization

The development of an Amharic news text classification dataset is described in a publication by Azime and Mohammed (2021). The dataset consists of 50,000 sentences and is classified into six categories, including local news, sports, politics, international news, business, and entertainment. Fesseha et al. (2021b) created a Tigrigna text classification dataset with manual annotation, consisting of 30k news sentences categorized into six classes, including sport, agriculture, politics, religion, education, and health. To enhance their analysis, the authors investigated the use of various word embedding techniques such as CNN, bag of words, skip-gram, and fastText. The dataset used for these experiments was made publicly available, as shown in Table 7. The work by Megersa (2020) utilized a dataset collected from the Ethiopian News Agency to experiment with 8 and 20 classes, but unfortunately, both the model and datasets are not publicly available.

Hasan et al. (2021) created an abstractive summarization dataset for 44 different languages using BBC articles collected via crawling. The resulting dataset comprises 5461 Amharic, 4827 Tigrinya, and 5,738 Afaan Oromo samples, which can potentially be employed for various Ethiopian language-related tasks. The authors fine-tuned mt5 models using this dataset and subsequently reported the outcomes. All publicly available data and code are listed in Table 7 for exploration. In general, news classification and text summarization has not yet been properly researched for Ethiopian languages.

6 Summary of Challenges, Opportunities and Future Directions

Challenges: Based on the findings of the above studies, we identified the following challenges: **(i)** A scarcity of publicly available data for Ethiopian languages. As the data and resources are not mostly publicly available, researchers are going to "re-inventing the wheel" by trying to address the problem. This leaves the low-resource language research usually 'in limbo', as it is not clear if the problem is addressed or not. This further makes it difficult to train different NLP tasks for Ethiopian languages and limits the scope of NLP applications. Moreover, it is very difficult to reproduce results since the benchmark datasets are not maintained. **(ii)** A lack of resources, tools, and infrastructure for NLP research in low-resource Ethiopian languages, can make it difficult to attract funding and talented researchers to work on the problem. **(iii)** Few people are interested in NLP for low-resource Ethiopian languages. This can make it difficult to attract resources and support for NLP research in these languages.

Opportunities: Here are some suggestions and ideas for the future that will help get more Ethiopian languages into NLP research: **(i)** There needs to be more work done to collect and label data in Ethiopian languages. This will require collaboration between linguists, NLP experts, and native speakers of the languages. **(ii)** As the results of the addressed NLP tasks are not comparable since the datasets are different, one big issue to address in the future is the release of benchmark datasets on which researchers can work on improving performance and developing new approaches. This will require sustained funding and collaboration among researchers. **(iii)** The development of machine translation systems for low-resource Ethiopian languages can help bridge the language

Author(s)	Task	Language	dataset link
Gezmu et al. (2021)	MT	Amh-Eng	http://dx.doi.org/10.24352/ub.ovgu-2018-144
Belay et al. (2022a)	MT	Amh-Eng	https://github.com/atnafuatx/EthioNMT-datasets
Abate et al. (2019)	MT	Amh-Eng, Orm-Eng, Tir-Eng, Wal-Eng	http://github.com/AAUThematic4LT/
Lakew et al. (2020)	MT	Amh-Eng, Orm-Eng, Tir-Eng	https://github.com/surafelml/Afro-NMT
Vegi et al. (2022)	MT	Amh-Eng, Orm-Eng	https://github.com/pavanpankaj/Web-Crawl-African
Tedla et al. (2016)	POS	Tir	https://eng.jnlp.org/yemane/ntigcorpus
Belay et al. (2022b)	QC	Amh	https://github.com/uhh-lt/amharicmodels
Nega et al. (2016)	QC	Amh	https://github.com/seyyaw/amharicquestionanswering
Adelani et al. (2021)	NER	Amh	https://github.com/masakhane-io/masakhane-ner
Jibril and Tantğ (2022)	NER	Amh	https://github.com/Ebrahimc/
SAY project NER dataset	NER	Amh	https://github.com/geezorg/data
Yimam et al. (2020)	SA	Amh	https://github.com/uhh-lt/ASAB
Ayele et al. (2022)	hate	Amh	https://github.com/uhh-lt/amharicmodels
Minale (2022)	hate	Amh (dataset only)	https://data.mendeley.com/datasets/p74pfhz3yx/
Abebaw et al. (2022)	hate	Amh	https://zenodo.org/record/5036437
Fesseha et al. (2021b)	news	Tir	https://github.com/canawet/
Azime and Mohammed (2021)	news	Amh	https://github.com/IsraelAbebe/
Hasan et al. (2021)	text summ.	Amh, Orm, Tir	https://github.com/csebuetnlp/xl-sum

Table 7: Available datasets for Ethiopian languages.

gap and enable communication across different languages. **(iv)** Transfer learning techniques can be used to leverage pre-trained models in high-resource languages to improve the performance of models in low-resource languages. **(v)** The involvement of local communities and stakeholders is critical for the success of NLP research in low-resource Ethiopian languages. People in the community can give researchers and developers important information about the language and culture.

Impact of this work and future directions: The results of this survey could be used to support future research initiatives in the field of NLP in Ethiopian Languages. Researchers can use the findings of the survey to identify areas that require further investigation and to develop research proposals that address the challenges and opportunities identified in the survey. This work also helps to conduct more surveys and develop a low-resource language demarcation. The demarcation helps to identify languages that need more NLP research attention. Adding more Ethiopian languages to NLP research will require researchers, linguists, and native speakers of the languages to work together, hence, at some point, these languages will be not considered low-resource languages anymore. Moreover, we point out with caution that not all the gaps and challenging problems can be instantly and readily fixed by researchers and research teams alone. Some of these problems call for sustained community cooperation as well as significant research funding from academic funding organizations. The difficulties we discussed in this paper are based on what we have learned from published research work and a quick scan of available corpora. Further studies with more comprehensive analysis, such as questionnaires directed to resource authors and users, or a more systematic inspection of the available data, can provide a deeper understanding of the causes of these problems and suggest effective solutions.

7 Conclusion

In this work, we investigated the most common NLP tasks and research works carried out in four Ethiopian languages. We explored the main NLP research directions, progress, challenges, and opportunities for Ethiopian languages. Our findings revealed that a significant amount of research has been centered on English or Amharic-centric machine translation tasks. Despite there being a plethora of written languages in Ethiopia, only a few of them have been explored in common research studies. Additionally, we observed a low prevalence of valuable resource publications in international conference venues. The majority of works are master's theses. The publicly available datasets, models, and tools are released in a centralized GitHub repository[2]. In the future, we plan to conduct a survey on more African languages and try to come up with an NLP resource demarcation line that could help funders to prioritize research topics and languages.

References

Teshome Mulugeta Ababu and Michael Melese Woldeyohannis. 2022. Afaan oromo hate speech detection and classification on social media. In *Proceedings of the Thirteenth Language Resources and Evaluation Conference*, pages 6612–6619.

Abdo Ababor Abafogi. 2021. Boosting afaan oromo

[2]Link to the survey GitHub repository

named entity recognition with multiple methods. *International Journal of Information Engineering and Electronic Business (IJIEEB)*, 13(5):51–59.

Solomon Teferra Abate, Michael Melese, Martha Yifiru Tachbelie, Million Meshesha, Solomon Atinafu, Wondwossen Mulugeta, Yaregal Assabie, Hafte Abera, Biniyam Ephrem, Tewodros Gebreselassie, et al. 2019. English-ethiopian languages statistical machine translation. In *Proceedings of the 2019 Workshop on Widening NLP*, pages 27–30.

Sani Genemo Abdi. 2015. *Afaan Oromo Named Entity Recognition Using Hybrid Approach*. Unpublished master thesis, Addis Ababa University.

Zeleke Abebaw, Andreas Rauber, and Solomon Atnafu. 2022. Multi-channel convolutional neural network for hate speech detection in social media. In *Advances of Science and Technology: 9th EAI International Conference, ICAST 2021, Hybrid Event, Bahir Dar, Ethiopia, August 27–29, 2021, Proceedings, Part I*, pages 603–618. Springer.

Bekalu Tadele Abeje, Ayodeji Olalekan Salau, Habtamu Abate Ebabu, and Aleka Melese Ayalew. 2022. Comparative analysis of deep learning models for aspect level amharic news sentiment analysis. In *2022 International Conference on Decision Aid Sciences and Applications (DASA)*, pages 1628–1633. IEEE.

Sisay Fissaha Adafre. 2005. Part of speech tagging for amharic using conditional random fields. In *Proceedings of the ACL workshop on computational approaches to semitic languages*, pages 47–54.

David Ifeoluwa Adelani, Jade Abbott, Graham Neubig, Daniel D'souza, Julia Kreutzer, Constantine Lignos, Chester Palen-Michel, Happy Buzaaba, Shruti Rijhwani, Sebastian Ruder, Stephen Mayhew, Israel Abebe Azime, Shamsuddeen H. Muhammad, Chris Chinenye Emezue, Joyce Nakatumba-Nabende, Perez Ogayo, Aremu Anuoluwapo, Catherine Gitau, Derguene Mbaye, Jesujoba Alabi, Seid Muhie Yimam, Tajuddeen Rabiu Gwadabe, Ignatius Ezeani, Rubungo Andre Niyongabo, Jonathan Mukiibi, Verrah Otiende, Iroro Orife, Davis David, Samba Ngom, Tosin Adewumi, Paul Rayson, Mofetoluwa Adeyemi, Gerald Muriuki, Emmanuel Anebi, Chiamaka Chukwuneke, Nkiruka Odu, Eric Peter Wairagala, Samuel Oyerinde, Clemencia Siro, Tobius Saul Bateesa, Temilola Oloyede, Yvonne Wambui, Victor Akinode, Deborah Nabagereka, Maurice Katusiime, Ayodele Awokoya, Mouhamadane MBOUP, Dibora Gebreyohannes, Henok Tilaye, Kelechi Nwaike, Degaga Wolde, Abdoulaye Faye, Blessing Sibanda, Orevaoghene Ahia, Bonaventure F. P. Dossou, Kelechi Ogueji, Thierno Ibrahima DIOP, Abdoulaye Diallo, Adewale Akinfaderin, Tendai Marengereke, and Salomey Osei. 2021. MasakhaNER: Named Entity Recognition for African Languages. *Transactions of the Association for Computational Linguistics*, 9:1116–1131.

Sisay Adugna and Andreas Eisele. 2010. English—oromo machine translation: An experiment using a statistical approach. In *Proceedings of the Seventh International Conference on Language Resources and Evaluation (LREC'10)*.

Girma Neshir Alemneh, Andreas Rauber, and Solomon Atnafu. 2020. Negation handling for amharic sentiment classification. In *Proceedings of the The Fourth Widening Natural Language Processing Workshop*, pages 4–6.

Besufikad Alemu. 2013. *A named entity recognition for Amharic*. Unpublished master thesis, Addis Ababa University.

KIBROM HAFTU AMARE. 2016. *TIGRIGNA QUESTION ANSWERING SYSTEM FOR FACTOID QUESTIONS*. Unpublished master thesis, Addis Ababa University.

Yeabsira Asefa Ashengo, Rosa Tsegaye Aga, and Surafel Lemma Abebe. 2021. Context based machine translation with recurrent neural network for english–amharic translation. *Machine Translation*, 35(1):19–36.

Abraham Gizaw Ayana. 2015. Towards improving brill's tagger lexical and transformation rule for afaan oromo language. *Department of Geographic Information Science, Hawassa Universty, Hawassa*.

Abinew Ali Ayele, Skadi Dinter, Tadesse Destaw Belay, Tesfa Tegegne Asfaw, Seid Muhie Yimam, and Chris Biemann. 2022. The 5js in ethiopia: Amharic hate speech data annotation using toloka crowdsourcing platform. In *2022 International Conference on Information and Communication Technology for Development for Africa (ICT4DA)*, pages 114–120. IEEE.

M Azath and Tsegay Kiros. 2020. Statistical machine translator for english to tigrigna translation. *Int. J. Sci. Technol. Res*, 9(1):2095–2099.

Israel Abebe Azime and Nebil Mohammed. 2021. An amharic news text classification dataset. *CoRR*, abs/2103.05639.

Weldemariam Bahre. 2022. *Hate Speech Detection from Facebook Social Media Posts and Comments in Tigrigna language*. Ph.D. thesis, St. Mary's University.

Emuye Bawoke. 2020. *Amharic text hate speech detection in social media using deep learning approach*. Ph.D. thesis.

Tadesse Destaw Belay, Atnafu Lambebo Tonja, Olga Kolesnikova, Seid Muhie Yimam, Abinew Ali Ayele, Silesh Bogale Haile, Grigori Sidorov, and Alexander Gelbukh. 2022a. The effect of normalization for bi-directional amharic-english neural machine translation. In *2022 International Conference on Information and Communication Technology for Development for Africa (ICT4DA)*, pages 84–89. IEEE.

Tadesse Destaw Belay, Seid Muhie Yimam, Abinew Ayele, and Chris Biemann. 2022b. Question answering classification for Amharic social media community based questions. In *Proceedings of the 1st Annual Meeting of the ELRA/ISCA Special Interest Group on Under-Resourced Languages*, pages 137–145, Marseille, France. European Language Resources Association.

Zemicheal Berihu, Gebremariam Mesfin Assres, Mulugeta Atsbaha, and Tor-Morten Grønli. 2020. Enhancing bi-directional english-tigrigna machine translation using hybrid approach. In *Norsk IKT-konferanse for forskning og utdanning*, 1.

Yohanens Biadgligne and Kamel Smaïli. 2021. Parallel corpora preparation for english-amharic machine translation. In *Advances in Computational Intelligence: 16th International Work-Conference on Artificial Neural Networks, IWANN 2021, Virtual Event, June 16–18, 2021, Proceedings, Part I 16*, pages 443–455. Springer.

Yohannes Biadgligne and Kamel Smaïli. 2022. Offline corpus augmentation for english-amharic machine translation. In *2022 5th International Conference on Information and Computer Technologies (ICICT)*, pages 128–135. IEEE.

Sidamo Biruk. 2021. *Named Entity Recognition for Wolaytta Language Using Machine Learning Approach*. Unpublished master thesis, Adama Science and Technology University.

Sisay Chala, Bekele Debisa, Amante Diriba, Silas Getachew, Chala Getu, and Solomon Shiferaw. 2021. Crowdsourcing parallel corpus for english-oromo neural machine translation using community engagement platform. *arXiv preprint arXiv:2102.07539*.

Fita Elanso Chaltu. 2016. *Afaan Oromo List, Definition and Description Question Answering System*. Unpublished master thesis, Addis Ababa University.

Endale Daba. 2021. *Improving Afaan Oromo question answering system: definition, list and description question types for non-factoid questions*. Unpublished master thesis, St. Mary's University.

NB Defersha and KK Tune. 2021. Detection of hate speech text in afan oromo social media using machine learning approach. *Indian J Sci Technol*, 14(31):2567–78.

David M. Eberhard, Gary F. Simons, and Charles D. Fennig. 2022. Ethnologue: Languages of the World. Twenty-fifth edition. Dallas, Texas: SIL International. Url: `http://www.ethnologue.com`.

Awet Fesseha, Shengwu Xiong, Eshete Derb Emiru, Moussa Diallo, and Abdelghani Dahou. 2021a. Text classification based on convolutional neural networks and word embedding for low-resource languages: Tigrinya. *Information*, 12(2):52.

Awet Fesseha, Shengwu Xiong, Eshete Derb Emiru, Moussa Diallo, and Abdelghani Dahou. 2021b. Text classification based on convolutional neural networks and word embedding for low-resource languages: Tigrinya. *Information*, 12(2).

Björn Gambäck, Fredrik Olsson, Atelach Alemu Argaw, and Lars Asker. 2009. Methods for amharic part-of-speech tagging. In *First Workshop on Language Technologies for African Languages, March 2009, Athens, Greece*.

Björn Gambäck and Utpal Kumar Sikdar. 2017. Named entity recognition for amharic using deep learning. In *2017 IST-Africa Week Conference (IST-Africa)*, pages 1–8. IEEE.

B Gardie and Z Solomon. 2022. Afan-oromo named entity recognition using bidirectional rnn. *Indian Journal of Science and Technology*, 15(16):736–741.

Ibrahim Gashaw and H L Shashirekha. 2020. Machine learning approaches for amharic parts-of-speech tagging. *arXiv preprint arXiv:2001.03324*.

Michael Gasser. 2011. Hornmorpho: a system for morphological processing of amharic, oromo, and tigrinya. In *Conference on Human Language Technology for Development, Alexandria, Egypt*, pages 94–99.

Binyam Gebrekidan Gebre. 2010. *Part of speech tagging for Amharic*. Ph.D. thesis, University of Wolverhampton Wolverhampton.

Ebisa A Gemechu and GR Kanagachidambaresan. 2021. Machine learning approach to english-afaan oromo text-text translation: Using attention based neural machine translation. In *2021 4th International Conference on Computing and Communications Technologies (ICCCT)*, pages 80–85. IEEE.

Fantahun Gereme, William Zhu, Tewodros Ayall, and Dagmawi Alemu. 2021. Combating fake news in "low-resource" languages: Amharic fake news detection accompanied by resource crafting. *Information*, 12(1):20.

Andargachew Mekonnen Gezmu, Andreas Nürnberger, and Tesfaye Bayu Bati. 2021. Extended parallel corpus for amharic-english machine translation. *arXiv preprint arXiv:2104.03543*.

Saron Habtamu. 2021. *Amharic Question Classification System Using Deep Learning Approach*. Unpublished master thesis, Addis Ababa University.

Tahmid Hasan, Abhik Bhattacharjee, Md Saiful Islam, Kazi Samin, Yuan-Fang Li, Yong-Bin Kang, M. Sohel Rahman, and Rifat Shahriyar. 2021. Xl-sum: Large-scale multilingual abstractive summarization for 44 languages. *CoRR*, abs/2106.13822.

SINTAYEHU HIRPSSA and GS Lehal. 2020. Pos tagging for amharic text: A machine learning approach. *INFOCOMP: Journal of Computer Science*, 19(1).

Ebrahim Chekol Jibril and A Cüneyd Tantğ. 2022. Anec: An amharic named entity corpus and transformer based recognizer. *arXiv preprint arXiv:2207.00785*.

Krishna Prakash Kalyanathaya, D Akila, and P Rajesh. 2019. Advances in natural language processing–a survey of current research trends, development tools and industry applications. *International Journal of Recent Technology and Engineering*, 7(5C):199–202.

Lata Guta Kanessa and Solomon Gizaw Tulu. 2021. Automatic hate and offensive speech detection framework from social media: the case of afaan oromoo language. In *2021 International Conference on Information and Communication Technology for Development for Africa (ICT4DA)*, pages 42–47. IEEE.

Dorothy Kenny. 2018. Machine translation. In *The Routledge handbook of translation and philosophy*, pages 428–445. Routledge.

Lidia Kidane, Sachin Kumar, and Yulia Tsvetkov. 2021. An exploration of data augmentation techniques for improving english to tigrinya translation. *arXiv preprint arXiv:2103.16789*.

Surafel M Lakew, Matteo Negri, and Marco Turchi. 2020. Low resource neural machine translation: A benchmark for five african languages. *arXiv preprint arXiv:2003.14402*.

Mandefro Legesse. 2012. *Named Entity Recognition for Afan Oromo*. Unpublished master thesis, Addis Ababa University.

Xin Li and Dan Roth. 2006. Learning question classifiers: the role of semantic information. *Natural Language Engineering*, 12(3):229–249.

Fanta Teferi Megersa. 2020. Hierarchical afaan oromoo news text classification.

Moges Ahmed Mehamed. 2019. *Named entity recognition for Amharic language*. LAP LAMBERT Academic Publishing.

Habtamu Mekonnen. 2019. Amharic-awngi machine translation: An experiment using statistical approach. *International Journal of Computer Sciences and Engineering*, 7:6–10.

Million Meshesha and Yitayew Solomon. 2018. English-afaan oromo statistical machine translation. *International Journal of Computational Linguistic (IJCL)*, 9(1).

Samuel Minale. 2022. Amharic social media dataset for hate speech detection and classification in amharic text with deep learning.

Zewdie Mossie and Jenq-Haur Wang. 2018. Social network hate speech detection for amharic language. *Computer Science & Information Technology*, page 41.

Zewdie Mossie and Jenq-Haur Wang. 2019. Vulnerable community identification using hate speech detection on social media. *Information Processing & Management*, page 102087.

Adane Nega, Workneh Chekol, and Alemu Kumlachew. 2016. Question classification in amharic question answering system: Machine learning approach. *International Journal of Advanced Studies in Computers, Science and Engineering*, 5(10):14–21.

Megersa Oljira. 2020. Sentiment analysis of afaan oromo using machine learning approach. *International Journal of Research Studies in Science, Engineering and Technology*, 7(9):7–15.

Omer Osman and Yoshiki Mikami. 2012. Stemming tigrinya words for information retrieval. In *Proceedings of COLING 2012: Demonstration Papers*, pages 345–352.

Jaruwat Pailai, Rachada Kongkachandra, Thepchai Supnithi, and Prachya Boonkwan. 2013. A comparative study on different techniques for thai part-of-speech tagging. In *2013 10th International Conference on Electrical Engineering/Electronics, Computer, Telecommunications and Information Technology*, pages 1–5. IEEE.

Wondwossen Philemon and Wondwossen Mulugeta. 2014. A machine learning approach to multi-scale sentiment analysis of amharic online posts. *HiLCoE Journal of Computer Science and Technology*, 2(2):8.

Surangika Ranathunga, En-Shiun Annie Lee, Marjana Prifti Skenduli, Ravi Shekhar, Mehreen Alam, and Rishemjit Kaur. 2021. Neural machine translation for low-resource languages: A survey. *ACM Computing Surveys*.

Megersa Oljira Rase. 2020. Sentiment analysis of afaan oromoo facebook media using deep learning approach. *New Media and Mass Communication*, 90(2020):2224–3267.

Binyam Ephrem Seyoum, Yusuke Miyao, and Baye Yimam Mekonnen. 2018. Universal dependencies for amharic. In *Proceedings of the Eleventh International Conference on Language Resources and Evaluation (LREC 2018)*.

Birhanesh Fikre Shirko. 2020. Part of speech tagging for wolaita language using transformation based learning (tbl) approach.

Utpal Kumar Sikdar and Björn Gambäck. 2018. Named entity recognition for amharic using stack-based deep learning. In *Computational Linguistics and Intelligent Text Processing: 18th International Conference, CICLing 2017, Budapest, Hungary, April 17–23, 2017, Revised Selected Papers, Part I 18*, pages 276–287. Springer.

Yitayew Solomon, Million Meshesha, and Wendewesen Endale. 2017. Optimal alignment for bi-directional afaan oromo-english statistical machine translation. *vol*, 3:73–77.

Martha Yifiru Tachbelie, Solomon Teferra Abate, and Laurent Besacier. 2011. Part-of-speech tagging for underresourced and morphologically rich languages—the case of amharic. *HLTD (2011)*, pages 50–55.

Martha Yifiru Tachbelie and Wolfgang Menzel. 2009. Amharic part-of-speech tagger for factored language modeling. In *Proceedings of the International Conference RANLP-2009*, pages 428–433.

Mikiyas Tadele. 2014. Amharic named entity recognition using a hybrid approach.

Tilahun Abedissa Taffa and Mulugeta Libsie. 2019. Amharic question answering for biography, definition, and description questions. In *Proceedings of the 2019 Workshop on Widening NLP*, pages 110–113, Florence, Italy. Association for Computational Linguistics.

Yemane Tedla and Kazuhide Yamamoto. 2016. The effect of shallow segmentation on english-tigrinya statistical machine translation. In *2016 International Conference on Asian Language Processing (IALP)*, pages 79–82. IEEE.

Yemane Tedla and Kazuhide Yamamoto. 2017. Morphological segmentation for english-to-tigrinya statistical machinetranslation. *Int. J. Asian Lang. Process*, 27(2):95–110.

Yemane Keleta Tedla, Kazuhide Yamamoto, and Ashuboda Marasinghe. 2016. Tigrinya part-of-speech tagging with morphological patterns and the new nagaoka tigrinya corpus. *International Journal of Computer Applications*, 146(14).

Abrhalei Frezghi Tela. 2020. Sentiment analysis for low-resource language: The case of tigrinya. Master's thesis, Itä-Suomen yliopisto.

Senait Gebremichael Tesfagergish and Jurgita Kapociute-Dzikiene. 2020. Deep learning-based part-of-speech tagging of the tigrinya language. In *Information and Software Technologies: 26th International Conference, ICIST 2020, Kaunas, Lithuania, October 15–17, 2020, Proceedings 26*, pages 357–367. Springer.

Atnafu Lambebo Tonja, Olga Kolesnikova, Alexander Gelbukh, and Grigori Sidorov. 2023. Low-resource neural machine translation improvement using source-side monolingual data. *Applied Sciences*, 13(2):1201.

Atnafu Lambebo Tonja, Michael Melese Woldeyohannis, and Mesay Gemeda Yigezu. 2021. A parallel corpora for bi-directional neural machine translation for low resourced ethiopian languages. In *2021 International Conference on Information and Communication Technology for Development for Africa (ICT4DA)*, pages 71–76. IEEE.

Pavanpankaj Vegi, Sivabhavani J, Biswajit Paul, Abhinav Mishra, Prashant Banjare, Prasanna K R, and Chitra Viswanathan. 2022. WebCrawl African : A multilingual parallel corpora for African languages. In *Proceedings of the Seventh Conference on Machine Translation (WMT)*, pages 1076–1089, Abu Dhabi, United Arab Emirates (Hybrid). Association for Computational Linguistics.

Negessa Wayessa and Sadik Abas. 2020. Multi-class sentiment analysis from afaan oromo text based on supervised machine learning approaches. *International Journal of Research Studies in Science, Engineering and Technology*, 7(7):10–18.

Getachew Mamo Wegari and M Meshesha. 2011. Parts of speech tagging for afaan oromo. *International Journal of Advanced Computer Science and Applications*, 1(3):1–5.

Michael Melese Woldeyohannis and Million Meshesha. 2018. Experimenting statistical machine translation for ethiopic semitic languages: The case of amharic-tigrigna. In *Information and Communication Technology for Development for Africa*, pages 140–149, Cham. Springer International Publishing.

Tariku Birhanu Yadesa, Syed Umar, and Tagay Takele Fikadu. 2020. Sentiment mining model for opinionated afaan oromo texts.

Seid Muhie Yimam, Hizkiel Mitiku Alemayehu, Abinew Ayele, and Chris Biemann. 2020. Exploring amharic sentiment analysis from social media texts: Building annotation tools and classification models. In *Proceedings of the 28th International Conference on Computational Linguistics*, pages 1048–1060.

Seid Muhie Yimam, Abinew Ali Ayele, Gopalakrishnan Venkatesh, Ibrahim Gashaw, and Chris Biemann. 2021. Introducing various semantic models for amharic: Experimentation and evaluation with multiple tasks and datasets. *Future Internet*, 13(11):275.

Seid Muhie Yimam and Mulugeta Libsie. 2009. TETEYEQ: Amharic question answering for factoid questions. *IE-IR-LRL*, 3(4):17–25.

Hailemariam Mehari Yohannes and Toshiyuki Amagasa. 2022a. A method of named entity recognition for tigrinya. *ACM SIGAPP Applied Computing Review*, 22(3):56–68.

Hailemariam Mehari Yohannes and Toshiyuki Amagasa. 2022b. Named-entity recognition for a low-resource language using pre-trained language model. In *Proceedings of the 37th ACM/SIGAPP Symposium on Applied Computing*, pages 837–844.

A MT Summary

Figure 6 shows the MT progress per year. As it can be seen from the figure in recent years MT research for Ethiopian languages getting attention.

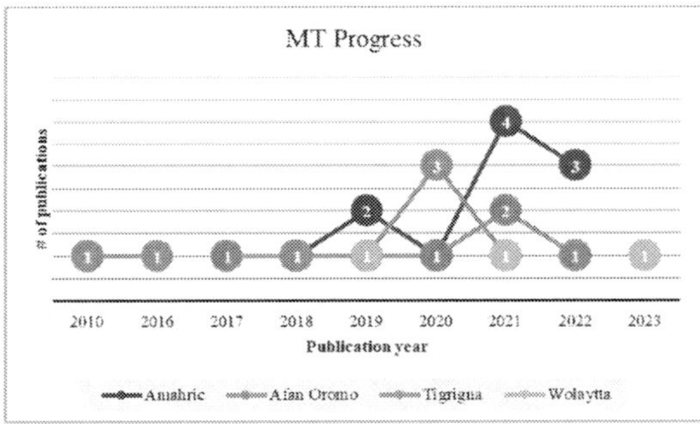

Figure 6: MT progress per year

Figure 7 shows the dataset availability per publication year. It can be noted from the table that in recent works there are attempts to make datasets available for Ethiopian languages but this still needs more effort.

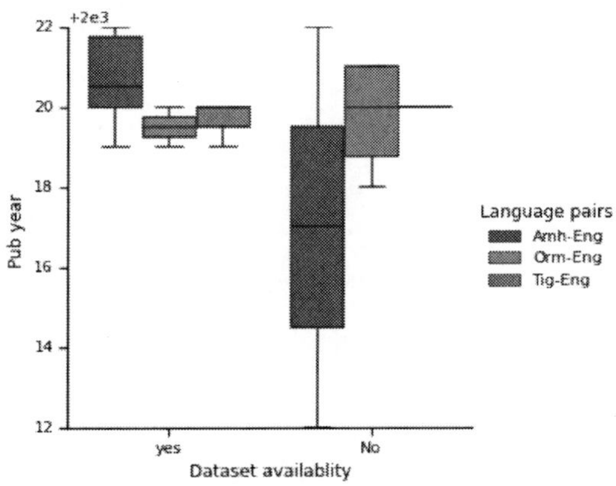

Figure 7: (**MT=>English centeric**) Dataset availability per publication year

Figure 8 shows the publications and methodologies used. It can be seen from the figure that before 2021 the dominant methodology used by different researchers was SMT, but in recent years different researchers have applied a neural network-based approach even if its performance depends on the availability of parallel datasets.

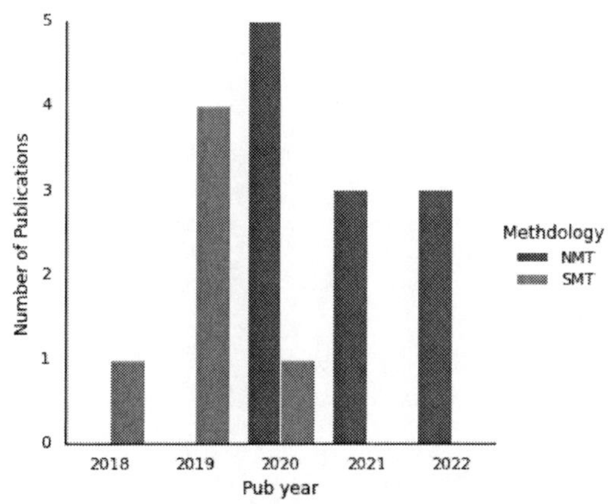

Figure 8: (**MT=>English centeric**) Methodology per publication year

Author Index

Association for Computational Linguistics
209 N. Eighth Street
Stroudsburg, Pennsylvania 18360

ISBN 978-1-7138-9061-4

9 781713 890614